Ron Weber

BLACK PUFF POLLY

AND OTHER FLIGHTS TO ETERNITY

BLACK PUFF POLLY

AND OTHER FLIGHTS TO ETERNITY

Edited by
ROLAND O. BYERS
LT. COLONEL USAFR (RET.)

Pawpaw Press
P.O. Box 9191 Moscow ID 83843

This Book Is Dedicated

To those men of the 457th Bombardment Group
who made the supreme sacrifice by giving
their lives for their country

Copyright © 1991 by Roland O. Byers

All rights reserved under Pan-American and International Conventions. Published in the United States by Pawpaw Press, P.O. Box 9191, Moscow, Idaho 83843

Library of Congress, Card Number 90-092116

ISBN 0-9614563-2-9

Manufactured in the United States of America

Cover and book designed by North Country Book Express, Inc. Printed by McNaughton and Gunn

Contents

Introduction 1
Prelude 3

Black Puff Polly 9
Mission No. 53 to Dessau .... 28 May 1944
   S/Sgt. William F. Bemus
   S/Sgt. Sheldon E. Moore
   2nd Lt. John O. Millham
Mission No. 1 to
Lippstadt/Gutersloh .... 21 Feb. 1944 33
   2nd Lt. Samuel L. Kalman
Mission No. 4 to Augsburg .... 25 Feb. 1944 57
   1st Lt. Edward J. Reppa
   2nd Lt. Aaron J. Ayres
Mission No. 23 to Gdynia .... 9 April 1944 65
   S/Sgt. Ralph E. Smith
   T/Sgt. Amos T. Bunch
Mission to Merseburg (recalled) ... 21 April 1944 71
   War Department report Lt. Coffman's crash
   Eye Witness Report
Mission No. 44 to Lutzkendorf .... 12 May 1944 75
   2nd Lt. John Akers
Mission No. 46 to Berlin .... 19 May 1944 81
   2nd Lt. Paul V. Owens
Mission No. 50 to Berlin .... 24 May 1944 85
   S/Sgt. Walter H. Osika

Mission No. 52 to Ludwigshafen...27 May 1944.........91
   S/Sgt. John L. Toney
Mission No. 53 to Dessau ....28 May 1944.........99
   2nd Lt. Clyde Knipfer
Mission No. 66 to Paris ....14 June 1944........101
   T/Sgt. Milton E. Bunch
   2nd Lt. Roy W. Allen
   2nd Lt. Charles R. Blackwell
   2nd Lt. James La Paze
Mission No. 71 to Hamburg ......20 June 1944........117
   2nd Lt. William B. Bomar
Mission No. 73 to Berlin ....21 June 1944........125
   S/Sgt. Frank X. Heekin
   1st Lt. Edward J. Reppa
Mission No. 79 to Leipzig ....29 June 1944........133
   2nd Lt. Harry Will, Jr.
Mission to No. 91 Augsburg ......19 July 1944 139
   2nd Lt. Wesley C. Akins
Mission No. 133 to Peenemunde...25 Aug. 1944 143
   S/Sgt. John A. Roe, Jr.
Mission No. 123 to Nijmegen .....17 Sept. 1944 153
   1st Lt. Douglas L. Grantham, Jr.
Mission No. 128 to Magdeburg....28 Sept. 1944 157
   2nd Lt. Angelo A. Archiopoli
Mission No. 133 to Politz......... 7 Oct. 1944........165
   1st Lt. William A. Morrow
   1st Lt. Ernest T. Salzer
   2nd Lt. Richard R. Garland
   2nd Lt. Leo J. Higgins
Mission No. 136 to Cologne ......17 Oct. 1944........185
   T/Sgt. Marshall T. Windham
Mission No. 139 to Hamburg .....25 Oct. 1944........195
   1st Lt. J. Francis Angier
Trap! Lt. Col. Roland O. Byers......................203

1st 457TH B/G crew to complete tour.

Mission No. 143 to Merseburg .... 2 Nov. 1944 203
   1st Lt. Jerome Silverman
   T/Sgt. Clifford A. Upton
   T/Sgt John C. Bruggeman
Mission No. 154 to Bohlen .... 30 Nov. 1944 219
   2nd Lt. John F. Welch
Mission No. 172 to Euskirchen .... 10 Jan. 1945 225
   2nd Lt. Aurthur Fitch
Mission No. 228 to Oranienburg .. 10 April 1945 233
   1st Lt. Gerald Zelikosky (Selig)
   2nd Lt. Ralph H. Hall
Luftwaffe Fighter Pilot 239
   Col. Douglas Pitcairn
Bits and Pieces 249
   Capt. Clarence Schuchmann
   W/O Allen Yates (RAF)
B-17s Lost by 457th Bomb Group in WWII 269

Introduction

The contents of this book are, for the most part, composed of first-person stories by 457th Bomb Group, B-17 aircrew members of the 8th Air Force who were shot down and became casualties of aerial combat over occupied Europe and Germany during World War II. Included also is supporting information taken from the records of the 457th BG concerning the combat mission—the track chart narrative—on which the crewman was determined to be a casualty. Also included are eye witness accounts, by other B-17 crewmen flying on the same mission, of what they thought happened to the missing crew, as told to intelligence officers during critique back at the base after a mission.

Research by the author of the records of the 457th Bomb Group reveals that from 21 February 1944 through 20 April 1945, during 236 combat missions, ninety-one aircraft were lost directly to enemy action and did not return to base. Of this number, seventy-two aircraft were lost over enemy territory. Nineteen other aircraft either ditched in the English Channel/North Sea, landed in liberated Europe(after D-day), or were interned in the neutral countries, of Sweden or Switzerland. A list of these crews and the date of their loss is included. Many of the lost and missing crews will be further identified in the first person stories related by a member of the crew. The author wrote a letter of invitation to at least one member of each crew for which he had a name and address. Some crewmen declined to answer the invitation; however, over forty stories have been compiled and are part of this book. Needless to say, the book is an incomplete history of the lost and missing crews of the 457th Bomb Group.

In an attempt to provide the reader with some information about WWII from the German viewpoint, a chapter is included which was provided by a German Luftwaffe fighter pilot who fought against the American bomber crews. To him I express my appreciation for this information.

The author wishes to thank those men who provided the narratives which made this book possible. Each person who provided a story has been identified with the story. Photographs of the lost and missing crews and aircraft are included where they could be obtained. Appreciation is here extended to Wayne Zemper, group photography officer, for the photographs he provided, without which this book would be a lesser publication.

To Homer and Mickey Briggs, of Bentonville, Arkansas, who have dedicated a large part of their lives to nurturing the 457th Bomb Group Association, I express my appreciation for their help in providing a sounding board for many of this author's efforts. To Irving Lewis, go thanks for the compiled track chart narratives, which were very useful in imbellishing this publication.

A special thanks to Ms. Kathy Probosco, who edited the authors' often garbled phrases, making them a more intelligible offering.

Appreciation is also extended to the English members of the FOTE (Friends of the Eighth) who have contributed so much to the success of the 457th Bomb Group Association; Bernard Bains, John Wilson, Gordon Townsend, George Townsend, John Walker and Eric Brumbry.

It is hoped by the author that this collection of stories has provided for the reader and for posterity, a descriptive picture of how the American youth faced death during World War II, without regard for their own well- being, to provide the opportunity for future generations to be born into a free society. Considering there has not been a major war in over forty five years, this effort has considerable credibility. This statement does not purport to minimize the service and valor of those veterans who fought in the Korean and Vietnam Wars. The author was recalled from civilian life at considerable sacrifice to a professional career and served in the Air Force during the Korean War.

Prelude

Dawn forces its way almost furtively through the grey mist hovering over the 'Fens' of East Anglia. The mist wets down the 'tarmac' hardstands as well as the dispersed B-17 bombers squatting expectantly on them. The lingering darkness is shouldered away by the sun's emanations, ever so slowly during the long days of June 1944, at 52 degrees 27' 53" north latitude. The sun rises as a huge orange orb to the southeast, at a time when the hour hand points to the wee hours of the clock and seems to roll along the flat unbroken horizon that surrounds the 'Fens.'

The ghosts of a phalanx of Roman soldiers, which sixteen centuries earlier (circa 43 to 400 AD) strode to the count of cadence..uno..due..tre..quattro.. ...hut...hut...hut...hut... along the rock-paved Great North Road connecting Londinium (London), north to Hadrians Wall, can be imagined on such a misty morning in this ancient civilization. The now 'tarmac'-covered road forms the western boundary of this mile-square United States Army Air Force base in England that is named for the nearby village of Glatton. The Air Force designation for the base is Station 130.

But the pastoral setting does not contravene the purpose of the drama that is unfolding on the air base, as a swarm of O.D. (olive drab) clothed soldiers, the unheralded maintenance, supply, and service personnel, enlisted men, and officers of the 457th Bombardment Group (H), of the United States Air Force, scurry about and ready the instruments of war — the four engine heavy bombers — for a grisley "FLIGHT TO ETERNITY" in the German Reich.

The relative quiet is broken by a cacophony of sounds, including the intermittent, staccato backfires of a cold Wright Cyclone R-1820-97 radial air-cooled engine, four of which power the B-17 'Flying Fortress' that the crew chief is attempting to start. He and the three-man crew have spent the better part of the sleepless night working on the engine and they expectantly listen, hoping their dedicated efforts have not been futile. The engine alternately backfires and runs, smoke and flame curling out of the

Glatton AAB—457th Bomb Group

blackened exhaust stack. A fatigue suit (coverall) clad member of the maintenance crew stands nearby with a fire extinguisher at ready, in case the primed 100 octane gasoline erupts into excessive flame and ignites the gasoline and the ever-present leaking oil and hydraulic fluid, along with the non-metallic components of the engine, or possibly even the airplane itself.

The day begins like hundreds of others for the B-17 and B-24 bomber ground and flight crews of the United States Army Air Force, since the first heavy bomber mission to Rouen-Sotteville in German-occupied France on 17 August 1942.

The young bomber flight crews selected to complete the 'impersonal' manning list, necessary to fly the airplanes which the 457th Bombardment Group must 'put up' for the day's mission, as mandated by the 8th Air Force commanded by Lieut. Gen. James

Doolittle, are awakened from sleep on their cold, biscuit-mattressed steel cots by duty officers and NCOs, four hours before the mission is scheduled to take off.

The men who make up the flight crews have slept fitfully during the night, knowing 'their' crew had been alerted and would fly on the next day's mission. The evening before the day of the mission some crewmen had written, on v-mail stationery, prophetic words of apprehension to their wives, girl friends or relatives. Others wrote only of their sterile non-military coming and going in a strange land among people with strange habits, never alluding to the fear and apprehension which 'gripped their guts,' not wanting to tell the truth about the danger. Not all flight crewmen spent their time writing letters, for some attempted to drown their fears by consuming alcohol of any brand, be it 'arf 'n arf,' orange gin, Irish whiskey, or white lightning, for cold beer, bourbon, or common stateside products were hard to obtain. Yet others turned to religion for strength and guidance. Whatever the means of attempted escape from the suppressed fear and apprehension, it was not allayed until the mission was 'on' and the assigned duties necessary to pilot the plane, plot the course, arm the bombs, man the guns, and monitor the radio pushed aside the fears. Anger was not the usual stimulus which 'pumped' adrenalin, rather it was fear and apprehension which motivated the flight crewman in this detached non-contact environment of air combat, where the man did not see the killing and destruction caused by the bomb blast, or even the death of an enemy fighter pilot. While some crewmen were killed while flying missions, there were only a few crewmen who ever saw death unless they were shot down.

There is, by those who make up a bomber crew, a feeling of need to appear intrepid, even in the face of possible death. Few men succumb to the fear which engulfs them as they face the lurking spectre of death. Whether it was the need for them to perform well for the family back home in the States, his buddy in the bunk next to his, or the comradery as a member of a close-knit bomber crew. A man feels he must do his best to perform his duties to the best of his ability. There are very few situations in life where the individual is as dedicated to a group as are the members of the crew of a bomber in combat.

There are, however, those men whose neurological makeup could not cope with the daily deluge of pressure on their psyche. These men did not 'measure up,' could not perform their assigned duties under combat stress and were 'grounded'-relieved of their flying duties and reassigned to other duties, usually at a location other than where they had been flying. As far as the author knows, none were executed for exhibiting cowardice under fire. The rules were somewhat different in the world of aerial warfare than in the ground forces where 'don't fire until you see the whites of their eyes' almost demands that cowards be court-martialled and possibly shot.

A particular bombardier was assigned to fly with Lt. Robert Krumm's crew of which the author was a member. During the mission, while under head-on attacks by German fighters, the man repeatedly failed to return fire with the chin-turret because of paralyzing fear, displaying cowardice in the face of the enemy. Needless to say, that bombardier, who shall go un-named, did not fly any more missions with Lt. Robert Krumm's crew. A crew member who has displayed cowardice is viewed by other members of the crew as if he were afflicted with the 'plague' and is an outcast. The feeling is that if I must face death every day, I will not associate with anyone who is afraid to do the same.

A bomber crew was made up of all nature of men, technically trained at the many schools operated by the Army Air Force. As in the case of any mass selection from the general population, some men performed their duties well, while others were incompetent. The schools 'washed out,' eliminated, from their program those who did not perform satisfactorily. However, very little psychological testing was done to determine how a man would perform his duties under the stress of combat. Many crews, including that to which the author was assigned, completed their required number of missions—a tour—with different personnel than that with which they began even disregarding the physical casualties of aerial combat.

The stories listed hereafter are told by men who experienced the extremes of aerial combat during bombing missions over Germany and occupied countries, were 'blooded,' and 'met the test.' While many of us experienced the onslaughts of the German Luftwaffe fighters and flew through flak 'you could walk on,' we returned to base after each mission and did so repeatedly to complete a number of missions to satisfy the theatre 'tour' requirement. It was those who were shot up badly, or were shot down and taken as prisoners of war, that experienced the extremes of the rigors of aerial combat and participated in a 'FLIGHT TO ETERNITY.' Many men died on these flights and it is up to those who survived to tell their story.

Although the articles of the Geneva Convention supposedly protected those who parachuted to earth from a disabled aircraft, men were killed by being beaten to death by infuriated civilians. It was usually the German military who protected the American airmen, if they arrived on the scene before civilians had a chance to vent their anger and frustration. These people had on that day watched their homes destroyed, and their relatives and friends killed by the men who were shot down. Because we were aware of this danger from civilians, many airmen carried a .45 cal. automatic pistol in a shoulder holster when flying on missions. Although it is possible that the possession of a gun may have caused the death of some men, it also saved some lives. The author always carried the weapon while flying on a combat mission, feeling that the advantages outweighed the disadvantages. Capture and subsequent incarceration in a German prison camp for the duration of the war was often the least agonizing result for the crew of a shot-down aircraft. Often some of the crew were killed and others badly wounded. Those who were wounded depended on the enemy to put aside their idealogical differences and treat their wounds. In many cases the treatment was humane, while in others the dead are silent. Some German physicians treated medically and did perform surgery on men which was as professional as they would have treated their own countrymen.

Flying through a barrage of flak 'you could walk on.'

Fighters at 4 o'clock.

Nose Insignia

457th Bomb Group
Mission No. 53
28 May 1944

Target — Dessau Junkers Aircraft
jet engine factory

Crew of the B-17G No. 42-96067 'Black Puff Polly'

1st Pilot	2nd Lt.	Rudolph M. Stohl	
Co-Pilot	2nd Lt.	David W. Schellenger	
Nav.	2nd Lt.	John O. Millham	
Bomb.	2nd Lt.	James E. Thomas	
Engr.	T/Sgt.	Robert C. Kriete	
Radio Op.	T/Sgt.	Walter W. Wagoner	KIA
LW Gun.	S/Sgt.	Irvin A. Welling	
RW Gun.	S/Sgt.	William F. Bemus	
B. Turret	S/Sgt.	Sheldon E. Moore	
Tail Gun.	S/Sgt.	Charles L. Stewart	

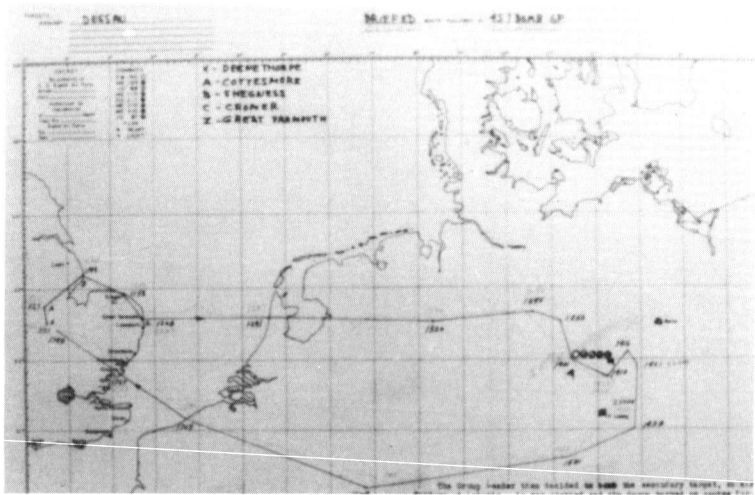

Track Chart, Mission No. 53, 28 May 1944.

457th Bomb Group Mission Narrative

With the first good visual bombing weather since May 12th and 13th, the 8th Air Force today resumed its campaign to destroy German synthetic oil production. Rotheinsee, Lutzkendorf, Luena, Ruhland, and Zeitz-Troglitz were targets for twelve CBW's while three CBW's, including the 94th were assigned the parent Junkers aero engine and aircraft factory at Dessau. The works was primarily engaged in the design of new aircraft and was turning out jet propulsion units. This target has the highest priority of all the remaining targets of this type.

The 457th formation led by Major Hozier in a PFF (radar) ship took off at 1030 hours to form the lead box of the 94th CBW. After assembly the formation made its penetration of the enemy's territory through Holland across northern Germany, the common route for all fifteen CBW's in today's aerial assault. The 94th was the last CBW in the 1st division formation. The flight was uneventful until a point northeast of Brunswick had been passed where the fifteen wings took up separate courses, in a south-easterly direction, to their various targets. As the 457th Group approached its I.P. near Magdeburg it was attacked again and again by large forces of both single and twin engine fighters. First an enmasse saturation attack was made by about 50 Me-109's and FW-190's. Lt. Clyde B. Knipfer, No. 6 in the low squadron dropped out of the formation with No. 1 engine burning. He was last seen several thousand feet below, under control, flying a course toward

England. At least four other B-17's from the low and high groups went down in the first fighter attack. A second mass frontal attack was made and then waves of Ju-88's and Me-109's attacked from the side firing cannons, followed immediately by the Me-109's and FW-190's. Lt. Rudolph M. Stohl's plane was hit and he was last seen lagging behind the formation. Other planes in the high and low groups went down. There was no friendly fighter escort in the immediate vicinity. The enemy had thrown in his fighters, 200 in number, at what he believed to be the weakest link in the chain of bomber wings, at a time when the fighter escort was spread out the most. It occurred at a time when the wing formation had separated to reach their assigned targets. The 94th CBW for the second successive day bore the brunt of the German fighter attacks. Twelve of its planes were lost in this 20-minute attack. Our gunners fought back savagely spending 42,000 rounds of ammunition (.50 cal.) and claiming 14 enemy fighters destroyed. One man was killed by a 20mm shell, S/Sgt. Harry Bernstein, engineer on Lt. Brackley's crew. During these attacks the formation took up the bomb run but Dessau was obscured by thick haze and industrial smoke. The lead bombardier, Lt. Fast, was unable to pick up the Junkers works until they had passed the BRL. The low box dropped into the smoke and haze and the high box salvoed their bombs when the leader had to jettison his.

The 457th then made a wide circle to the left and came back over the target a second time, with anti-aircraft bursts enveloping the formation. The target could not be picked up again. In the meantime the low squadron dropped its bombs when the lead of the high squadron salvoed his. The lead bombardier in this plane, Lt. Gides, had received a wound in the head by a .303 machine gun bullet.

The group leader then decided to bomb the secondary target, an aircraft factory in Leipzig. The target was sighted and the group turned on course for a two-minute bomb run. The six planes in the group that still had bombs dropped them in the western edge of the target area.

By this time there was friendly fighter cover and the formation took up a heading for home, after having spent 30 minutes in the target area.

A fire developed in Lt. Emanuel Hauf's No. 4 engine which burned all the way back to the English Channel coast. There he left the formation as if to ditch. Lt. Green B. Poore went with him. At about 10,000 feet Lt. Hauf's wing exploded and broke off. The plane went into a spin, hit the water and exploded. No chutes were seen. The rest of the formation arrived at the base at 1750 hours.

Two hours later Lt. Conners, who had been given up for lost, came limping in with one engine functioning properly. Two engines had burned out in the target area and three cylinders in the third had been punctured by enemy fire. He had dropped out of formation, thrown everything possible out of the airplane on any convenient German town and flew all the way home at 12,000 feet at an airspeed of 115-135 m.p.h.

Only 50 out of 296 planes in the 1st division were able to attack their primary targets, due to the poor visibility and fighter attacks. One thousand and twenty-seven heavy bombers were dispatched, including one wing, glider bombing the Cologne M/Y, but only 863 had attacked thirty-two had failed to return to base.

S/Sgt. William F. Bemus' story of the 28 May 1944 mission to Dessau, Germany.

"This was my nineteenth mission and it was flown in the silver B-17, 'Black Puff Polly/Georgia Peach,' A/C Number 42-97067. 'Black Puff Polly' was the second airplane our crew had been assigned. Our first B-17G was an olive drab (o.d.) camouflaged airplane which we had flown overseas from the States. We had landed in Ireland for gasoline and then flown on to the air base at Glatton. We had named our first plane, 'What's Next?'

"Well anyhow, we flew about eight or nine missions to Germany in 'What's Next?' and then were assigned the silver, no camouflage, airplane.

"Well I'll tell you what. — Whoooeee! — I never will forget that day. It was on a Sunday, the 28th of May 1944. The target was the Focke Wulf-190 aircraft factory in Dessau, Germany. I was the right waist gunner and also the assistant engineer. Well, on that day I switched positions with the engineer, T/Sgt. Robert C. Kriete, who normally operated the top turret. As the assistant engineer, I was qualified to operate the top turret. Well, as you know, you always test fire the guns when you fly over the North Sea or English Channel. Well, I test fired the two guns in the turret and in doing so found out the left .50 cal. gun was not firing! I checked the turret over and it seemed the solenoid on the right gun was not working correctly. On our previous missions we had not had much trouble with Luftwaffe fighters, so I told the pilot, Lt. Stohl, "Let's go to war anyway." There was nothing we could do about the gun without some new parts, which we did not have with us. So we followed the formation back there in our assigned position 'Tail End Charlie.'

"Well, if I remember right, we had some P-38's and some P-51's escorting us into Germany that day, and if I'm not mistaken the P-51s were supposed to pick us up after the P-38s turned for home. Well, we were heading for the I.P., when the fighters hit us! There was a cloud bank over to our left and—well, I want to tell you something! I had never seen as many enemy fighters in my life as came out of that cloud bank! As the old saying goes; 'They looked like bumblebees boiling up out of the nest!' I had seen Luftwaffe fighters before and had been in a couple of good fights, one was over Schweinfurt, where we got into one hell of a battle. But I want to tell you, I had never before seen the likes of fighters out there in front of us! There were Me-109's, FW-190's, JU-88's Me-110's and Me-210's and I don't know what else. Well, you know our fighter cover had left and—I remember this as well as the day is long. The old co-pilot, Lt.David W Schellenger, was saying, 'Here they come, conserve your ammo, conserve your ammo.' Well, anyway here they came, headed right for us, all lined up shootin' white puff balls at us! [Ed. 20mm cannon bursts] There was an Me-109 came at us, I could see the flashes of the guns firing along the leading edge of the wings and, as you know, they were all bunched up. Well, I had only that right .50 cal. working, oh man, how I wished I'd a' had that left '50' workin', cause you know how that Sperry sight jumps up and down anyway. Boy, when you get one gun pulling the turret to the right and with the sight jumpin', its hard to hold the sight on a 'bandit.' In other words, you've got hell! Anyway, there was nothing I could do about it but do the best I could. Well anyway, here came that old Me-109—we gave him hell, boy! I'll tell you, he trailed out and down, just a' smokin'. Well, then an old Focke Wulf came in hot dang, he came barrellin' straight in at us. Well, we hit him and, well, he just went ass over tea kettle! I don't think he ever knew what hit him!

"Well, at about two o'clock high, there was an Me-210 that came at us, and I mean he really came in! And he hit us head on! He was the old boy that put us out of commission. I'm going to tell you something, Col. Byers, I'm going to tell the story the way I remember it. And I always stick to this way: What I am referring to is the way the engines were operating after the Me-210 shot us up. Lt. Stohl says he does not remember exactly what happened, but our difference of opinion is concerning the two engines on the one side of the airplane. But here goes anyway. Well, anyway that old Me-210 came at us and I'm rakin' him with that one .50 it would drift off to the right and I would pull it back and he hit our No. 3

and No. 4 engines on the right side of the airplane with 20mm fire! He also blew a big hole in the side of the airplane just behind me! I can remember the air, just whistlin' in. I didn't get hit with any of the shrapnel but the shock of the explosion dropped the tail wheel down (I learned this later). The co-pilot feathered the propeller on No. 3 engine but he could not get the propeller on No. 4 feathered and it continued to windmill. Well, I don't need to tell you, if you have ever been in a ship like that, you know how they 'somp' and 'balk,' and they drag some. Whooeee...like I said, we were in the lower right hand corner of the formation — Tail End Charlie — and I think we were the first plane to be hit! Ooooh, man! There were a lot of fighters hittin' those bombers! I don't know whether I shot a flare or not; you know there are some red flares up there in the top turret to shoot, when you are in trouble. Anyhow, that old Me-210 really hit us hard, that old ship just rocked. Well the Me-210 went straight up and behind us — well, I know I followed him up, shooting at him with that one .50. I turned the turret around and was giving him all I could get out of that one .50 — pouring it to him. That Me-210 went up, circled around and headed for us again! I lined him up and started shooting at him again. Then he peeled off to the right and I don't know if he followed the other bombers or not. I lost him and I don't know why he gave up on us, because we were sure a wounded duck! We had dropped out of formation and were floundering out there in no-man's land, all by our lonesome. He must have run out of ammunition or was getting low on gasoline, for we didn't see him again. Well, we were in bad shape, with only the two engines on the left side running and the wind whistling through the big hole behind me. I had not noticed the temperature as long as the fighters were after us, but now I could feel the cold.

"Now that we were not being shot at, the pilot talked with the bombardier, Lt. James E. Thomas, and they decided to drop the bombs to get rid of all that weight, and possibly we could make it back to base on the two engines. The bomb bay doors were opened and the bombs were dropped; however, they would not close. Kriete and I got together in the bomb bay and tried to crank the doors closed but we could not budge them. Of course the open bomb bay doors put a lot of drag on the airplane, but we could do nothing about it."

"Then Lt. Stohl gave the order to lighten the ship by throwing out everything that was loose. We threw out the flak suits, the guns and ammunition, and also dropped the ball-turret. Well, the old girl was still losing altitude. 'Black Puff Polly' was a' goin' down!

"I remember the intercom was all shot to pieces because I had to

S/Sgt. William F. Bemus

crawl down through the hatchway into the nose to ask the navigator, Lt. John O. Millham, for a heading to give to the pilot. Later, Lt. Millham would stand up and look back at the pilot through the celestial dome and motion to the pilot the direction to go. Well, I'll tell you, we were losing altitude and to tell you the truth, we were getting awfully low but I wasn't looking at the altimeter. For a time everything was real quiet — and I'll tell you something, up to then no one had a scratch on him, even though there had been a lot of lead thrown at us! Well, we kept flying, 'limping in', so to speak. Well, we flew over Bremen and with the bomb bay doors open, I suppose they thought we were about to bomb them. Oooweee! All hell broke loose again! Man, we got into some awful flak. That's where the radio operator, T/Sgt. Walter W. Wagoner, was killed. I was up on the flight deck behind the pilot, and heard a big explosion, and was later told that an anti-aircraft shell exploded right in the radio room. Some of the control cables to the rear of the airplane were cut and the pilots had almost no control of the airplane! I want you to know they were flakin' that airplane something awful! And they were throwing up everything they could get loose! Then there was an explosion right under No. 3 engine, the one that had been windmilling, and the propeller on the engine just dropped off! The pilot's windshield was also blown out on the left side. Hot damn! I never will forget that, the old wind was really 'whistlin' Dixie' through the airplane. Hey, I remember that as if it had been yesterday! When that happened, Lt. Stohl rang the bail out bell. Old 'Black Puff Polly' was a' comin' apart! She was a' goin' down!

"The engineer and I headed down through the crawlway to the nose hatch and I opened the hatch — I never will forget the old nose hatch. Well, as I said, I opened the hatch and looked down and noticed I had my chute snapped on backwards. I had a little old chest chute on, you know? I am right handed and I had the pull cord handle to the left. So I motioned for the engineer to jump as I was changing the chute end for end. Old Lt. John O. Millham, the navigator, he came out of the nose, and I could see John O. — I always called him John O. — had been hit! Blood was running down over his face! He was bleeding pretty good! He had been hit in the forehead by a piece of flak, when the shell exploded under the No. 3 engine. (I later learned the wound was a flesh wound and had not fractured his skull. He told me he remembered he had heard a hell of an explosion and something hitting him in the head that really made the spark's fly.)

"Well, Kriete, Millham, and Thomas all bailed out and there I was trying to change the chute. Kriete was hollerin' for me to jump but I kept motioning to my chute. That wasn't all though, for— Hey! Hey! That was the hardest thing I have ever done in my life, was to leave that airplane! Even though she was a' comin' apart. This was my home and, besides, I had never jumped out of anything before! Well, I knew I had to go. I had changed my chute around and just as I went through the hatch there was a big explosion and a piece of flak hit me in the back, about — it turned out — an inch to the right side of my spine and about three inches up from the crack in my butt. Well, I'll tell you, it went through me and came out my left groin! Wowee! I was glad the old chute straps were holdin' the 'family jewels' away from harm! Oh, man! that piece of flak tore a hell of a' hole in me! Everything was happening so fast, the only thing I remember was just a burning sensation! Well, I had jumped out and I guess it was a good thing I had changed my chute around, because when I dove out underneath that plane, the slip stream from the No. 2 engine hit me and I was wearing my little good luck overseas cap and I remember it a' flyin' away. Then I went underneath the tail plane and when I pulled the handle of the rip-cord, the chute didn't open! What happened was the little old pilot chute popped out and just 'set there' and went 'flop, ---- flop, ---- flop, ---- flop, flop! I never will forget that! Boy! I forgot all about the pain in my butt and grabbed the pilot chute and began jerking! I gave it a good jerk and the main chute popped open! Well, I looked down and — hot damn! — the old blood was a' runnin.' I was bleeding bad!

"Well, I'll tell you, as I drifted down, some German soldiers on the ground were shooting at me! Those bullets were coming up by me! — I'll never forget that! — zip!--zip!--zip!-- Well, on top of it all, I looked up and there came old 'Black Puff Polly.' She was circling. Now if I remember correctly, the No. 2 engine had stopped. Now this is my version of what happened. There I was floating in the chute and I looked up and I saw old 'Black Puff Polly' turning toward me. 'Oh my God!' I thought, 'here I am all shot full of holes, over Germany, and my old ship is going to run over me!' She just kept coming at me. Woweee! And when I was just about to start counting beads, she was only about a' hundred yards away. Then she straightened out and flew away as straight as an arrow! I don't know where she crashed.

"Now my attention came back to those bullets that were still flyin' around me! I guess I'll always remember one thing. Old Hotaling [Ed. — Capt. Monroe J. Hotaling, Group Gunnery Officer, who was KIA on 10 April 1945 on a flight to Berlin] had told me; 'One thing about bailing out at high altitude, let her go, boy, let her go! until you get down to where the oxygen will sustain you. Another thing: Those civilians, and sometimes the soldiers, will shoot at you. If they do, slump in your harness and act like you have been hit!' Well, those bullets were just missing me! That's all I needed was another hole in me! So I slumped in my chute and glory be! It must have worked, for they quit shooting at me. Well, I looked down and saw I was heading for the cemetery by a church. In it were some of those big old tombstones, they have some of those big 'jobbers' over there. I thought I was going to hit one of them! Anyway, we had been taught how to steer our chute, to spill air out of one side of the chute and to drift in that direction. I saw this opening, it was right in front of the church, so I steered the chute and came down right in the opening. Remember, it was Sunday and all the people in the church came outside when they heard all the ruckus. That was the ugliest, meanest, bunch of 'Christians,' I've ever seen in my life! Well, I'll tell you, they came out of the church and circled around me! Man! They had clubs and rocks and anything they could pick up! They were spittin' and throwing rocks at me and one fellow yelling and making motions to hang me! You know, we, on occasion, carried our .45 pistol with us when flying missions, but I didn't carry mine, but I reached inside my flying suit and made a motion like I was about to pull one out. This, I found out, would back them up. I was afraid they would grab me, and it's hard to say what they would have done to me.

"About that time a Catholic nun came over to me and she gave me some kind of a pill. I never will forget that. She also backed the people up away from me. I spit the pill out, not knowing what it was. An SS officer showed up about that time, and he came over to me and stuck his old Lugar pistol against my head and said in English, 'pistol,' 'pistol,' I opened up my flying suit and showed him that I did not have a pistol. Well, he searched through my heated flying suit and my fatigue suit and found my escape kit, with money, morphine and maps in it. He took all of that and motioned to a big old German soldier—he was an ugly son of a gun—to load me in a horse-drawn wagon which they had brought up. This soldier was laughing and said something like, 'sheisen.' Well I knew I had been gut-shot, you know, and now I could smell it. I was still bleeding all over the place and I told him I was gut-shot. Then, that 'big ugly' grinning corporal hit me—hot damn!—and then he slapped me across the face. I think he broke my nose, but, I'll tell you what, I shut up after that."

"The wagon they brought up (this is my version of the story) they pulled the wagon up beside me, and a civilian picked me up by the feet and the 'big ugly' grabbed me by the collar and they threw me over the side-boards, into the wagon. Boy! I hit the bottom of the wagon hard, the blood just flew! Well, there in the wagon was old John O. Millham, the navigator! He had broken his leg when he parachuted down and had hit one of those big old tombstones in the cemetery. He also had that flesh wound in his forehead—more superficial than anything—however, it was still bleeding.

"Well, I told him, 'John O. I'm gut shot, and damn! I'm bleeding bad! and I don't think I'm gonna' make it!' I'll always remember that. John O. put his arm around me and said, 'Bemus, you're going to be all right, just hang in there.' And I said 'Damn, I'm bleedin', damn, I'm bleedin'.' Years later we met at a 457th BG reunion and I said to him, 'I sure was bleeding badly.' And he said, 'I know you were and before long you were lying in a pool of blood and I really thought you would bleed to death!'

"Anyhow, they threw us in this old, high-sided, horse-drawn wagon, the old civilian and the 'big ugly,' and they took us to a little old Luftwaffe base. I was told about this later. There was a

German doctor there; I do remember that. He was a Luftwaffe doctor. He looked at me and he got some bandages and he put them between my legs where I was shot through the groin. There was a hydrant nearby — I never will forget this, as long as I live — with a tin cup hanging on it. I kept motioning toward the water and he said, 'Nein' 'Nein.' Well, naturally with a gut shot wound like I had, I didn't need any water! After I persisted, he finally motioned for an aide, to bring me a little water. Well, he probably thought I was not going to make it anyway, so he handed me the water. I gulped it down and asked for more and he said; 'Nein' 'Nein.' Later they loaded John O. and me up in an old ambulance. If I'm not mistaken, the ambulance came from the hospital to which we were taken — St. Joseph's Catholic Hospital. They had no more than loaded us up than an air raid siren wailed. It had been raining and the ambulance slipped off of the road and got stuck. I said, 'Holy cow, that is all I need, here I am all shot to hell and trying to get to the hospital, and we have an air raid.' The driver managed to get the ambulance out of the mud and away we went. Things got a little foggy for me about this time, for I was conscious only part of the time, but we did go to St. Joseph's Hospital in Bremen. There was a doctor there — Captain Barteles was his name. He was a German military officer, a big old guy, and I understand he had taught surgery at a medical school, for the people referred to him as Professor Barteles. He was the doctor who operated on me. He performed a colostomy on me, and I remember going in and out of consciousness while the operation was being performed. I do not know what anesthetic I was given. It was not a spinal and I don't know whether or not it was ether. I did, at one time, remember looking down and the doctor was working on my stomach. What had happened was the piece of flak had hit me in the back and gone through the lower part of my rectum and among other things had cut the sphincter muscle, and then gone out through my groin.

"I heard this later from John O. Millham. The doctor had said to him that he would be all right. 'You have only a flesh wound on your forehead and your broken leg should mend all right. But your friend here, probably will not make it through the night! He has lost so much blood and I am not permitted to give blood to prisoners because it is very scarce.' Well, it was more than 40 years before I learned that diagnosis!

"Like I said, I fooled them! I never did have a transfusion or have any intravenous feeding at any time. Well, as the old saying goes: being nineteen years old and full of piss and vinegar, I made it. "They kept me at St. Joseph's Hospital for nearly four months and then transferred me to Dulag Luft where I was interrogated as were all prisoners. The interrogator at one time said to me, 'I guess you know that S/Sgt. Wagoner, the radio operator, had been killed?' I guess I must have jumped when he said that, and he knew that I was a member of that crew. They kept asking me a lot of different things. There were two interrogaters questioning me, both psychiatrists, and they spoke perfect English. You wouldn't have known they were German. The only thing I told them was my serial number: 18189010 and that my name was William F. Bemus. Finally they told me that Wagoner had been killed, and I knew then that they knew more than I did about the loss of 'Black Puff Polly.'

"From Dulag Luft they sent me to a hospital in Nienburg and from there to a hospital at Annaburg. I was repatriated through Switzerland to Marseilles, France, loaded on the Swedish ship, 'Gripsholm,' and sailed for the good old USA, all courtesy of the International Red Cross.

"I landed in New York City on the 20th of February 1945 and was sent to Brooks General Hospital, San Antonio, Texas. There they operated on me again and put the old pipes back together again.

"Lt. John O. Millham was patched up and sent to prison camp. I did not see any of the crew again, but they were all captured and sent to prison except the radio operator, Wagoner."

S/Sgt Sheldon E. Moore's story of the 28 May 1944 mission to Dessau, Germany.

Our crew had just been assigned a ship which so far was just a number and as did most crews we were casting about for a suitable name for her. One night we sneaked off the base like all 'good soldiers' and visited a nearby 'pub' for a little relaxation and refreshment. The 'pub' was located in a residence along the 'Great North Road' which ran along the west side of our airbase and led to Peterborough, 8 miles to the north. In the little 'pub' were some games—darts and draughts—and a piano, along with the usual warm, 'mild and bitters,' the excuse the English sold for beer, which, surprisingly, I liked. I didn't like bubbles in beer.

The radio operator on our crew, T/Sgt Walter W. Wagoner, who in civilian life had been a 'disk jockey,' often played the piano for our entertainment. He would play and spontaneously make up songs. On this night, after a few draughts of 'bitters,' Wagoner started playing and singing;

Mission No. 53

> Black Puff Polly flies again,
> Ee-I, Ee-I, O.
> Black Puff Polly flies again,
> Ee-I, Ee-I, O.
> With a black puff here
> And a black puff there,
> Here a puff, there a puff,
> Every where a black puff.
> Black Puff Polly flies again,
> Ee-I, Ee-I, O.

Wagoner made up many verses, describing machine guns, fighters, bombs, and crew members. After a time during which we had temporarily forgotten about the horrors of war, we reluctantly remembered we had been alerted to fly the following day and we headed back toward the base. On the way back to base, tripping over our feet, barbed wire, and 'sloshing' through the perpetual mud, we decided we would christen our new airplane 'Black Puff Polly.' A day or so later we managed to 'scrounge' some paint, black and yellow, and I painted on the nose of the airplane a big, black burst of flak and inside the burst, the words, in yellow doughnut-shaped letters, 'Black Puff Polly.'

Ironically the symbolism was precursory of what would be the ultimate fate of the plane and crew in the not too distant future. Thinking later about the name, I would have named the plane something like 'Go Gettem' for the only man on the crew to die was T/Sgt. Wilbur W. Wagoner, who was the man who really named her.

When we went down, the plane had first fallen into a spin and, as we learned later, had recovered from the spin without a pilot's help, as all the crew in the forward part of the plane had bailed out. Those of us in the back were not aware they had jumped and thought we were 'sailing along' on the way home. We were saying, "Oh boy, we will have steak in England tonight."

About that time an 88mm anti-aircraft shell exploded in the bomb bay/radio room and Wagoner was killed. Black smoke from the explosion filled the airplane. Shrapnel hit me in the head and face, as well as it did Irvin Welling, the left waist gunner there with me. I could see that Wagoner's clothes were on fire, and also see that the lower part of his torso had been emasculated. I grabbed a fire extinguisher and tried to put out the fire but my efforts were fruitless, as he was already dead. I yelled to Welling to jump, while I tried to pull Wagoner's body over to the hole in the airplane where the ball turret had been, but I couldn't budge him. The plane fell into a spin again and it took all my strength to push myself free of the spinning plane, out through the ball turret hole. I pulled the ripcord, of my chest chute and felt the upward jerk as the canopy opened but I did not see the chute opening as my feet hit the ground almost immediately. I was 'scrunched' downward, my head below my knees, by the force of hitting the ground so hard. My flying boots had flown off my feet when the chute opened, had hit the ground, and bounced nearly 40 feet from me. I was dazed by the shock and ended up flat on my back. My chute was still inflated and was pulling me backwards along the ground. I attempted to get up and 'shuck' my parachute harness, oblivious of what was going on around me. As I scrambled to my feet, I became aware of a soldier pointing a rifle at a location between my eyes. I had landed in the middle of four 88mm anti-aircraft guns. We were in a field on the outskirts of Bremen and I heard my captor say, "Halten Sie Soldaten," or something in that order. While I did not know anything about the German language, I raised my hands over my head, as the voice was commanding and the intent was obvious. I was directed over to a little guard-post house, where they sat me down and a ground Luftwaffe sergeant cut the hair away from my head wounds and wiped the blood from my face with a wet cloth. He then handed me a glass of beer from a barrel in the corner of the room. I looked at the sergeant and asked him, "Do you have a cigarette?" I was still in shock from my experience and was not really cogent — the sergeant looked at me for quite a while and then reached inside his blouse and took out a cigarette, lit it, and handed it to me.

Later I learned that the German soldiers were rationed — limited — to two cigarettes each day. He had given me, an enemy, one-half of his daily ration of cigarettes.

After I had finished smoking the cigarette, another Luftwaffe soldier motioned for me to follow him. We walked over to a nearby GI truck that was waiting on the road. I climbed into the back of the truck and there in the truck were six other members of my crew: pilot, co-pilot, bombardier, engineer, tail gunner and waist gunner. We were taken to an air base, which was in shambles as it had been recently bombed by our airplanes. Strangely this was the second time I had been involved with the air base as I had been on the bombing raid that had bombed the base. I would later, during the 'Black Hunger March,' return to this same base when I escaped from Stalag 357 and was making my way west to the Allied lines. That would make three times I would have something to do with the base.

From Bremen Air Base we were taken by train to Vetslar, a staging depot where prisoners of war were separated, (non-commissioned officers and commissioned officers) and sent to different prison camps.

We were all sent to Dulag Luft for interrogation and then assigned to our permanent camp. I was sent to Stalag Luft No. 4. We traveled by train through Berlin and northeastward to Grosstichow, a small railroad station near our camp. The camp was located geographically about 30 kilometers south of the Baltic Sea and one hundred and twenty kilometers west of the Polish border.

From the railroad station we were marched for 8 miles, to a new 'virgin' camp. We were the first POW's assigned to the camp. We were alphabetically assigned to barracks and I was in the second room in the second barracks in the compound. Twenty-four prisoners with names beginning with M through P were assigned to my room. There were four compounds in the camp, however there were no prisoners at the time in the other compounds. Later the compound next to ours was filled with Russian prisoners. Eventually all the compounds were filled with prisoners.

We were shot down on 28 May 1944 and for the first three months, during the summer, it was warm and it wasn't so bad not to have enough to eat. We usually had a bowl of lentils or a few — three — small potatoes, once a day. We did not receive any Red Cross packages until fall. The rumor making the rounds of the compound was that the Germans were treating the Americans better than anyone else because the war wasn't going well for the Germans. Whether that was true or not I don't know. But for a time we were receiving one Red Cross package each week. We also received some books and some musical instruments.

The first Red Cross packages to arrive contained sweaters, pants, shirts, sox, soap, tooth brushes, combs, razors and cascarra tablets. We made balls out of the unraveled sweater yarn and bats out of bed slats. Teams were formed of men from each barracks and we had a regular ball league of teams from 10 barracks. We were playing ball one day and a player threw the ball beyond the wooden guardrail built to prevent us from approaching the wire fence around the compound. We were not allowed, on threat of death, to trespass in the zone between the guardrail and the fence. The ball player looked up at the guard in the nearest tower, pointed to the ball and asked if it was all right to retrieve the ball. He thought he received an affirmative answer and stepped across the three-foot-high rail, whereupon he was immediately shot by the guard.

Some time later, a German electrician was working on a power pole in the compound and was electrocuted. Some of the prisoners cheered the event, feeling there was some retribution involved. The

Germans took a dim view of our actions and called us all out in the center of the compound and then sprayed the area with machine gun bullets, seriously wounding several men.

As in most prison camps there was an escape tunnel project being carried on. The Germans knew of the project and when some men tried to escape, the Germans were waiting at the end of the tunnel for them.

Previous to that, when we received the musical instruments from Denmark, we formed an orchestra. I, along with a man from Dallas, Texas, a guitar player, who helped me, wrote the arrangements of the songs we played. He became very good at arranging music and I have wondered all these years if he followed a musical career after he was released from the service. That is, if he did get back, as many men died in the 'Black Hunger March.'

Winter came and the days grew shorter and the nights longer. It was dark almost all day, it seemed. You got up in the morning — 0500 hours was roll call — and it was dark when you ate your three-potato dinner. 'Time hung heavy on your hands' during those long days. My musical arrangement work for the orchestra helped a lot to pass the time.

Around Christmas time, I started a lottery and for it I collected over one thousand cigarettes. The 'Grand Prize' was to be 600 cigarettes. All the barracks contributed to the lottery as 'the committee' used cigarettes to bribe the guards, for they liked American cigarettes and were willing to grant special favors, on occasion.

The prisoners in the Russian compound did not receive anything from anybody and, for Christmas, we gave them about five hundred of the cigarettes.

The medium of exchange in the prison camp was usually cigarettes. A cigarette was equal to a $20.00 bill. The commodity of exchange in the poker games was cigarettes. The cigarettes came from the Red Cross packages along with various kinds of food. During the early winter months we were receiving a package per man each week and some of the men were actually gaining weight on the food in the packages. The packages we received around Christmas time contained plum pudding, canned turkey, and all sorts of good food. We planned to have a good Christmas dinner and on Christmas eve, when we were to open our packages, there was an abortive escape. Well, the German guards called us all outside the barracks. They then went through the barracks, dumped the straw from our beds in a pile, and took all the food, opened it up, and dumped it on the straw and mixed it all up together. Well, there went our Christmas celebration.

Back during the summer, about a month after we arrived at the

S/Sgt. Sheldon E. Moore

camp, the camp administration 'in their magnanimity' announced that we would be provided beer. We thought, boy that would be great! It turned out that each barracks received a bucket of beer, one glass for each room of 24 men. We had a raffle in our room for the glass of beer and a fellow by the name of Perry, whose father owned a restuarant in San Francisco, won the raffle. Anyway, we watched him drink the beer. He said it was very good. Having won the raffle this time, he was to be eliminated from future raffles. Well, that was the only time we were ever given any beer and I don't know to this day, what the motivation was for the first time.

We did many things to occupy our time in the prison camp. One 'kriege' was the son of a famous architect who had designed such structures as the 'Palladium' in Hollywood, department stores in Pasadena and buildings in New York City. He taught a course in architecture in which I 'enrolled.' He talked about the 'Old English' and 'Heidelberg' styles of architecture. I learned a great deal from his presentations.

Among the other things we tried was hypnotism. We hypnotized a fellow one day and told him he was in the 'Copacabanna' night club in New York. We gave him a piece of bread and a canteen cup of water and told him he was eating steak, drinking champagne, and watching the beautiful chorus girls. When we snapped him out of the trance, 'he was as happy as a bug in a rug.' He rubbed his stomach and acted 'giddy' and really thought he had eaten steak and drunk champagne.

On the serious side, later in the winter as things got tougher for the Germans, the Red Cross packages, which had originally been distributed once a week, were cut back to one every two weeks — then a half a box every two weeks. By January we seldom received any boxes at all, as the Germans were diverting the boxes to their troops in the 'Battle of the Bulge.' We had tried to get word out for the Red Cross to discontinue sending any more packages. Come February and the time of the 'Black Hunger March,' we were not receiving any more boxes.

In early 1945 the Russians were advancing toward Germany from the east and pushing the German Armies to the west. According to the Geneva Convention, prisoners of war are supposed to be quartered at least 125 kilometers from any ground fighting. Well, early in February, the camp administration informed us we were being moved to another camp. On 6 February 1945 we were marched out of Stalag Luft No. 4 and headed west. The temperature was well below zero degrees Fahrenheit. We were not told where we were going and thought we would be walking for only a short distance. Well, as we now know, the 63 day walk would cover over 400 miles, and farther than that for some of the prisoners. We made packs of our blankets and our other meager belongings. As we were not in good physical condition at the start, as conditions became worse many of our treasured belongings were discarded along the trail.

Our usual routine was to march during the day and stay in a barn each night. Baronial estates were common in rural Germany and the baron — landowner — usually lived on one side of the estate and the 'share croppers' lived in small cottages, near the farm buildings, on the other side. We would stop and stay the night and sleep in these barns. The Germans provided very little food for the first eighteen days of the march and all we had to eat was the food we had brought with us and the few potatoes they provided. We were losing about a pound of weight a day, even though we had almost no fat on our body when we started the march, only bone and muscle.

One night, about 35 or 40 days after the start of the march, I made one of the most terrible mistakes I had ever made in my life. My feet had been frozen on several occasions. I was wearing GI shoes and I had not removed the shoes since the start of the march. Finally the pain in my feet was so great I removed my shoes after we had bivouacked for the night. Well, I took my shoes off and almost immediately my feet swelled up to the size of footballs. They were badly infected and pus oozed out of ulcerous sores. They turned all colors, black, red, blue, and green. After that I could hardly walk. I wrapped strips of burlap, which I found in the barn, around my feet and walked the best I could for 10 or 12 days. The pain became so bad I could go no farther and I couldn't stand on my feet. Well, the Germans had three or four wagons pulled by horses on the march and they threw me up on one of them along with the other sick and maimed.

I had ridden on that wagon for about ten days, when we came to a railhead out in the middle of nowhere. There was a train of boxcars parked on the track into which we were loaded. Maybe a better word would be jammed, as 80 or 90 men were crammed into each box car so tightly you couldn't fall down even when you slept. The only consolation was that I got warm for the first time in two months. The train pulled out and after 8 days we arrived at Hamburg in the western part of Germany.

In Hamburg they opened the car doors and let us out. Beside the track was a water well in which there was a pump, and for the first time in three days we got a drink of water. Along the way to Hamburg a German had thrown a sack of rock salt into the car and, because we were so hungry, we had eaten it. Well, my tongue had swollen up so badly I could not keep it in my mouth. It hung out and I couldn't even push it back in my mouth with my fingers. Someone helped me get some water and I cannot remember anything tasting as good as that water.

By this time I had lost so much weight, I was 'skin and bones.' Later, when I was liberated, I was weighed and I was at 110 pounds. I had weighed about 172 pounds when I was shot down.

Unbelievably, some Red Cross women showed up where we stopped and handed out sausages to the prisoners. I guess they were salami but they were so fresh they were just raw sausage. We split the sausages up, four men to a sausage, about one-half a pound per man. Although I was ravenously hungry, I looked at the raw sausage and said to a fellow 'kriege,' an RAF bomber — Lancaster — gunner, 'I wonder how long it will be until we get something good to eat?' Between mouths full of sausage, he said, 'What's the difference? Wolf it up, Wolf it up.' So I Wolfed it up.

Hamburg the town was almost nonexistent as it had been literally flattened to the ground by bombing. The town had been repeatedly bombed by both American and English bombers and it was so badly destroyed it was hard to conceive how anyone had lived through the 'fire storms' which had ravaged the city. Even under these unbelievable conditions, here were these Red Cross Volunteers distributing sausages to POW's, some of whom had taken part in the destruction of the city.

I mused to myself, even in my terribly emaciated condition, of 'man's inhumanity to man.' How inconceivable, that these Red Cross women were here. From Hamburg, our train continued on until we came to an abandoned prison camp, Stalag 357. The camp had previously been a Russian prison camp but was now deserted. The story making the rounds was that 30,000 Russian prisoners were buried here. They had been forced to dig their own graves and then were shot and buried in the grave. Whether that was true or not, I do not know.

Well, they formed us up to continue the march and it was then that I decided I would go no farther, so I hid in a pile of straw in a big tent. A German guard with a pitch fork came by and plunged the fork into the straw a couple of times but fortunately missed on either side of me. I guess if he had hit me I would have terminated the march right there.

I waited for two or three hours, until I could not hear any sounds of marching and then poked a hole in the straw to breathe better. The following morning I crawled out of the straw and cautiously looked around. I could see no one and walked out of the tent. The camp covered a very large area and when I felt there was no one around I walked around for awhile. I was close to one of the compound gates and not knowing where to go, I walked over to the gate. When I got there I was unexpectedly confronted by an old German Luftwaffe guard. He looked at me and I at him, neither one of us saying anything for a moment or two. I didn't know whether he would shoot me right there on the spot or not. He then said, 'Sitten sie — nein mehr krieg' (there is no more war). I sat down near him and he took his lunch out of a bag, cut an apple in two parts and handed half to me. We tried to talk in broken English and German. Strange as it may seem, that is the way it was.

I walked around the camp and soon found that between 60 to 70 men had hidden as I did. The men had come from several different countries. There were Americans, English, Russians, Yugoslavians, and French.

After a day or so, one of the English soldiers left the camp to try to contact units of the English army which were in the vicinity. Members of an English regiment came to the camp and, in effect, liberated us. They gave us food which we were awfully glad to get. I had the first 'square' meal I had eaten for over two months. I had my first piece of white bread in eleven months and it was like eating angel food cake after having eaten black moldy bread, so hard you could not cut it.

We were taken by truck to a British regimental bivouac but I did not stay there long, as I hitched a ride to Brussels and from there to Paris, France. I wanted to see a little bit of Paris before I was sent back to the United States, and I wandered around Paris for a period of time.

For identification we had been issued a prisoner of war card and as I had no other means of identification I used that to ride the trains. After hostilities ceased in Europe, you could ride the trains anywhere in Allied liberated territory at no cost, so I traveled around for a time.

I found a food kitchen at North Station in Paris that was feeding GI's who were on leave and traveling, and in a relatively short time 'ate' my weight back up to 126 pounds. GI food never tasted so good as it did there.

I went to the airport in Paris and tried to get a flight back to England to the 457th Bomb Group, but was told the group had shipped out to New Guinea in the Pacific, which of course turned out not to be true.

So I traveled to the French coast near La Harve and from Camp Lucky Strike (there were four camps around La Harve: Chesterfield, Phillip Morris, Camel, and Lucky Strike), I was loaded on a ship and sent back to the United States.

Lt. John O. Millham's story of the 28 May 1944 mission to Dessau, Germany.

This was my twenty-second mission over enemy territory. We were on our way to bomb an aircraft engine plant in Dessau, Germany. Dessau is due south of Berlin in the Magdeburg area. As we turned onto the bomb run we were attacked by what seemed to be hundreds of German fighters. There was a mix of Me-109's, FW-190's and multi-engine aircraft. Some of them came at us head-on and I was shooting at them. We lost two engines in the attack. One of them would not feather. We were losing altitude and we couldn't keep up with the formation. We dropped our bombs but then we couldn't close the bomb bay doors.

My intercom was knocked out so the pilot talked to me through the engineer. I went up to the flight deck and he told me that we were in a shallow dive. I could see we were traveling at only 110 M.P.H. He asked me if we could we get to either Sweden or Switzerland. I thought we would be too low to cross the mountains into Switzerland and we would have to cross Berlin to get to Sweden. I thought it would be better just to continue on our present course and try to reach home base.

For ninety minutes we followed a westerly course. At first, I tried to communicate with the pilot by signalling through the celestial dome. That didn't work so every time I wanted a course correction, I crawled through the hatchway up to the flight deck. The rest of the crew, including the co-pilot and the bombardier, were in the waist of the airplane throwing out everything that would come loose. After a lot of effort they dropped the ball turret. The reduction in weight did not help the airspeed problem. We were also fighting a strong head-wind. A P-51 approached us and flew along with us for a short time. He must have had a hard time maintaining flying attitude with our low airspeed of only 110 M.P.H. We thought that in debriefing he would report seeing us and our condition. Apparently he didn't, however; either that or the message was not relayed to our base.

As we approached the Zuider Zee, I informed the crew that we were approaching Holland and that we were not far from the North Sea. Almost simultaneously we were hit by flak. I could feel the plane taking hits. Shrapnel was coming through the nose section of the airplane. I was struck in the forehead by a piece of shrapnel. Within seconds I was covered with blood and I let out a yell! About that time the bail-out alarm sounded. I snapped on my chest-pack parachute and headed for the hatch escape door. When I left my position we were at 2000 feet elevation. Sgt. Bill Bemus was at the hatch door when I got there. Something caused him to back off and he told me to go first. I got down on my knees and did a somersault out of the plane.

I didn't wait to pull the rip-cord. After the shock of the parachute opening, I felt as if I was gaining altitude and moving horizontally. Then I realized that the plane was spiralling down around us. The Germans were still shooting at it. Some of the shells were coming close to me but I don't think they were shooting at me. As I looked down, I thought I was coming down in a tree, so I tried to collapse the chute to miss it. My chute did not have time to recover and I came down unusually hard. I landed on a tombstone. My leg broke with the sound of a board breaking. As soon as I landed, a young boy jumped astride me.

28 May 1944 was Whit Sunday, a big religious holiday in Europe, and I had come down in a churchyard. The church had been full of people who were out watching the excitement. They were all around me. Some of them were threatening, but they backed off when some soldiers appeared and cocked their rifles. I had tried to give my escape-kit away but no one would accept it. I couldn't speak German and none of the people seemed to be able to speak English. However, we could still communicate fairly well, maybe because I was trying so hard to do so. One lady knew I had a first aid kit. She asked me where it was and I showed her. She took it and bandaged my head wound. I did have a hard time convincing them I was not armed. Although my leg was at an odd angle from where it should have been, they tried to make me walk. When they realized I could not walk, they let me stay where I was until a small wagon was brought up. They picked me up and threw me into the wagon, on top of Sgt. Bemus.

Bill (Sgt. Bemus) told me that he had been wounded badly and he thought that he might die. I remember trying to comfort him and then I realized that the bottom of the wagon was covered with his blood. He told me that when he got to the escape hatch, he realized he had put his chest-pack on so that the rip-cord was on the wrong side. He had told me to go ahead and he backed away to put the chute on correctly. When he did, he was hit at the base of the spine by a piece of shrapnel. As the shrapnel emerged from his groin, it left a large wound in the area of his rectum.

It was a short ride to what I believe was the anti-aircraft post that shot us down. There was an army doctor there that put my leg in a splint. He also tried to do something for Bill, but there wasn't much he could do. The boy who had jumped on me when I hit the ground in my parachute was there watching everything. In a short time they put Bill and me in an army ambulance, the driver of which told me they were taking us to a hospital. Several times along the way, the driver stopped to check on Bill. He was unable to do anything other than see if he was still alive.

We were taken to St. Joseph Stift's Hospital in Bremen. We were both taken to surgery. When I woke up, they had taken care of my head wound and put my leg in traction. I laid there outside of surgery until the doctor came out to talk to me. He told me that it would take some time but that I would be all right. He told me that my sergeant was wounded badly and he did not think he would survive. He said that Bill had lost too much blood and he could not give an enemy prisoner any blood. He also said he had done all he could that day, but he was going to operate on him again the next day. He had repaired the wound and stopped the bleeding. The next day he fixed Bill up with a colostomy. He lay there in his bed, near death, for almost two months.

We were in a civilian hospital and they really didn't know what to do with prisoners of war. We were in a room at the end of the ward, near where there were bunkers that were as big as the hospital. Anytime there was an air raid all the people in the neighborhood would come to the hospital. Although I was a POW, I got to talk to hundreds of Germans of all ranks and social status. The German doctors and nurses were not mean to me. They took as good care of me as they did of their own people. Many of the patients were wounded very badly. Some of them had been experimented on by 'Fraulein doctors.' They were part of the Hitler regime, trained as doctors, however did experimental work on prisoners. They would cut tendons in the legs of prisoners to see what would happen — to see if the body would develop new replacement tendons. I knew a man that they had experimented on.

I was in traction for two months after which they put me in a walking cast. I was then sent to Dulag Luft near Frankfurt. I was transported by train and assigned to a compartment in which were an older man and his wife. My uniform had not been cleaned and was still covered with blood. When the man figured out who I was, he got up and started beating me up. The woman started crying and pulled him off of me and we had no further trouble. The soldier who accompanied me showed no sign of caring what they did to me.

Although I had been a prisoner for two months, they wanted to interrogate me. I was kept in solitary confinement for some time. Also, they threatened that I would not get any medical help if I didn't tell them anything they asked. In the end, and after I had not told them anything but some information about baseball, they told me they knew all about me anyway.

I was sent to Obermassfeld, which was a prison hospital run by English doctors who had been captured at Dunkirk. Considering what they had to work with, these doctors did an amazing job. When I arrived there the doctor told me that I should never have been put into a walking cast and they took it off and put a big cast on me.

I was transferred to Stalag Luft 3 on 28 November 1944. Later, I ended up at Mooseburg, and was there at the end of the hostilities in Europe.

Mission No. 1
21 February 1944
Target — Lippstadt-Gutersloh A/F

Crew of the B-17G, No.42-31596

1st Pilot	2nd Lt.	Llewellyn G. Bredeson
Co-Pilot	2nd Lt.	George Barnes
Nav.	2nd Lt.	Robert A. Whitby
Bomb.	2nd Lt.	Samuel Kalman
Engr.	T/Sgt.	Howard R. Collins
Radio Op.	T/Sgt.	Leonard V. Luchonok
LW Gun.	S/Sgt.	Louis P. Rigaud
RW Gun.	S/Sgt.	John F. Lewis
B. Turret	S/Sgt.	Walter J. Jutze
Tail Gun.	S/Sgt.	William H. Schenkel

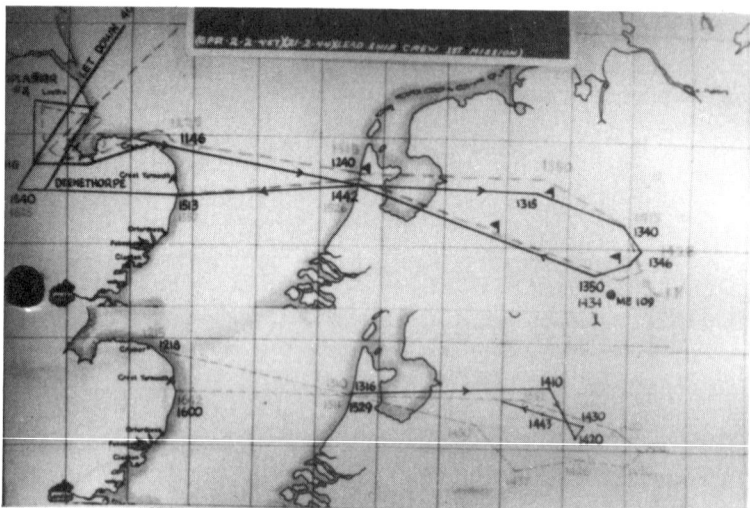

Track Chart, Mission No. 1, 21 Feb. 1944.

457th Bomb Group Mission Narrative

The first mission of the 457th Bomb Group took place on the second day of the final pre-invasion campaign of the 8th Air Force to destroy German air power. On the previous day, the 20th of February 1944, a thousand heavy bombers with 823 escorting fighters devastated aircraft factories at: Leipzig, Bernberg, Oschersleben, Gotha, Brunswick and Tutow in the greatest and most successful air operation in the war to date.

The operation of 21 February 1944 was directed against Brunswick, Diepholz, Achmer with the 457th Bomb Group sending an 'A' box to Gutersloh and a 'B' box to Lippstadt. Both targets were air-parks for the storing of enemy fighters. The 457th 'A' box, led by Lt. Col. James Luper/Lt. Smith, was airborne at 1042 hours, failed to assemble with the 94th CBW (combat wing), but joined with the 41st CBW at Egmont, Holland which was missing its high group. Its target was the Werl Airdrome near Hamm. 10/10ths clouds obscured the airdrome and, when the wing leader dropped on a target of opportunity in the vicinity, 12 of our crews released their bombs. The group leader with 6 other planes of the 457th Bomb group held their bombs and, failing to find a better target, returned to Glatton.

Enemy fighter opposition on the day's operation was weak. The 'A' box sustained fairly heavy losses. Lt. Llewellen Bredeson was shot down in the target area. Lt. Edward Dozier's ship received 8,

20mm cannon bursts and came home alone, badly shot up, with no rudder control. His radio operator, Sgt. Seymour Pliss, was killed and ship No. 588 never flew again.

The 'B' group, led by Major Wilson/Lt. Mays, made assembly with the '94th' CBW after taking off at 1028 hours. The flight to Lippstadt was uneventful and, after taking bomber interval, the target was found to be completely overcast. As no PFF ship (blind bombing, radar) was provided, the wing leader searched for a target of opportunity. None was found on the withdrawal course to the Dutch border and the 17 planes in this box jettisoned their bombs in the North Sea.

There were no fighter attacks on this group and only two planes sustained minor flak damage.

The operation was an interesting introduction into the many factors that can complicate and affect a bombing mission in this theatre.

Lt. Samuel Kalman's story of the 21 February 1944 mission to Lippstadt-Gutersloh.

[Ed. This was the first mission for the crew and their loss was the first for the 457th Bomb Group.]

FIRST MISSION, LAST MISSION

"It is a tale told by an
idiot, full of sound and fury
and signifying nothing..." William Shakespeare

"SNAFU...Situation normal
all f_____ed up!" —any World War II G.I.

by 1st Lt. Samuel Kalman, USAFR(Hon.Ret.)

WELCOME TO THE 457TH! I was stunned by the welcome extended my crew and other crews of the "Hutchinson Provisional Group." We had only that 7 December 1943 morning come down from off the cold, barren Wendover, Utah, gunnery range where we had been isolated in quarantine for four days.

This was to be our first meeting with the leadership of the 457th Bomb Group (H), something we had all looked forward to with great anticipation.

The welcome went like this. First the Squadron C.O. got up and chewed us out. Then the Squadron Operations Officer got up and chewed us out. Then the Squadron Bombardier got up and chewed us out. It was, to put it mildly one hell of a welcome. Especially after it followed four miserable days of isolation in quarantine on the gunnery range because of a single outbreak of meningitis. The disease had struck a bombardier named Guest who was taken from our less-than-luxurious troop train during our three day journey from Rapid City, South Dakota.

There are few places on earth that God has forsaken. The Wendover gunnery range is one of them. And what God had forsaken, the Army Air Force chose as an ideal location to put an air base. Such was Wendover Field. The gunnery range distinctly outranked the field on the uglyness scale.

Our gunnery range quarters with their outdoor latrines and outhouses could easily have been the role model for the ramshackled wooden buildings of the fishing village in Robin William's movie "Popeye." Except that the gunnery range was landlocked. Instead of looking out to sea, our quarters looked into the side of what I believe is the ugliest mountain in the world.

The mountain had absolutely no redeeming qualities. It wouldn't have made even a first class slag heap. It wasn't overly tall. It was too big to be classed a hill. Yet amongst mountains, it ranked in stature to just a little more than a mole hill. Nothing green grew on it. Its sides were mostly rubble. It had no distinguishing features except one. On its slopes facing our quarters was lettering we saw each time we ventured outdoors. Someone creative must have thought the message was appropriate to our situation. The letters were white and seemed larger than the lettering of the famous Hollywood sign in Beverly Hills. The message was much terser. On the side of that ugly, barren mountain, near the top, spelled out letter by letter was this message: "KILL OR BE KILLED."

It was a helluva slogan! But that was the business we were in.

So there we were in the briefing room, just about an hour after leaving the mountain behind, getting chewed out by the entire welcoming committee. The Squadron C.O. reamed us for shooting the tow lines off the tow target sleeve and shooting up the tail of the tow ship in aerial gunnery practice. The Squadron Operations Officer chewed out our enlisted men for not saluting officers in town. And the Squadron Bombardier chewed us generally for having "a chip on our shoulders" and for being uncooperative.

I waited for someone to speak up, one of the pilots, or one of the others who had been an officer longer than I. No one did and my sense of fair play and outrage came to the fore. I had had enough when the Squadron Bombardier got in on the play, even though I was a 2nd Lt. and he was a 1st Lt.

As Bombardier on our crew, I was also the morale officer and I took that job seriously. We had a good bunch of enlisted men on our crew and I felt they and our officers were being maligned. So I jumped up.

"Lieutenant," I said, "Your the one with a chip on your shoulder. If you check, you'll find that as a group we have an outstanding record and are competent and cooperative. We couldn't have shot the cable off the tow target or shot up the tail of the tow plane because we haven't been in the air. Our enlisted men haven't been in town and if they had they have enough military bearing to salute officers. We've been in quarantine, isolated on the gunnery range for the last four days. This is our first time here on the base."

Having said my piece, I sat down. I learned later that I had made a friend of nearly every enlisted man in the room. A number of those I knew came over and thanked me. Others I did not know came over and pounded me on the back. "Attaboy Lieutenant," they said. Many of my fellow officers also expressed their approval.

But guess whose list (and what kind) I was now at the top of.

It seemed to be my crew's destiny to participate in the 457th's preliminary research leading to the discovery of Murphy's Law: i.e. "If anything can go wrong it will."

On completing training the "Hutchinson Provisional Group" ordinarily would have been split up into replacement crews for operational groups already in combat. However, because of the Hutchinson group's excellent training record, the decision was made higher up to merge it with the 457th whose training record was less than brilliant. Thus, instead of 36 crews, the 457th now had 71 crews.

The theory behind the merger was to create a better, more proficient group. The facts, however, proved otherwise. Instead of getting an improved group by merging the two groups, the Air Force simply got a larger not so good group. This is not meant to reflect on any of the crews that flew combat with the 457th. It never was the fault of the crews. The fault lay in the inept early leadership of the 457th and Murphy's Law.

The Squadron leaders who chewed out my crew and other crews who had been in quarantine simply made a mistake. They chewed out the wrong people. By doing so, they set the wrong tone of welcome for which, incidentally, they never apologized.

Our training was nearly over when word came down that only

half of the crews in the group would get "fly-aways" — brand new B-17G's fresh from the Boeing factory. The half who got new planes would fly them to the 457th's new base in England. The other half would leave Wendover early and go by ship to England.

My crew was one of the lucky ones. Destination: Grand Island, Nebraska. After eight hours of flying, fog at Grand Island forced us to land at North Platte. Many came out to the airfield in their cars to drive us into town to the hotel whose accomodations were luxurious by comparison to what we had at Wendover.

We were grounded for two days at North Platte because of heavy snow. It was like a paid vacation. There were 14 bars in town. In addition to our B-17 group, the only other soldiers in town were two M.P.'s.

Obviously, it was with reluctance that we left North Platte.

On 5 January 1944, we arrived in Grand Island which was a modification center. While at Grand Island, I checked out the bomb racks, guns and other related equipment.

It was there that Bill Shenkel, our tail gunner, asked if he could be my assistant. I'm not sure how the table of organization reads, but I said yes and appointed him assistant bombardier. Since the bombardier was also the armament officer on the crew, I put Shenkel in charge of the ship's guns. I knew that my own gunnery training was no match for the training the crew's gunners received.

On 19 January 1944, we resumed our journey to England. We left Grand Island and headed for Presque Isle, Maine. Weather forced a detour to Grenier Field, Manchester, New Hampshire, where we spent a day and one-half.

On 21 January, we left Grenier Field at 1900 hours, destination Goose Bay, Labrador.

The flight over Canada to Labrador was in cold, overcast conditions. It began at night and continued into the next day. Whenever there was a break in the clouds, the snow covered countryside below showed an occasional sign of human existance, evidenced by plumes of smoke from fireplace chimneys. Tall pines, ice covered streams, and snowy hills and valleys gave the landscape a picture postcard albeit lonely look.

On landing at Goose Bay at 1000 hours, we were immediately cautioned not to stay outdoors longer than 20 minutes at a time. To do otherwise, we were told was to risk having our lungs seared by the super sub-zero temperatures.

The living quarters at Goose Bay were well heated and comfortable. Nearly all buildings were linked by heated corridors. The food was good. Except for the sub-zero cold, our stay at Goose Bay was pleasant.

One of the mysteries I have pondered even to this day is how the walls of the ramps were cut so perpendicularly in the snow. The snowy sides of the ramp walls were smooth and straight from top to bottom. To look into a perpendicular wall of snow that towered at least 10 to 12 feet above the surface on either side of the ramp had a strange effect. It humbled the inherent humanity each of us possess.

At 2000 hours on 22 January 1944, we left Goose Bay for the British Isles. Our destination: Nutts Corner, Ireland.

We took off in a blinding snow storm. The tower informed us that we would hit a band of clear weather at 8,000 feet.

Our plane had been serviced and checked out for our trip across the Atlantic Ocean. We had a full load of gasoline, a full crew of 10 plus their baggage, and 20 rounds of ammunition in each gun. Each crew member stored his baggage at his own station. Pilot Lew Bredeson cautioned us not to move around too much because to do so could effect the ship's center of gravity.

Before leaving Goose Bay, we attended a briefing at which the pilots were warned not to follow the radio beam. Reason: the Germans were known to bend the beam with the nefarious purpose of having it lead unsuspecting planes to Nazi occupied France. There were several instances, we were told, where American crews unwittingly wound up in France and were captured.

At that time flying the ocean was still relatively new. In addition we were flying the Northern Route which ordinarily was closed in winter. Here we were, a brand new aircraft, a pilot and co-pilot who had never flown the ocean before, and a navigator who had never navigated the ocean before.

All of that crossed my mind but once we were in the clear, I put those thoughts aside and settled back in my seat in the nose. I dropped off to sleep now and again. Just before dawn, I awoke and caught sight of a red glow on the horizon out ahead. As a precaution, I aimed my guns in that direction. I watched the red glow for some time until I realized it was Venus. I called off my personal alert and tried to get back to sleep.

The trip was uneventful until we passed the point of no return and were about 400 miles from our destination.

It was now daylight and the ship had climbed to 21,000 feet. We were about to hit a storm over the ocean and Lew, and George Barnes the co-pilot, were trying to get above the murky weather.

As we climbed higher, the wings began to pick up ice. As luck would have it, number 4 engine conked out. Lew feathered the propeller but it continued to windmill. High winds were beginning to buffet the ship.

The pilots tried to bring the ship above the bad weather, but the higher we went, the more the wings iced up. At about 24,000 feet, they decided to go to a lower altitude to try to escape the icy conditions.

As we started down, we skimmed the top of the storm clouds that were black bottomless whirlpools of violent looking turbulance. It was one of the few times that I was aware of how high we were.

As the plane passed over them, I looked down into these eerie, swirling black whirlpools and could never see bottom.

The windmilling propeller and the buffeting winds tossed the ship about the sky with some violence. At one point, my chest chute which hung on a hook made from a coat hanger, shook loose from its place on the bulkhead leading to the cockpit. It fell near Bob Whitby's feet. He kicked it over in my direction. I picked it up and snapped it in place on my harness.

As we were letting down, storm clouds buffeted the ship about the sky. At this point, it crossed my mind that all altimeters at that time had a built-in error, especially over long distances. If the altimeter read too high, then our altitude would be lower than we thought.

If it read too low, we would be higher than we thought. It took a long time to break out of that storm mess. When we finally did, it was at a reading of 200 feet. And we were above the sickliest green choppy water I'd ever seen.

The ice was gone from our wings and we flew the rest of the way at about 200 feet above the ocean which pitched and swirled below us.

During all this time the navigator couldn't get any new fixes and was working with information several hours old.

The ship settled down. The ice was gone and the buffeting had subsided. It was at this point that Whitby noticed I was wearing my chute. He looked quizzically at me. I pointed to the windmilling propeller on number 4 engine. He immediately put on his own chute and asked me on the intercom why I hadn't told him before. I said I thought you knew when you kicked my chute over to me. He said he was too busy trying to keep track of our course to realize we had lost an engine.

Anyway, it wouldn't have mattered much with or without a chute. Survival time in the icy North Atlantic was measured in minutes. Finally, we reached land and all of us throughout the ship gave a great silent sigh of relief.

At my first sight of Ireland, I had mixed emotions. I was glad to be over land but at the same time I was homesick for the good old U. S. of A.

The Irish landscape reminded me very much of illustrations in fairy tale books that I read as a child. The heather colors of the fields in rich dark tones of browns and greens were pleasing to my eye. The quilted patchwork of the fields, aged by time, wind and rain passed peacefully beneath the ship. The Irish landscape was like a soft natural blanket, warm and comforting. Yet I was stranger to this charming land.

Fasten safety belts! Back then they were called "safety belts." Today, they are called "seat belts." Then as now I was a little lax in fastening my safety belt.

The Nutt's Corner airfield was in sight. Bob Whitby the navigator had hit it right on the nose. Lew and George, the pilots had brought the ship and crew safely across the ocean and we were about to land. I relaxed as I watched the beautiful Irish landscape pass beneath the ship as we were gradually reducing speed and altitude.

I looked forward to getting on the ground and stretching my legs. We were now on the final letdown, some 500 or 1,000 feet over the end of the runway when without warning, I was literally

Glatton AAB — Home of 457th B.G.

hurled from my seat and thrown spreadeagle into the plexiglass nose.

At the same moment, the noise and thrust of the engines at full power came roaring at me as the pilots dropped the nose and gave the engines full throttle.

I found myself pinned in the nose by the centrifugal force and looking straight down at the ground which was coming up fast. I wasn't sure that I wouldn't go flying out nose and all and I hoped the Boeing riveters had used plenty of strong rivets to keep that plexiglass nose in place.

The ship picked up airspeed and did a go-around. I was able to get back in my seat. This time I fastened my safety belt. I completely understood now why the Air Force's policy said bombardiers should not sit in the nose seat while landing. Instead, we were to stand in the cockpit behind the seats of the two pilots. Ordinarily I followed that procedure. Baggage and other equipment prevented me from doing so on this trip.

When the ship landed, I learned the reason for my near catastrophe.

As we were about to touch down and land, the engineer after a routine check, rushed to tell the pilots that the tail wheel had not come down. Had we landed with the wheel up, the ships back would have been broken and the plane would have split in two. The pilots took the only action they could to gain altitude and get back into the air. They dropped the nose and gave the engines full throttle. There was no time to warn the crew.

At 1100 hours, 23 January 1944, we landed at Nutts Corner. The flight had taken some fifteen hours. Except for number 4 engine, the aircraft had performed well.

When I got out of the ship and felt the earth beneath my feet, I let myself relax for the first time since we left Goose Bay. And had someone said to me "Okay, Kalman, you can go home now." I would have replied, "Fine, except I want to go by boat, thank you."

When the crew heard what had happened to me in the nose, we had a few good laughs and some good-natured ribbing. Naturally, at my expense. But it was good and it broke the tension for all of us.

At Nutts Corner, we got our first taste of English food. It was good but not plentiful.

We were quartered out on a farm and we had to go by the farmer's house to get to our hutment. The farmer's chickens nearly always blocked the road as we went by. The weather was poor — damp, windy and cold.

The next day we left at 0800 hours for our new base at Glatton.

Mission No. 1

We were escorted by a British Beaufighter light bomber and a B-17. The weather was clear.

We were among the first American crews at Glatton. The mess hall was run by English personnel who were on temporary duty until our own mess cadre arrived. Among the changes in diet was a switch to sow belly instead of bacon for breakfast, strong tea instead of coffee and slices of heavier English white bread with margarine instead of butter. We looked forward to the arrival of our own mess personnel.

The routine of training and ground school continued.

The break from the routine came on 1 February 1944, when the crews who had come by ship arrived at the base.

My buddy, Bob Horn and my friend, navigator Roland Byers, were in that group. The officers of my crew and theirs were quartered in adjoining metal Quonset huts.

Having time off the next night, I went into nearby Peterborough for the first time. Visited several pubs. The only available "hard" drink was "gin and orange (juice)." The beer was served warm which didn't offend me. I was never much of a beer drinker.

The tempo of ground school training and practice missions seemed to intensify on the arrival of the second group of crews.

During the first ground school gunnery session at Glatton, we were told to forget everything we had been taught in the States. "Don't lead the target. Repeat: don't lead the target. In air to air gunnery, the bullet's trajectory changes. Now you aim between him and your tail." The instructor said. "And no more tracer bullets. They don't work."

Another change based on the Eighth Air Force's combat experience: "Only the lead ship and the two deputy lead ships have bomb sights. The rest of the bombardiers toggle their bombs when the lead ship drops its load.

"Fly tight formations. Don't straggle. The Germans love stragglers. Call out fighters."

In parachute class, we were told that if we had to bail out, count ten before pulling the rip-cord to make sure you clear the ship. Jump head first! The reason: "If you strike the ship, it will be your feet not your head that gets broken." We were also told that it was unnecessary to hold on to the risers (lines) of the chute. "The longer you delay opening your chute the better your chances of not being seen in the air and of evading capture."

We were ordered not to carry sidearms because intelligence reports said the Germans were following the Geneva Convention in the treatment of Prisoners of War.

We were also reminded that if captured by the Nazi enemy, we

Flak!

were duty bound to give no information other than our name, rank and serial number. And we were told, it was our duty to escape if possible. We were also told that if captured, we were to continue to resist the enemy in whatever way possible.

Air and ground training kept moving us closer to combat. 14 February was typical. We were awakened at 0300 hours for our first mission. We got as far as the truck to the mess hall and the mission was scrubbed.

The night of 16 February 1944, we were alerted again for a mission the next morning. The mission also was scrubbed. Instead I reported to Operations at 0800 hours. No ground school. I was duty bombardier from 1800 to 2200 hours. We were stood down that evening which meant no mission the next day.

AERIAL GUNNERY PRACTICE! 19 February 1944, I reported to Operations at 0800 hours for briefing on a practice gunnery mission. At last I would get to fire my new twin .50's. Since the bombardier was also the crew's Armament Officer, it was my responsibility to see that our ship's guns were in good working order. (When I made Shenkel my assistant, I put him in charge of the guns. We were told not to leave our gun barrels in the ship overnight because the damp English weather rusted them. Shenkel and all our gunners were conscientious about taking care of the ship's guns. All of us knew that our lives might depend on them. The barrels were always cleaned, oiled and stored indoors at Armament. Periodically, I walked over to the ship at night, which was no easy task in the blackout, to make sure that the guns were not left outside.)

When we reached the rendezvous point for the tow target ship, it wasn't there. We circled around for awhile, hoping it would show. Finally it became apparent that it wasn't coming. Another snafu. Instead we practiced local formation flying. I still hadn't properly tested my guns.

Later that evening, the Officers Club had its Grand Opening. I left the celebration early because we were alerted for a mission the next day. I hit the sack at 2200 hours.

The mission was scrubbed and I slept until 0930 hours.

During this stretch of training, we flew three or four so-called "diversionary raids." The group would fly in formation up to the English Channel and scoot back to the base. We had 20 rounds of ammo in our guns. Purpose of the raids: to fox-up the German radar in an attempt to divert Luftwaffe fighters away from the 8th's main bomber thrust that day. I don't know if it worked. But that was the idea.

Later, I wondered how much defense we could mount with just 20 rounds if the German fighters had taken the bait.

During one of our earlier get-to-gethers, Bob Horn and I stood outside in the blackout and watched a Luftwaffe raid on London that was miles to the south of our base. We could see the orange glow and hear the rumble of the exploding bombs. We saw bursts of anti-aircraft fire amid the bright shafts of searchlights in the blackness of the distant London night sky.

We were both much aware that we would be in combat in raids over enemy territory. Among close wartime friends facing a common danger, there is a tendency to hide fear behind a macabre kind of humor. Such was the case with Horn and me.

"You sumbitch," Horn said, "you'll never get past your fifth mission." "If I don't, you won't," I said.

Neither of us realized at the time that we had predicted our own futures.

On the night of 20 February 1944, my crew was not put on alert status for the mission the following day.

Since we were stood down and not alerted for a mission, I went to the Officers Club. Turned in my laundry. Relaxed. Had a few drinks with friends. Played blackjack with a fellow bombardier. Not my night. I lost 27 pounds (approx. $108.00 American). I came back to the hut and wrote letters home. I looked forward to the week-end when I planned to go to London to meet Joe Levitt, another friend from St. Louis, at the American Red Cross. Joe was a combat engineer. His outfit had only recently arrived in England. Hit the sack later than usual.

21 FEBRUARY 1944. I awoke to the sound of the Operations Officer's southern accented voice. It sounded almost as if he was crying. As I became more awake, what he was saying began to register. He was standing just inside the doorway of the Quonset hut where Lew Bredeson, the pilot, George Barnes, the co-pilot, Bob Whitby, the navigator, and I lived.

"I forgot to wake you," he said. "You guy's are to go on today's mission." "The group is already at the flight line. Take off is at 0830 hours."

I looked at my watch it was 0800 hours.

"You've got to get going. There's no time for briefing. Only the navigator will br briefed. You won't have time for breakfast. I'll have sandwiches waiting down at the ship. You'll have to hurry," he said and left.

The four of us dressed quickly.

When we arrived at the flight line, Shenkel and the rest of the crew were already there. Shenkel was upset. "Some other crew got our gun barrels and the one's we got are as rusty as hell," he told me.

"That's a bunch of shit!" I said. Let's go to Armament. When we got there I chewed butt. "Where in the f_____ are our barrels? These are not ours. They're rusty. Give us some better ones than these m/f things."

"I can't Lieutenant. These are all we have. There ain't no more barrels." There wasn't time to argue so I said, "When I get back, I'm gonna ream some butt. You can bet your ass on that!"

"Let's go," I said to Shenkel. "I still have to get my chute. Take these s.o.b.'s back to the ship while I go for my chute."

Mission No. 1

I got to Quartermaster and asked for my chute. It was a chest chute. They couldn't find it. Look, I said, "I want my harness. Just find my harness and give me another chute."

My harness was important to me because I had equipped it for the possibility of having to bail out. It was actually a jungle type, which unlike others, had a large zippered pocket on the back. In it I had put a trench knife, some extra "K" ration, a change of underwear and some clean socks — all in case I got shot down and needed these things to escape capture.

I also carried my G.I. high-tops at my station in case I ever needed them to escape. The electric heated shoes and fur-lined zippered boots I ordinarily wore when flying were not meant for running.

Those guys at Quartermaster couldn't find my harness and my chute even though my name was printed in large letters all over both pieces.

Time was running out so I said, "Give me a G____ D____ chest chute so I can get going. You can bet your ass, I'm gonna chew butts when I get back."

It seemed like the whole damned organization had fallen apart with the worst yet to come in the air.

I hurried back to the ship where breakfast was waiting — two slices of English brown bread spread with some tasteless margarine. Nothing to Drink.

When I got into the nose, Whitby the navigator, relayed the briefing he got. It consisted of two coordinates and the name of the target, a Luftwaffe airfield near Guttersloh. That was it.

He got no information on where to expect flak or fighters, what our course was to be, how far it was to the target, or what time we would be over it. We had no information about our own fighter escorts, if any.

This mission was one of the first 1,000 plane raids mounted by the 8th in the battle called the "Air Offensive." The goal of the Air Offensive was to destroy the Luftwaffe in the air and on the ground. Our strike force was to include more than 500 bombers and 500 fighter aircraft.

The pilots, Lew and George, warmed up the engines of our B-17 then headed for the flight line. We were the last ship to take off. Our position in the formation: "Tail-end Charlie."

As the plane left the runway and climbed into the air, I could sense that the ship was enclosed in an invisible envelope of fear.

By being denied briefing, we were denied the bonding that takes place between crews on a dangerous mission. We were denied the repartee, the kidding and friendly needling between each other individually and as crew's. The briefings served more than just detailing a mission. They were an important escape valve for the tension and apprehension that existed before a mission.

By being denied proper briefing, we were isolated from the group. Although we flew in formation with the other planes, we were denied the essential contact with other crews to give us the feeling of being part of the group heading out on the same mission.

To break the tension aboard, someone started singing the Army Air Corps song on the intercom. Soon we were all singing "we live in fame and go down in flame, nothing can stop the Army Air Corps."

We flew across the North Sea, our course taking us a mile or so north of Amsterdam. As we were tangential to the Dutch city, black smoke bursts of flak flared up through the clouds into the sky over Amsterdam. The flak was some distance from where we were. On the intercom, someone commented matter of factly, "that's flak to the right over Amsterdam."

By this time we were under oxygen and climbing to altitude as we penetrated into Germany proper. Clouds obscured the ground below.

Now and again, the lead ship of our element was slip sliding in and out of formation. At one point we were so far behind and below the rest of the formation that I sensed that Lew and George both were prodding the element leader to catch up by flying in tight to his wing and tail.

It was about at this point that I caught sight of a B-17 a thousand feet or so below us heading back for England. It was aborting the mission for reasons known only to the crew aboard. I hoped they would make it.

The cloud deck was still with us and by elapsed time I knew we were probably over Germany. I had no idea exactly where that was.

As we continued our flight, I saw a Luftbury Circle of fighters off in the the distance to my right, slightly above 2 o'clock level. They were too far away to tell whether they were friend or foe or a mix of both. The Luftbury Circle was an aerial maneuver carried over from World War I.

Now in addition to the solid cloud deck below, we were getting contrails. These plumes of white vapor streamed from every engine of every four-engined B-17 in the 18 ship formation. They pointed like arrows to their source — the bombers.

To add further negatives to the ill-fated mission, the group began circling. I can only surmise that the lead ship was lost. They didn't know where the hell they were and they were making 360's over enemy territory.

Mission No. 1

For the life of me, then and now, I don't understand how the lead ship could get lost. We started out from England together with at least a thousand other planes. It doesn't require any great shakes of navigating when all you need do is tell the pilot to "go with them." The rest of us will follow.

But there we were, in formation, following the lead ship as it circled, contrails streaming out behind every ship. And below us a solid cloud deck. We might as well have hung out a huge sign saying "Here we are!" and extended an engraved invitation to the Luftwaffe to "come and get us!" Which they did.

Six enemy fighters came zipping out of nowhere. They flew head on and parallel to the formation. They were slightly to the right of 12 o'clock level.

I opened fire on the third, fourth, fifth and sixth aircraft as they came streaking past. I didn't worry too much about the WEFT system of aircraft identification. My survival instincts told me that "friendlies" don't fly head on into B-17 formations.

They followed up their frontal assault with a pass from behind and below. The six FW-190's came at us from six o'clock low. They came up through the clouds, hidden under and in the contrails. This time they zapped us good. As "Tail-end Charlie," we caught the full brunt of the attack.

In this pass they knocked out two of our four engines, wrecked our intercom, our oxygen system, shot up the top turret and tail guns.

They wounded both respective gunners. Tail gunner Bill Shenkel was mortally wounded.

With the top turret and tail guns out of commission, they continued to hammer away at us from this avenue of attack. On another pass they shot up the cockpit, virtually destroying it. Miraculously, neither the pilot nor the co-pilot was wounded.

They knocked us out of the formation and continued to attack like angry hornets, pumping lead and firing exploding 20mm shells into our stricken ship.

Meanwhile I sat up in the nose with two perfectly good guns, cursing a blue streak. I was no longer an "Officer and a Gentleman." I was a terrified street-wise kid brought up in the slums of Soulard, a melting pot South St. Louis neighborhood. Yet, I was where I wanted to be when I first enlisted into the Air Corps— face to face with a Nazi s-o-b. Scared? Your damned right I was scared. But as a kid, I learned in street fights that the other guy was just as scared as I was and that usually whoever landed the first good punch won the fight.

The FW's were pouring it on. The noise of our engines, out of sync and running away, along with the exploding 20mm shells was horrendous.

The engine's vibrations were shaking the ship apart. But we were still in the air and fighting back.

Out of nowhere, from underneath our plane, an FW came into my line of fire. He was no more than 100 feet from where I sat in the nose. I could clearly see the markings on his ship. He was that close.

The instant I saw him, I pointed my guns at him and cut loose. He was so close there wasn't time to use my gun sight. I just moved my chin turret handles in his direction and fired away. I paid no heed to gunnery class instructions to fire short bursts. What the hell, the ship was on her last legs. (Lew had salvoed the 12 armed 500lb. demolition bombs to keep the ship in the air. I have no idea where the bombs landed. My best guess is they plowed up a German farmer's field.) I fired one long continuous burst until the FW wheeled up and to the left toward 9 o'clock, out of my line of sight. As I fired I could see puffs of gray smoke coming off the tops of his wings. After he disappeared from sight, I wondered if I got him.

During all the din, I sensed rather than heard the bail-out bell. Whitby, the navigator handed me my chute. About that time the co-pilot, George Barnes, poked his head out of the hatchway and yelled "You fellas better get out of here." The wide eyed look on George's face told me what my face probably looked like.

Whitby and I were the only crew members wearing flak vests. Two were issued to our crew. Pilot Lew Bredeson decided that Whitby and I should get them because there was no protective armor in the nose. Other stations in the ship had some kind of armor protection.

At this time I was unaware that Whitby had been wounded. I got out of my seat to put on my chute. But first, I had to take off the flak vest so I could hook the chute to my harness. The flak vest had an emergency release that when I pulled would make the vest drop off. I pulled the release cord and nothing happened. I pulled it harder. It still didn't drop off. At that point I panicked. I could see myself going down with the ship because I couldn't get my chute on. I literally screamed, "Whitby! Help me!"

With all the ear bursting noise going on, Whitby couldn't hear me much much less help me. It was at this point that the self discipline that comes with military training took hold. I yelled loud to myself, "Don't panic! Think! Try taking it off over your head like you would a sleeveless sweater."

I did. It came off. A few seconds later, I felt a hot sting in my back near my left shoulder blade. I had no idea what it was. I shook

Dulag-Luft. Kriegsgefangenenkartei.	Gefangenen-Erkennungsmarke Nr. 294780-1	Dulag-Luft Eingeliefert am: 28.2.44.
NAME: KALMAN	Vorname des Vaters: *Abraham*	
Vornamen: Samuel Louis	Familienname der Mutter: *Rose Brittler*	
Dienstgrad: 2/Lt. Funktion: bomb.	Verheiratet mit:	
Matrikel-No.: O-749 639	Anzahl der Kinder:	
Geburtstag: 22.2.21.		
Geburtsort: St. Louis, Mo.	Heimatanschrift:	
Religion: Jewish. *Lebensmittel*	Mr. Abraham Kalman: 1326 Shawmut Pl. St. Louis, 12, Mo.	
Zivilberuf: Clerk *Großhandel*		
Staatsangehörigkeit: U.S.A.		

Abschuß am: 21.2.44. bei: Bruckenburg, Oldenburg. Flugzeugtyp:
Gefangennahme am: wie oben bei:

Nähere Personalbeschreibung

Figur: schlank		Augen: braun	
Größe: 5,9 ¾		Nase: groß gebogen	
Schädelform: oval		Bart: ohne	
Haare: braun		Gebiß: 1 Kunstzahn	
Gewicht: 60 kg			
Gesichtsform: eckig		Besondere Kennzeichen: Kleine Narbe r. Daumen, Mal rechte Bauchseite.	
Gesichtsfarbe: blass			

2nd Lt. Samuel Kalman's prison camp identification.

it off and thought no more about it at the time.

The flak vest came off so easily that I broke out in a cold sweat. Dealing with that problem was the supreme test in my life. Up until that moment of panic, I had, in my own mind, performed well. Even after I panicked, I was able to conquer my fear and regain control. I now knew the depth of my own mettle: that I could deal with anything that came down the pike, regardless of what lay ahead. I believe it was at that moment that I grew up.

Whitby was saying something but the noise was too great for me to hear him. Still I understood what he was saying. He motioned for me to go first because he had charts and other classified material to destroy. Since I had no bombsight, there was nothing for me to get rid of. I grabbed up my G.I. shoes and headed for the escape hatch.

I dangled my feet out the hatch, sitting there long enough to tie the laces of my G.I. shoes to the leg strap of my parachute harness. Whitby looked at me and yelled, "are you going?"

I couldn't hear him because of the noise. I understood his question. I answered him by diving out the escape hatch head first.

To make sure I cleared the ship, I counted ten. After that I stopped counting. I had pre-planned to delay opening my chute as long as possible in order to improve my chances of evading capture.

Back in the States, I used to worry about whether I would have the guts to jump if it became necessary. Now, I had the answer, simple and uncomplicated: Jump and live. Don't and die.

It was 1515 hours when I bailed out at about 12,000 feet. As I fell free of the ship, I felt myself tumbling. I experienced no sensation of falling because I didn't pass anything as a reference point. Its the same with speed. Only when you pass things, do you realize how fast you are going. At least, that was my experience.

Once away from the horrendous noise of combat, runaway props and vibrating engines out of sync, things got extremely quiet. There was also a physical reason for the quiet. As I fell the denser air pushed on my eardrums making me temporarily deaf.

I continued tumbling and I feared I might black out. I said aloud, "try a little aileron." I did. I stretched my arms out wide, flattened my hands, turning them so they would catch the wind. It worked. The tumbling stopped. I pulled my arms back in and continued to free fall until I felt myself tumbling again. I put my arms/ailerons out again and the tumbling stopped. (At that time there was no name for what I was doing. Years later I realized I had been sky diving.)

The cloud deck below hid the ground.

Finally, I said aloud, "You'd better quit foxin' around and pull the rip-cord." Which I did.

I was in a sitting position when my chute opened and caused me to grunt involuntarily.

What a beautiful sight that big, white silk canopy overhead

made. Once my chute opened, I grabbed the risers and held on.

Drifting slowly earthward, I looked up and saw our ship in the distance still in the air. "God!" I thought, "I jumped too soon."

As I watched the plane move further away, a body came hurtling down from her. The body waved its arms and kicked its legs as it fell.

"That's Whitby," I thought. "I hope his chute works."

A little later, I drifted through the clouds into the clear. The groundscape below appeared in miniature. I made out a windmill on the horizon, a church steeple, a clump of bare trees, and barren farm land.

The windmill gave me the false hope that I might be over Holland. While still in the air, I decided I would head for the woods where I could hide and get my bearings. I had no idea of where I was. I wanted to look at the maps I knew I had in my escape kit.

In the last 300 feet of my descent, the ground seemed to come up and meet me. Everything on the landscape that previously appeared in miniature now seemed to grow larger in a big hurry.

I made a three point landing in a barren field, hitting on my heels, my butt and the back of my head. I collapsed my chute, gathered it up and looked for a place to hide it. I found a depression in the field, put my chute, my harness, and my May West in it. I hurriedly covered them with dirt and took off.

I spotted a drainage ditch along the side of the road. I climbed down into it only to find that it was ice covered. I broke through the ice with my first step and got one foot wet.

Climbing back out of the ditch, I ran down the narrow road with difficulty because I was still wearing my clumsy flying boots.

I remember being briefed by S-2 to get off the road and get into the middle of a field as soon as possible. Following that recommendation, I crawled under a barbed wire fence face down that had been freshly manured.

I made my way to the woods I had spotted, moving into the center of it. I hoped to find a hiding place with some cover. The trees were bare of leaves. I came to a tiny ice covered stream that had a break in the ice.

I changed to my G.I. shoes. Since I was wearing two pairs of socks (my feet were always cold in winter), I took one of the dry socks from my dry foot and put it on the other foot after I took off the two wet socks.

I hid my flying boots under the ice. I opened my escape kit. I found cloth maps, a small compass the size of a dime, escape photographs and an emergency "D" ration chocolate bar.

I hid the compass in the top sock of the two I had gotten wet.

The sock was a white, heavy woolen sock. The second one was a regular G.I. sock. When the socks had gotten wet, the white one was discolored by the dye of my wet flying boots. It was a dirty

Guard tower at Barth Prison Camp.

looking mess. I figured the toe of that sock would be a good hiding place for the compass if I should get caught.

I spread the maps out on the frosty ground and tried to get oriented to where I was and what direction to go in. As I did this, I heard shouting all around me.

I saw that I was surrounded by perhaps 15 or 20 German male civilians, including some teen-age Hitler Jungen in uniform. The men were armed with clubs and closed in on me. I was unarmed and outnumbered. I stood up and held my hands over my head, signifying surrender.

As our British Allies used to say: "I'd 'ad it."

The Germans had some words for it, too. "All ist kaput. For you der var ist over."

Epilogue

Usually it is the Generals, like Patton and others, who get the glory in wars. But it wasn't Patton whose blood and guts were spilled in battle. It was the soldiers on the battlefield who fought the enemy on land, sea and in the air. It was their blood and their guts that were spilled. It was their lives that were destroyed. It was their lives that were taken from them in the prime of their youth. No combat soldier, physically wounded or not, ever truly escapes the wounds and hurts of war. All are casualties in one way or another of man's inhumanity to man and the cruel disease called war.

S/Sgt. William H. Shenkel, the tail gunner of my crew, died a hero's death. Except there was no one there to see it. He died alone in a German farmer's field somewhere in enemy territory.

Other members of my crew who were also wounded included S/Sgt. Howard R. (Pop) Collins, top turret gunner and engineer on the ship: 2nd Lt. Robert A. Whitby, navigator; Sgt. Walter T. Jutze, waist gunner, who broke an ankle on landing after bailing out. There may have been others but these are the ones I know about.

Later I learned that one of Shenkel's two tail guns had frozen up and wouldn't fire; and that waist gunner Sgt. Louis P. Rigaud's oxygen mask had frozen up, forcing him to stay in the radio room. Only recently, I learned that mortally wounded Shenkel came into the radio room to ask that he be parachuted out on a static line in hopes of getting help from the Germans on the ground. The crewmen who bailed him out said that they saw his chute open.

The hot sensation I felt in my shoulder when we were under attack turned out to be a sliver of a 20mm shell. I had forgotten about it until I got to POW camp at Barth, Germany. It had festered and come to the surface. One of my fellow POW's dug it out with a pin.

The parachute I bailed out with belonged to — Capt. Dickinson.

I spent nearly 15 months as a POW, mostly at Stalag Luft 1, Barth, Germany. During the last four months, some 105 to 115 of us who were American Jews, were segregated and forced to live in an all Jewish barracks. According to the S.S. who ran the camp at this time, "the worst that could happen to us was that we would be sent to a 'central camp'" — a Nazi euphemism for concentration camp. The Russians liberated the camp on 1 May 1945 before the S.S. could carry out their plan.

My buddy, Bob Horn, was shot down on his first mission three days after I was. He was substituting for a bombardier on a crew other than his own.

In addition to Lew Bredeson, George Barnes and myself, other 457th group members who lived in North Compound 1, included Amos W. Shepard and William H. Good. Good who was on Shepard's crew, hailed from St. Louis.

A fellow POW who had been on the 21 February Guttersloh raid from another group and was shot down later told me that the 457th led the 8th Air Force that day. [ED. The 457th flew the high box. The 351st BG flew lead.]

It wasn't until January 1990 that I read Col. Byers' book "FLAK DODGER" and learned that there were two names to the target, "Lippstadt/Guttersloh." The significance of Lippstadt escapes me other than to further verify the p_____ poor briefing my crew got for that first mission on 21 February 1944. [ED. The 457th put up two boxes of 18 a/c that day. One to Lippstadt and the other to Guttersloh. Lt. Col. James Luper led the box to Guttersloh. He was famous for making 360's.]

On 22 February 1944, the next day after being shot down, I turned 23. I celebrated my birthday in a bare cell in solitary at a German disciplinary jail, the Nazi version of a "guard house" for their own delinquent troops.

Some 25 years after being shot down, Lew Bredeson came to the St. Louis area on a business trip. We got together one evening. He told me for the first time that the FW-190 I shot at had come in underneath our ship, wheeled up to the left and blew up at 9 o'clock. He didn't know that I had fired at it. Because of security reasons, we never discussed military subjects in POW camp at Barth. I told him that now, 25 years later, I was going to put in for a "kill."

Mission No. 4
25 February 1944
Target — Augsburg Messerschmidt A/C Plant

Crew of B17G, No. 42-97458

1st Pilot	2nd Lt.	Edward J. Reppa
Co-Pilot	2nd Lt.	Aaron J. Ayres
Nav.	2nd Lt.	Robert E. Jackson
Bomb.	2nd Lt.	George H. Stateman
Engr.	T/Sgt.	Stephen F. Billisits
Radio Op.	T/Sgt.	Ivan W. Browning
LW Gun.	S/Sgt.	John Harmke
RW Gun.	S/Sgt.	Irving Feldman
B. Turret	S/Sgt.	Francis Boyson
Tail Gun.	S/Sgt.	Charles W. Mehring

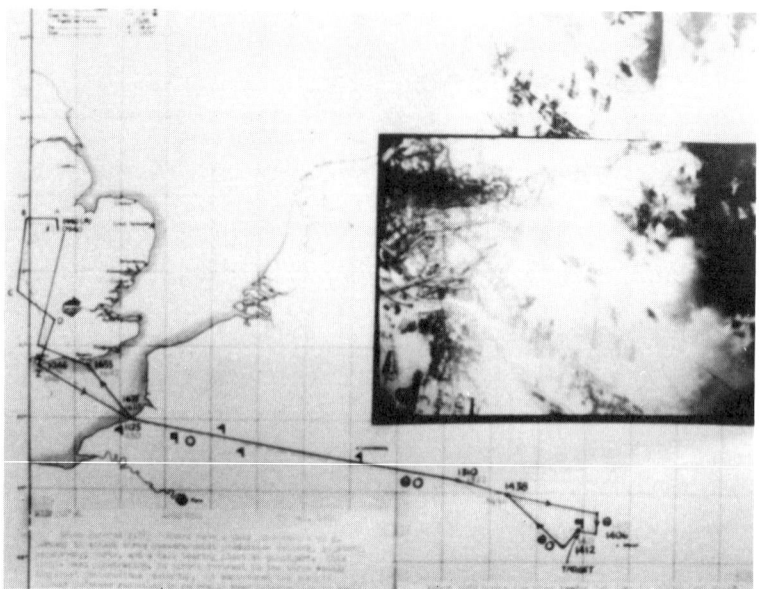

Track Chart, Mission No. 4, 25 Feb. 1944

457th Bomb Group Mission Narrative

Seven hundred and fifty bombers made a mass penetration of southern Germany to attack three Messerschmidt production centers, Augsburg, Regensburg, and Furth, and a ball bearing plant at Stuttgart. This single mass penetration, in direct contrast to the three widely dispersed penetrations on 24 February 1944, out maneuvered the enemy's fighter defense resulting generally in weak interception by small forces.

The 457th Bomb Group, whose target was the Messerschmidt plant at Augsburg, flew low box in the 94th Wing, the second wing on the target. In addition six planes were provided for the low squadron of the high box. The formation took off at 0900 hours and, after the wing assembly was completed at the French coast, proceeded on the briefed course through northern France, crossing the Rhine River between Mannheim and Karlsruhe to the I.P. at Ingolstadt, northeast of Augsburg.

Just inside the French coast, intense and accurate flak was encountered which knocked out one engine of Lt. Reppa's plane and one engine on Lt. James Chinn's plane. Lt. Chinn left the formation over Boye, France, to salvo his bombs. He could not regain the formation and was shot down by enemy fighters. Lt. Reppa continued with the formation to the target.

The 500-pound general purpose bombs were released on the Messerschmidt plant at 1412 hours with excellent results although about thirty seconds before bombs away a piece of flak crashed through the plexiglass nose directly in front of the bombardier Lt. David B. Jones, glanced off the bombsight, and narrowly missed Jones. Three minutes later flak knocked out the No. 2 engine of the lead plane flown by Lt. Lady, with Lt. Col. Luper as Air Commander. The deputy lead plane, flown by Capt. Raymond A. Syptak with Major Leroy Watson, Jr. in the right seat, took over and led the group home. Lt. Archie Bower's plane was hit by flak, dropped out of the formation, and was attacked by enemy fighters.

About 1500 hours the wing leader let down to 15,000 feet which resulted in the group receiving flak from the airfields along the route from Laon to Amiens. This flak became very accurate, causing considerable damage to the 457th BG planes in addition to the damage from flak at Augsburg. Lt. Reppa came out from 70 miles inside France with only two engines, having lost one engine on the way into the target. His plane was demolished in a crash landing at another base. Lt. Green B. Poore, badly shot up, landed at another base with only 25 gallons of gasoline in the tanks. Lt. Robert Lane also landed at another base with two engines knocked out. Flak from the French airfields knocked out three engines on Lt. Clarence E. Schuchmann's plane; as he was coming in to land at Deenethorpe the fourth engine quit and he made a dead stick landing in the B-17.

Twenty-three of the twenty-four planes completing the mission suffered battle damage. One A/C was destroyed on landing and two were lost over enemy territory. Six men received minor wounds and Lt. Gides, the bombardier of Lt. James crew, was seriously wounded.

Although the 457th BG suffered heavily, the entire operation was successful and the losses moderate. Thirty-one of the dispatched 750 A/C were lost.

Lt. Edward J. Reppa's story of the 25 February 1944 mission to Augsburg.

This was our second mission and I remember we assembled at about 10,000 feet and started climbing on our route to our target, the Messerschmidt airplane factory at Augsburg, Germany. We crossed the English Channel and the coast of occupied Europe at the relatively low altitude of 14,000 feet. Near Amiens, France, one battary of anti-aircraft opened up on us. Shrapnel hit and injured the ball turret gunner S/Sgt. Francis Boyson in the leg and a

Lt. Edward Reppa's A/C No. 42-97458 crash landing.

piece just missed T/Sgt Steve Billisits, while another piece knocked out the supercharger in No. 3 engine, leaving the manifold pressure in that engine to be the atmospheric pressure at the altitude we were flying. The sudden loss of power caused us to drop back in the formation from the No. 3 position to the No. 6 position — purple heart corner — in the low squadron. The formation continued climbing on course and we had to use full power on the three good engines to maintain our position. The higher we climbed also reduced the power we got from engine No. 3 and it became increasingly difficult to keep up. When we reduced power settings to conserve the three good engines we would quickly fall back out of formation forcing us to use full power again. Lt. Aaron Ayres, the co-pilot monitored the engine temperatures, opening and closing the cowl flaps at times to cool the engines. This procedure increased the aerodynamic drag on the airplane which also caused us difficulty.

I remember that at one time Lt Col. Luper yelled at me over the VHF radio to 'close it up.' Since I was required to maintain radio silence I could not tell him of our mechanical problem. The thought ran through my mind to try to return to England for at the time we were only about 100 miles inside France but I knew the German Luftwaffe flew from French bases and I feared the consequences to my crew of returning home alone. There was also the fear of explaining to Lt. Col. Luper why we aborted and did not continue to the target. To this day I don't know what was the deciding factor to continue flying with the group.

Well we finally reached bombing altitude allowing us to ease up somewhat on the engines. There were no more incidents on our trip to the target. We dropped the bombs with the group and turned and headed for home. The return trip was somewhat easier as we had dropped our bombs and there was a slow descent by the group allowing us to 'throttle back,' putting less strain on the three good engines. Our problem now was one of conserving fuel as we had used so much on our trip to the target. Everything seemed to be fine until we approached the French coast where a small battary of flak guns opened up on us and we lost engine No. 2, which we immediately feathered. However, about a minute later the oil pressure on engine No. 4 dropped and we had to feather it, too. Since we were now down to about 14,000 feet the No. 3 engine was running better and it along with engine No. 1 was enough power to maintain a slow descent for home. We dropped out of formation as we slowed down from the reduced power.

We dropped down to about 2,000 feet and had managed to cross the English coast and looked about for a landing field. The usual cloud cover made it difficult to see any great distance ahead; however, we finally saw a landing strip, made a pattern, and decided to land on it. The flaps would not lower, neither could we get them down manually, so we came in hot and without any hydraulic pressure did not have any brakes to stop our roll. Our left wing hit a tree but we rolled on until we came to a deep ditch at the end of the runway. Just before we hit the ditch Lt. Ayres cut the master switch to prevent a possible fire and explosion. Fortunately there were no serious injuries to the crew resulting from the crash as all members had assumed a crash position in the radio room. Three crew members were hospitalized for a short time but recovered to fly again.

B-17G, No. 4297458, with a 'broken back.'

Not knowing how to contact the group we were listed as missing on that day. The British picked us up and we stayed at an army installation until our group was notified. Four days later the group sent a truck for us and we returned to base, 'somewhat bent but not broken.'

Lt. Aaron J. Ayres' story of the 25 February 1944 mission to Augsburg, Germany

The mission began well, the take off and the forming of the group was good. It wasn't until we crossed the English Channel and were deep into France that we ran into flak. We took a hit in the No. 3 engine which knocked out the supercharger. We decided to leave the engine running since it was pulling enough manifold pressure to equal being feathered. This turned out to be a good decision, as we later received more damage to the other engines on the aircraft on the return flight to England. However with the No. 3 engine damaged we had trouble keeping up with the formation. Having been instructed that our No. 1 priority was to drop bombs on the selected target, and the fact that German fighters liked to attack lone B-17's, we decided to continue on to the target with the group. With the cowl flaps closed we could stay in formation but the other engines would over-heat. It was then necessary to open the cowl flaps and cool down the engines, but with the extra drag we were not able to hold our position in the formation. After the engines were cooled I would close the flaps and try to regain our position in the formation. We repeated this procedure all the way to Augsburg.

We dropped our bombs on the target with the group and turned for home. We thought now our troubles were over. Not so! Having overworked the engines they were not running at full power. However, we were able to keep up with the formation as we were gradually descending. Then about fifty miles south of the location where we had been hit by flak on the way to the target we ran into heavy anti-aircraft fire again. The formation and particularly our plane was getting the hell shot out of it again. Lt. Reppa and I discussed leaving the formation to get out of the flak but before we could decide anything we took a direct hit in No. 2 engine, setting it on fire. We turned off the gasoline and feathered the engine, which extinguished the fire.

Ever since our first attack, our engineer, T/Sgt. Steve Billisits, had been tranferring gasoline from the poor to the good running

Mission No. 4

B-17G, No. 42-97122, dropping bombs.

engines. He would no sooner get the gasoline transferred when something would happen and he would have to start all over again. While doing this he counted over 200 flak holes in the bomb bay alone.

Now with two engines not running and two not at full power we had no choice but to leave the group and start a slow descent back to England. We knew we could not make it back to our base at Glatton but hoped to make it across the English Channel and not be forced to ditch.

At this point we began to jettison everything that was loose in order to lighten the airplane and extend our range. About this time No. 1 engine began to lose power.

One bright spot in the mission was that shortly after leaving the group formation, two RAF Spitfire fighters picked us up and escorted us down to about 7,000 feet where we flew into a solid layer of clouds.

Flying on instruments, we crossed the channel all right, remaining in the clouds. We began picking up signals from barrage balloons on our radio and, not knowing our exact position while still in the clouds and losing altitude, I advised the crew to get ready to bail out at 1,500 feet. Some did not like the idea and we decided to drop to 1,200 feet instead. However, just before dropping to

1,200 feet we spotted a hole in the clouds and let down through it. We broke out of the clouds at 300 feet near the town of Headcorn. We immediately looked for a place to land the beleaguered B-17 and saw a fighter strip that was under construction that apppeared to be our best bet under the circumstances. We could not assess all of our damage but did know that our flaps would not extend. We did have full brake pressure and assumed they were all right. We decided to make a 'wheels down' landing without flaps, since we did not have time to crank them down. At this time No. 3 engine, without a supercharger, was the only engine giving us an appreciable amount of power. Lt. Reppa made a good approach and landing, a little hot because of the lack of flaps. Still we were in good shape, plenty of time to stop on the short strip. However, when Lt. Reppa applied the brakes we discovered they had been also shot out below the last check valve and we had none.

I then tried to ground loop the plane but could not get enough power out of the outboard engines. By this time we were approaching the end of the runway. I saw there was a big drainage ditch across the end of the runway and I thought, good! that will strip off the landing gear and we will skid to a stop. The wheels hit the ditch three or four feet down and plowed a couple of furrows as we kept going. A big oak tree stood about 100 yards from the ditch which we were going to clip with the left wing. My thoughts, again, were that it would cause us to turn and stop and everything would be OK. We left about four or five feet of wing hanging in the oak tree and rolled merrily on toward a gravel pit that had been used for fill when building the runway.

We had now slowed down considerably but still could not control the plane. Just before landing in the pit, I cut the master switches to prevent any fires. Thus we ended our second mission.

Our ball turret gunner, S/Sgt. Francis Boyson, had been hit by flak early in the mission and had been given first aid by S/Sgt. George Stateman. However, he was so severely injured he never flew any more missions. Two other members of the crew had received scratches in the crash. The rest of us walked away from this one, and went on to complete 30 missions.

Experience seemed to be the best teacher as we had battle damage on twenty of the remaining twenty-eight missions and later made safe landings with either engines feathered or no brakes.

Mission No. 23
9 April 1944
Target Rahmel, Focke Wulf 190 Factory.
Near Gdynia, Poland.

Lt. Amos W. Shepard's A/C No. 42-97537.

Crew of B17G No. 42-97537

1st Pilot	2nd Lt.	Amos W. Shepard	
Co-Pilot	2nd Lt.	Ralph O. Hammerstrom	
Nav.	2nd Lt.	Herbert W. Spalding	
Bomb.	2nd Lt.	Kenneth Galyean	
Engr.	T/Sgt.	Joseph E. Fasone	KIA
Radio Op.	T/Sgt.	Jon E. Roberts	
LW Gun.	S/Sgt.	Andrew H. Kauffman	
RW Gun.	S/Sgt.	Amos T. Bunch	
B. Turret	S/Sgt.	Harold E. Smith	
Tail Gun.	S/Sgt.	William H. Good	

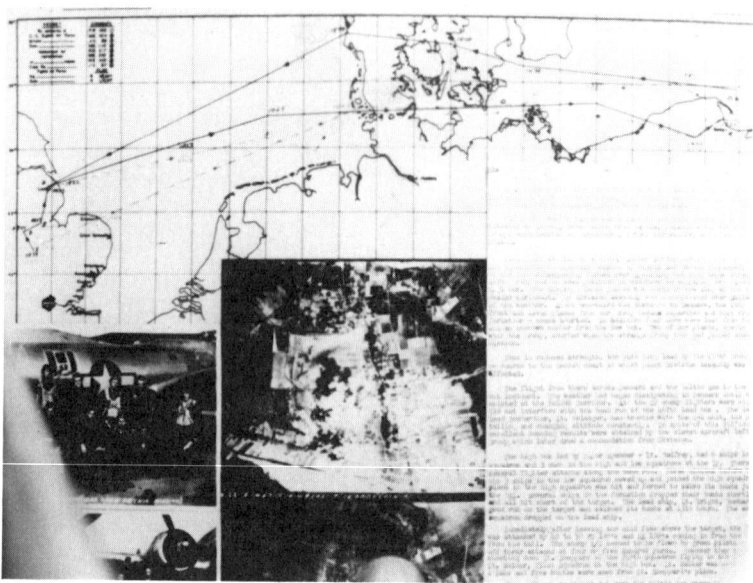

Track Chart, Mission No. 23, 9 April 1944.

457th Bomb Group Mission Narrative

In a large-scale attack against the FW-190 eastern complex of aircraft factories in north central Germany and western Poland, twelve combat wings were airborne today for the deepest penetration of the war into Germany.

The 457th Group's target for today was a factory airfield producing Focke Wulf-190 fighters situated at Rahmel, seven miles from Gdynia, Poland, while targets for other groups were located at Marienburg, Tutow, Warnemunde, and Posen in central Poland.

Taking off at 0740 hours on a cloudy Easter Sunday morning, the group assembly was impossible to maintain because of the clouds and became dispersed. Each group of the wing subsequently assembled over Spaulding but was much below strength. The 457th Group was in the lead position in addition to supplying two squadrons of six planes each to the high box. The missing planes joined the boxes in the wing at the coast as it headed northeast. Division formation was not accomplished over England because of the weather. About one-third of the distance to Denmark, the wing ran through a front and seven planes from our group became separated and lost from the formation and all subsequently aborted. In addition, four more planes were lost from the high group and an unknown number from the low box. Two of our planes, unable to assemble with the group, aborted when the strange group they had joined aborted the mission.

Thus in reduced strength, the 94th CBW led by the 457th Bomb Group continued to the Danish coast at which point division assembly was finally effected.

The flight across Denmark and above the Baltic Sea to the I.P. was without incident. The weather had been improving beyond Denmark and upon reaching the I.P. the clouds had dissipated and the visibility was clear. Enemy fighters were sighted by the lead group but did not attack the 457th on the bomb run. The lead bombardier, Lt. Lloyd T. Belanger, had difficulty with the C-1 unit, the plane fishtailing and changing altitude. In spite of this difficulty excellent bombing results were achieved by the eleven aircraft in the group and were later commended by the commanding officer of the division.

The high box, led by Major Spencer/Lt. Godfrey and composed of only twelve ships, experienced fighter attacks along the bomb run. Three minutes before bombs away the three ships in the low squadron and one plane in the high squadron were hit and forced to salvo their bombs just before reaching the BRL. Several ships in the formation dropped their bombs just after this and all hit short of the target. Lt. Wright, lead bombardier in the lead ship, made a good run on the target and dropped its bombs at 1316 hours. The lead squadron dropped their bombs with the lead ship.

Immediately after leaving the light flak above the target the formation was attacked by 40 or 50 FW-190's and Me-109's coming at the bombers from both the nose and the tail. The enemy aircraft seemed to be flown by green pilots as they broke off their attacks at 400-500 yards. However, they succeeded in shooting down Lt. Amos W. Shepard's plane of the 749th Squadron, flying in the lead box. Lt. Robert K. Walker was seen to ditch his airplane in a lake, while five chutes were seen coming from Lt. Shepard's plane.

Attacks by the enemy fighters continued out over the Baltic Sea where Lt. David P. Parks, flying in the high box, plunged nose down under a dense concentration of 20mm cannon fire with no chutes observed.

The formation was intercepted by enemy fighters as they crossed the Danish peninsula but no planes were lost to the attacks. Escorting P-51's did excellent work here. Our gunners claimed 12 enemy aircraft shot down in the continuing aerial battle and received credit for three destroyed, one probably destroyed, and one damaged. They expended 59,370 rounds of .50 cal. ammunition.

Lt. Karr crashed landed his badly damaged plane at another base in England. Only three planes incurred flak damage but several planes had 20mm damage. Because of low gasoline, Lt. Robert Krumm and crew landed at Tibbenham AFB, a B-24 base where Col. James Stewart was Commanding Officer.

The formation returned to base in very bad weather, landing at 1816 hours completing an eleven-hour mission.

S/Sgt. Harold E. Smith

Ball turret gunner S/Sgt Harold E. Smith's story of the 9 April 1944 Mission to Gdynia, Poland.

My feet had been frozen on my first mission, however I had recuperated and the flight to Gdynia, Poland, was my 4th and last mission. Both No. 3 and No. 4 engines were on fire and I decided to get the hell out of the ball turret. We were wearing chest pack parachutes; I could not wear the chute in the ball turret and had to leave it in the waist of the airplane. I was praying as I crawled out of the turret that my chute had not been shot full of holes. I was so nervous that I could not snap the chute to the harness, so Andy Kauffman, the left waist gunner, helped me buckle on the chute.

The tail gunner Bill Good was still in his position, shooting at enemy fighters, when I was heading for the waist door to bail out. I threw a spent .50 cal. shell at Bill to get his attention and he came forward in a hurry.

That was my first and only parachute jump. The one practice parachute jump we were to take while we were in training was aborted and we later discovered a lot of the chutes were incorrectly packed and probably would not have opened.

Anyway, I jumped out the waist door and hollered 'Geronimo' (for a ten-second delay) and believe it or not I guided that chute into an opening in a woods, just big enough to come down in and miss the trees.

I buried the chute in the woods and just sat and wondered what would be the best thing to do. I did not have an escape kit or any food so I just started walking and finally came to a small village. I was scared, but just walked around the village until I was picked up. People looked at me and spoke but did nothing.

Finally I just sat down on a street corner and it wasn't long before three soldiers in an old pick-up truck stopped and motioned for me to get in the back of the truck.

The soldier in charge was named Wilhelm Schmidt and when he looked at my dog tags he pointed to himself and said, "Schmidt."

I was taken to an interrogation camp and then to Stalag Luft VI at Heyde Krieg. I was soon evacuated to Stalag Luft IV and then to Keif Heide at Grosstychow. Later, near the end of the war, I was transferred to Nuremburg and then to Mooseburg, where we were liberated by General Patton's Fifth Army on 29 April 1945. I had been a POW for 13 months.

Lt. Amos W. Shepard

Enlisted crew members of A/C No. 42-97537

All the other members of Lt. Shepard's crew lived through the war except T/Sgt. Joseph E. Fasone. I do not know for sure what happened to Fasone, but it is believed that the German SS troops killed him. None of the other enlisted men were at any of the locations where I was imprisoned. I have not seen any of the crew since World War II but have been in contact with some of them by telephone and by mail.

S/Sgt. Amos T. Bunch 9 April 1944 story of Mission to Gdynia, Poland. Interviewed on 2 August 1944 by United States S2 officers.

I was injured when our plane was hit by anti-aircraft fire. I was wounded in the left leg between my knee and hip. I was knocked down by the piece of flak but I got to my feet and operated my gun, shooting at the enemy aircraft again. I heard someone on the crew holler, "The plane is on fire." We had lost our interphone and when the others bailed out, I did also. When I landed, I was picked up and carried to a hospital in Godning, Poland, where I was operated on by a German doctor who removed the piece of schrapnel from my leg.

I was sent to Stalag 17B, where I was hospitalized until 1 August 1944. Up to that time my wound had not completely healed, and is still giving me trouble.

457th Bomb Group critique report: 9 April 1944 Group Mission No. 23 to Augsburg, Germany.

Lt. Shepard's plane No. 537 was hit by flak and fighters at 1320 hours in the target area. While the ship was apparently under control 5 chutes were seen to open. Lt. Robert K. Walker's ship No. 456 was seen to go down over the target area and only two chutes were positively seen to open.

Mission Recalled
21 April 1944
Target — Merseburg/Luena refinery

Wreckage of Lt. Owen B. Coffman's A/C No. 42-97236.

Crew of B-17G No. 42-97236

1st Pilot	2nd Lt.	Owen B. Coffman	KIA
Co-Pilot	2nd Lt.	Stewart Barnes	KIA
Nav.	2nd Lt.	Joseph J. Peacock	KIA
Bomb.	2nd Lt.	Lowell D. Baker	KIA
Engr.	S/Sgt.	Leroy L. Logan	KIA
Radio Op.	S/Sgt.	Lloyd E. Larson	
LW Gun.	Sgt.	Morris R. Walker	
RW Gun.	Sgt.	Donald L. Moore	
B. Turret	Sgt.	James C. Hilty	KIA
Tail Gun.	Sgt.	John P. Medica	

War Department report of crash of B-17G No. 42-97236

Lt. Owen B. Coffman took off at 1419 hours to join the 457th BG assembling above the overcast. They entered the clouds at about 8,000 feet and continued to climb on instruments. The co-pilot had just completed an interphone oxygen check at 15,000 feet when the ship hit very turbulent air, probably prop-wash, throwing the ship into a dive. The pilot, who was flying the plane on instruments as they were still in the clouds, attempted a fast recovery putting such a strain on the tail section it broke off. The tail gunner, who parachuted to safety, felt one bump followed by a great pressure on him, no doubt caused by the fast recovery, and then another surging bump when the tail broke off. The fuselage broke apart between the tail wheel and the waist door. The crew had not attached their parachutes, and the ball turret gunner was in his turret while the ship climbed through the clouds. There was a scramble for parachutes when the ship broke apart and, although some of the men parachuted safely before it crashed, the right waist gunner and the engineer jumped too late to pull their rip-cords before the plane crashed. The tail gunner jumped out where the plane had parted. The radio operator and the left waist gunner went out through the waist door. The right waist gunner apparently was knocked out by the first bump and never got out of the plane. The pilot and co-pilot apparently stayed with the ship trying to get it under control. The ship went into the ground nose

Lt. Owen B. Coffman's crashed A/C No. 42-97236.

Tail section of crashed A/C No. 42-97236.

Crash site of A/C No. 42-97236

first at about a 45-degree angle with a full load of bombs and was full of gasoline, including tokyo's. The plane hit the ground with a terrific explosion. The radio operator, coming down in his parachute and at about 5,000 feet almost directly over the explosion, was pushed higher into the air by the force of the explosion. It is apparent that the pilot had inadequate instrument time and was not well versed in the possibility of over controlling the aircraft, especially with such a heavy load and performing such a quick recovery when coming out of a dive. Also if the crew had attached their parachutes while in the clouds more of them would have survived.

Eye witness of crash of A/C No. 42-97236

I was standing on a hardstand at Horham Air Base when racing engines overhead attracted my attention. About two miles to the north at about 8,000 feet a B-17 came spinning out of the clouds without a tail section. I could also see the tail section falling, just above the plane. Then I saw a chute open just above the tail section. The plane spiraled and then seemed to level out for a few seconds as the pilot manipulated the engines trying to bring the airplane under control. Two more chutes came out of the plane. Just before the plane hit the ground four more men came out of the plane but too late for their parachutes to open. The plane hit the ground and there was a terrible explosion. Flames roared up to 1,500 feet.

B-17 with broken back.

Mission No. 44
12 May 1944

Target — Lutzkendorf oil refinery

Crew of B-17G, No. Unknown

1st Pilot	2nd Lt.	John Akers
Co-Pilot	2nd Lt.	Charles T. Scott
Nav.	2nd Lt.	Lloyd C. Dell
Bomb.	2nd Lt.	Leo F. Kruszynski
Engr.	T/Sgt.	Edward White
Radio Op.	T/Sgt.	Robert J. Marsteller
LW Gun.	S/Sgt.	Harold T. Peterman
RW Gun.	S/Sgt.	Christopher W. Milgo
B. Turret	S/Sgt.	Austin F. Moore
Tail Gun.	S/Sgt.	Wallace V. Taft

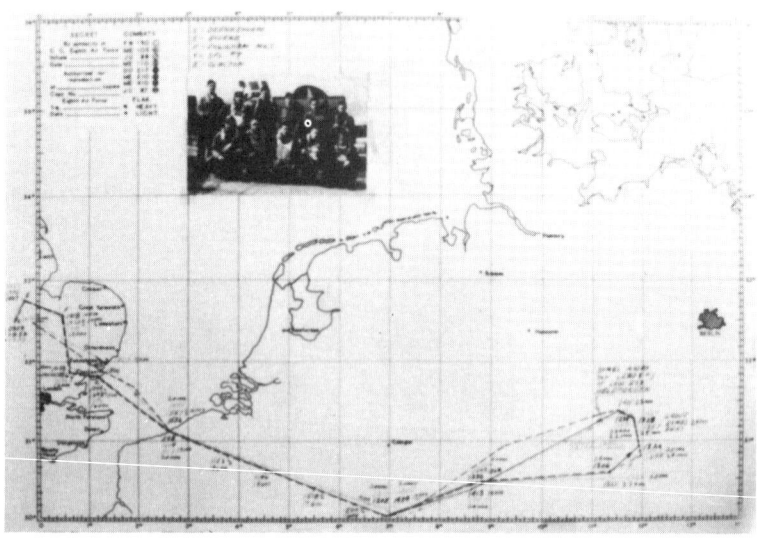

Track Chart, Mission No. 44, 12 May 1944

457th Bomb Group Mission Narrative

The opening punch of the long awaited aerial blitz of the German synthetic oil refineries was delivered today. Proper weather conditions existed at last. Fifteen combat wings, 806 bombers, were dispatched against the central German refineries at Brux, Merseburg/Luena, Zeitz, Leipzig-Bohlen, and Lutzkendorf.

The 457th BG furnished the lead and low boxes for the 94th 'B' CBW with two PFF ships in the wing lead position, 34 aircraft in all. The target was the refinery at Lutzkendorf, producer of 300,000 tons of petrol and diesel fuel annually and located 6 miles west of Merseburg.

Taking off at 0900 hours, penetration was along the southern route into central Germany, between the flak areas of the Ruhr Valley and Frankfurt, with five combat wings of the third division and the 94th 'A' CBW, spaced at two minute intervals, leading the procession out front. Behind at the same intervals were four more wings of the 1st division and four wings of the 2nd division.

Although our group saw no fighters, the leading wings of the 3rd division going to Brux had several attacks near Coblenz and Frankfurt from 150 enemy fighters, using en masse saturation tactics and even using suicide-ramming techniques. Thirty-two of the 34 heavy bombers lost to fighters were lost from these wings.

As visual bombing conditions existed, the PFF ships surrendered lead to the deputy lead Major Fred Spencer/Lt. Jerome E.

Godfrey at Saalfeld. The groups took interval in trail for bombing, the 457th BG going in first to the target. The I.P. was crossed on course at 24,000 feet and the bomb run began under excellent conditions with no interference from flak or fighters.

Several minutes before the bomb release line was reached, Lt. George Cahelo realized his synchronization was incorrect and decided not to drop the bombs but make another run on the target. When he turned off his rack switches one bomb accidentally released. At that point the other ships in the formation also released their bombs. Fortunately the bombs did cover one part of the target, scoring hits on the power house, ovens house, asnd other installations. The deputy lead A/C held its lead position until it had disposed of its bombs on a M/Y in the village of Buttstadt, near Gotha.

The 457th low box, led by Capt. J. McGavock Dickinson/Lt. Clarence Schuchmann, made a good run on the target. Two seconds before the BRL, the bombardier Lt. Warren H. Suddath gave the Aldis lamp signal to the deputy lead ship, and the deputy lead bombardier dropped his bombs, followed by the other ships in the box. The bombs in the lead ship would not release although the salvo handle was pushed twice. The bombs from this box fell two miles northwest of the target.

After the bomb run, Col. Henry B. Wilson in the lead PFF ship tried to reassemble the wing but could not contact the high and low boxes. The lead box returned to base alone and the high and low boxes returned home together.

The 457th BG lost one aircraft on this mission to causes unknown. Lt. John Akers, apparently having engine trouble, lagged behind the fomation near Eisenach on the return trip.

No fighters were met on the way home and the base was reached at 1630 hours, nine and one-half hours after departure. On the return trip a German operated B-17 joined our formation just west of Coblenz and continued with us as far as Brussels. Total bomber losses for the day was 44 A/C but on the whole a good start was made on the destruction of the German synthetic oil industry.

Lt. John Akers' story of the 12 May 1944 mission to Lutzkendorf, Germany.

I will write here my story of the 12 May 1944 mission when, unfortunately, I was shot down.

The mission was my fourth mission having gone to Nancy and

Leon, in occupied France, and on 8 May 1944 to Berlin, Germany. On the mission to Berlin my ship was badly damaged and my regular bombardier, Lt. M.F. Swerdlove, was in the hospital from injuries incurred on the mission and Lt. Leo F. Kruszynski, a substitute bombardier, from another crew, replaced him of the 12 May 1944 mission.

The mission started out normally and I was flying in 'purple heart corner' as 'Tail End Charlie' (No. 6 position in the low squadron). As usual, when we got over German territory we encountered some flak. I would assume we had crossed the Rhine River in the vicinity of Coblenz just south of 'Happy Valley,' when I lost oil pressure on my No. 3 engine presumably from a flak hit, as we had just seen some bursts of flak near our right wing. The engine started smoking so I feathered the propeller (turned it edgewise into the slipstream so it would not windmill and cause a lot of drag on the airplane). At this time we were possibly two or two and one-half hours into the mission and it seemed to me best not to abort (return to base), but to salvo my bombs, lighten our load, and try to stay with the group formation. Of course, at this time we were only at 21,000 feet and the field order had specified the bombing altitude to be at 25,000 feet with about one and one-half hours yet to go to the target at Lutzkendorf.

We salvoed the bombs and threw all non-essential items overboard, as was SOP (standard operating procedure). We had some difficulty getting the bomb bay doors closed since they must be manually closed when you salvo the bombs. This put an undue load on the aircraft; we were forced to drop lower and trailed behind the group. We joined for a time with other groups as they came along in the bomber stream and this probably accounts for no one reporting what had happened to us at the debriefing back at the base. We went all the way to the I.P. by following other groups; however, when we came to the I.P. I knew there was no use for us to go over the target, so we cut off at a 45-degree angle to try to intercept the groups on the way home. At this time my No. 1 and No. 4 engines started losing oil pressure and misfiring and to this day I do not know what caused them to malfunction as we had plenty of gasoline. With only one engine working we could not catch up or stay with any other formation as they departed the target area. I immediately broke radio silence and called 'mayday' on the VHF and asked for fighter support. I would say that within 5 or 10 minutes we had fighter cover and I set a long glide path and we flew at about 120 m.p.h. and for some two hours, I would estimate, we stayed airborne. I was told by the navigator that we had passed over the Rhine River and were over Belgium. We had an

Medical staff at Obermassfeld, Germany — mostly captured POWs at Dunkirque & Greece.

indicated altitude of 1,500 feet and I rang the bail-out bell and advised the crew to bail out. The No. 2 engine accommodated the automatic pilot, so I set the plane on auto-pilot and went down in the front hatch and pushed the co-pilot out the hatch door and bailed out myself. I cannot tell you what the altitude was at the time I bailed out but the co-pilot later said he never did see my chute open. When I started my first swing through, I hit the ground and blacked out. I remember nothing else until I recovered consciousness — it seemed to me to be about three o'clock in the afternoon. There were soldiers at the bottom of the hill where I had landed and they captured me. I could also see black smoke rising from a nearby hill and I presume that was where our plane had crashed. I had compound fractures in each of my ankles and the soldiers carried me to a nearby barracks, where I was kept under guard for a couple of hours. A white ambulance with an attendant came by and took me to a hospital in Coblenz. I spent one night in Coblenz where they gave me a thorough examination and put both of my legs in bucket splints. Although I had been somewhat apprehensive as to how I would be treated, I was not mistreated.

On the next day I was placed in a GI truck on a stretcher and taken to Frankfurt. This was the Dulag-Luft where they interrogated all the prisoners.

I will back-track a little bit. They did bring the co-pilot into the barracks where I had first been taken and he saw me dispatched in the ambulance. This was the last time I saw any of the crew, but they all landed safely and were captured. I stayed in Frankfurt for approximately 10 days, at which time they got very discouraged with me, slapped me around a bit, and brought in some high ranking officers along with a doctor. By this time I was running a temperature as my legs had never been set nor had I been given any medication. So they told me they were going to send me to the hospital facilities the next day. I was placed on a train and sent to a place known as Obermassfeld, located 80 or so miles from Frankfurt, where I was given treatment. They immediately set one of my legs and put the other in traction. My temperature continued to rise and they took off the cast and found the leg to be infected. The only drugs they had were sulpha which they used. They forgot about my left leg and tried to save my right leg, which they did. I recuperated there at Obermassfeld until late summer of 1944. In August or early September I was sent to a convalescent area where most of the prisoners who were ambulatory were sent. I was never able to walk while I was there so I was placed in a bed ward at Manigan. I stayed at Manigan until Thanksgiving day 1944 and they transferred us by rail to a place known as Annaberg, where Goering had his Luftwaffe headquarters at one time. It is northeast of Leipzig about 30 miles. I stayed at Annaberg until the end of 1944. Prisoners were accumulated there preparatory to exchanging them through the International Red Cross. Betweeen Christmas and the new year, I was sent by train across the German border into Switzerland. I was changed to another train which went to Marseilles, France where I was placed on a Swedish hospital ship which took me to New York City. I was then transferred to McClosky General Hospital at Temple, Texas. I was hospitalized until May of 1946, at which time I went before a retirement board which recommended I be retired as a First Lieutenant.

All the crew returned to the United States safely after VE day and I have corresponded and visited each of the officers except Lt. Kruszinski. I have not been able to find his address. I have not seen any of the enlisted men but have talked with them.

Each year on the 12th of May, I call the co-pilot and we count our blessings as to how we limped back on one engine when there were bandits reported in the area. With the help of the 'Little Friends,' we were not attacked.

The doctors and staff at Annaberg and Obermassfeld were British and Australians who were also prisoners of war and had been captured at Dunkirk and in Greece. They were very capable people and I am indebted to each and every one of them.

Mission No. 46
19 May 1944
Target — Berlin Friedrickestrasse Station

Crew of B-17G, No. Unknown

1st Pilot	2nd Lt.	Phillip H. Birong	
Co-Pilot	2nd Lt.	Robert A. Patty	
Nav.	2nd Lt.	Frank Partinjak	
Bomb.	2nd Lt.	Paul V. Owens	
Engr.	T/Sgt.	Max L. Hull	
Radio Op.	T/Sgt.	Norman Musial	
LW Gun.	S/Sgt.	Albert L. Missinger	KIA
RW Gun.	S/Sgt.	Sacco M. Pasquale	
B. Turret	S/Sgt.	William N. Farrar	
Tail Gun.	S/Sgt.	Franco H. Luis	

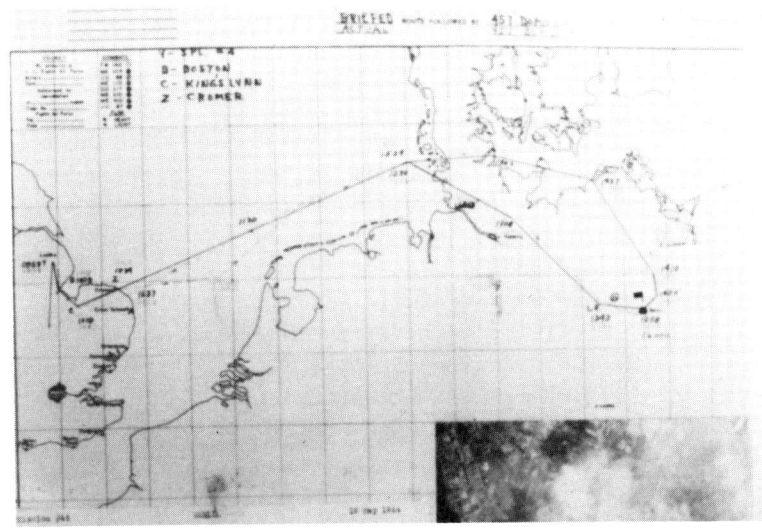

Track Chart, Mission No. 46, 19 May 1944

457th Bomb Group Mission Narrative

The city of Berlin again was the target for the bulk of the 8th Air Force bomber formations. Eleven CBW's, 663 heavies, were dispatched while 3 CBW's flew to Brunswick.

The 457th BG supplied 36 aircraft to compose the lead and low boxes of the 94th 'A' CBW. Lt. Col. Cobb led the wing in a PFF plane while Major George C. Hozier/Capt. Jerome E. Godfrey led the low box. The group took off at 0900 hours, assembled above the overcast, and headed out over the North Sea on the same course as the last mission to Stettin. After passing north of Helgoland, a turn was made to the southeast between Hamburg and Lubek. There was some difficulty with clouds and dense contrails after crossing the coast. Between Hamburg and Berlin a climb was made from 20,000 feet to the bombing altitude of 26,000 feet. The wing formation was spread out during the climb with the lead box maintaining a high speed and pulling away from the high and low boxes. Although the Germans massed a large concentration of over 200 fighters in front of Berlin, very effective United States fighter support diverted most of the attacking fighters away from the bombers. Almost 30 Me-109's and 10 FW-190's were seen at Wittenberg to the right of course. These Luftwaffe fighters paced the formation to Rothenow, the I.P., and then peeled off and attacked the low squadron of the lead group. Only the leading fighters fired their 20mm cannon, while those following seemed content with holding the mass formation — apparently new pilots being introduced to mass-frontal attacks. They succeeded in hitting Lt. Phillip H. Birong's plane. He left the formation with two engines burning and disappeared into the clouds, not to be seen again. By this time the turn to the I.P. had been made and while on the bomb run it was decided that bombing would be made by PFF if the lead bombardier could not see the target, as 7 to 9/10ths cloud cover existed. However, the bomb bay doors on the wing lead plane would not open and the radio man passed out trying to crank them open. The deputy lead PFF plane was notified to take over only one minute before the BRL was reached. The deputy lead dropped his bombs at 1354 hours and, as the lead box had pulled away minutes before dropping, partly obscured strike photographs showed the bombs hit 3 1/2 miles right of the center of the city, on the eastern edge of Lichtenburg district where the Frankfurter Allee crosses the Ringbahn.

Anti-aircraft fire on this group was much less than on previous missions to Berlin, as only seven planes were damaged. After leaving the city, excellent fighter support was picked up which brought the bombers north over Kiel Bay and out across the Danish Peninsula. An uneventful flight was made across the North Sea and the planes landed at 1800 hours.

Over 600 heavies participated in the operation with only 28 A/C lost, mostly to German fighters.

Lt. Paul V. Owens' story of the 19 May 1944 mission to Berlin.

I was the bombardier on Lt. Phillip H. Birong's crew that flew on the 19 May 1944 mission to Berlin, Germany. There were two substitutes on the crew that day, Lt. Robert A. Patty, as co-pilot, replaced Lt. Lloyd Miller and Lt. Frank Partinjak, as the navigator, for Lt. Carson. I have since learned that Lt. Miller completed his tour of duty safely and returned to the United States. Ironically, Lt. Carson was on a crew which was shot down later and ended up in Stalag Luft III, where Lt. Birong and I were enjoying [sic] our holiday.

We were shot down by German fighters and even among ourselves there is a slight disagreement as to the number of fighters that attacked us. We all agree there were at least three. Based on the

457th Bomb Group crossing the Channel into France, 1944.

pilot's recollections, two propellor governors were destroyed and two engines were set on fire by 20mm shell bursts. The plane became unmanageable and began to spiral down. When it became apparent that he was not going to be able to bring the airplane under control, Lt. Birong gave the order for the crew to bail out. All the crew bailed out except S/Sgt Albert L. Missinger, whose parachute became fouled and did not open. S/Sgt. Pasquale was the last man to see Sgt. Missinger alive. We were scattered over a large area and no two of us came down near one another. I landed by myself and was captured a few minutes later by three armed men including two members of the 'home guard' and the third, a policeman.

We were all taken to a military base by various members of the military establishment. Some time later we were processed through Stalag Luft. The officers of the crew were sent to Stalag Luft III and the enlisted men to another camp.

We remained at Stalag Luft III until January 28, 1945, at which time we were evacuated due to the Russian advance into Germany. By forced march and rail box cars we ended up in Stalag VIIA (near Munich). We were liberated on 29 April 1945 by Units of the 7th Army. We were then processed into France and returned to the United States.

As far as I know, all surviving members of the crew returned safely to the United States. I have not been in communication with any of them since the day we were released from prison. Also I believe I was the only one of the crew who stayed in the military and retired (1966).

We were a replacement crew arriving at the 457th BG on 1 April 1944. The mission was the third for the crew—the first for Lt. Partinjak—and we received no decorations.

Mission No. 50
24 May 1944
Target — Berlin, Friedrickestrasse Station

Crew of B17G, No. Unknown		
1st Pilot	2nd Lt.	Harry R. Stafford
Co-Pilot	2nd Lt.	Bernard J. Yavorsky
Nav.	2nd Lt.	Arthur E. Flack
Bomb.	2nd Lt.	Anthony G. Wodek
Engr.	T/Sgt.	Virgil D. Naylor
Radio Op.	T/Sgt.	Virgil R. Hook
LW Gun.	S/Sgt.	Reginal W. Buxton
RW Gun.	S/Sgt.	Francis M. Craven
B. Turret	S/Sgt.	Robert H. Ridge
Tail Gun.	S/Sgt.	Walter H. Osika

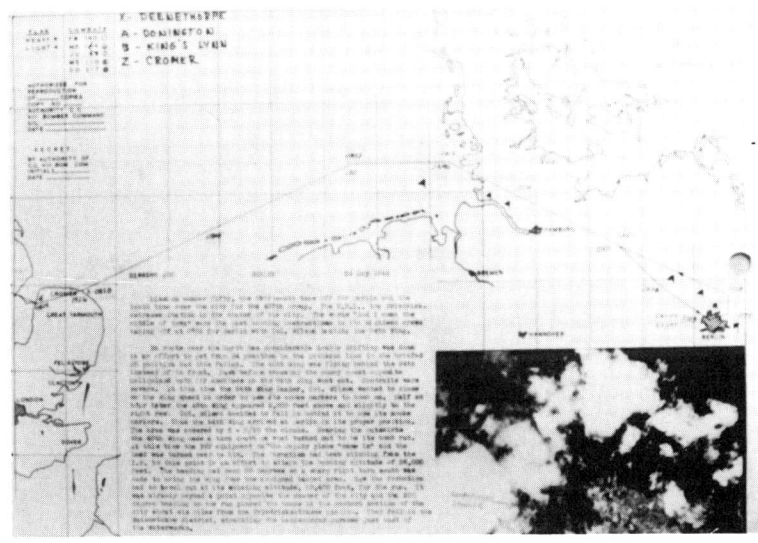

Track Chart, Mission No. 50, 24 May 1944

457th Bomb Group Mission Narrative

Mission number 50 and the thirteenth take off for Berlin by the 457th BG. The M.P.I., the Freidrickestrasse Station in the center of the city. The words 'And I mean the middle of town,' were the last bombing instructions to the eighteen crews taking off at 0706 hours for Berlin, with Col. Henry Wilson leading the 94th wing.

On the route over the North Sea considerable double drifting was done in an effort to get from number 4 position in the division line to the briefed number 5 position, but the effort failed. The 40th CBW was flying behind the 94th wing instead of in front. Just before crossing the enemy coast, just opposite Helgoland, both PFF units in the 94th wing became inoperative. Contrails were also severe. At this time the 94th CBW leader, Col. Wilson, wanted to close on the wing ahead in order to use its smoke bomb markers to bomb on. One-half hour later, the 40th CBW appeared 2,000 feet above and slightly to the right rear. Thus the 94th CBW arrived at Berlin in its proper position. The target was covered with 6-8/10 clouds. Nearing the target the 40th CBW turned south on what turned out to be its bomb run. At this time the PFF unit in the deputy lead plane 'came in' (became operative), and the formation lead was transferred to them. The formation had been climbing from the I.P. to this point in an effort to attain a bombing altitude of 26,000 feet. The heading had been 85 degrees, so a sharp turn was made to bring the wing over the assigned target area. Now the formation had to level out at its existing altitude, 23,400, feet for the bomb run. It was already beyond a point opposite the center of the city and the 200 degree heading on the run placed the bombs in the eastern section of the city about six miles from the Fredrickestrasse Station. The bombs fell in the Weissetaube district, straddling the Landsburger Strasse just east of the waterworks.

From there a left turn was made and the formation withdrew around the north of the city. Flak over Berlin was intense and accurate, and ten of the fifteen planes from the group sustained damage. No planes were lost until the group reached the North Sea, where Lt.Harry W.Stafford was seen to ditch. The formation landed at 1532 hours.

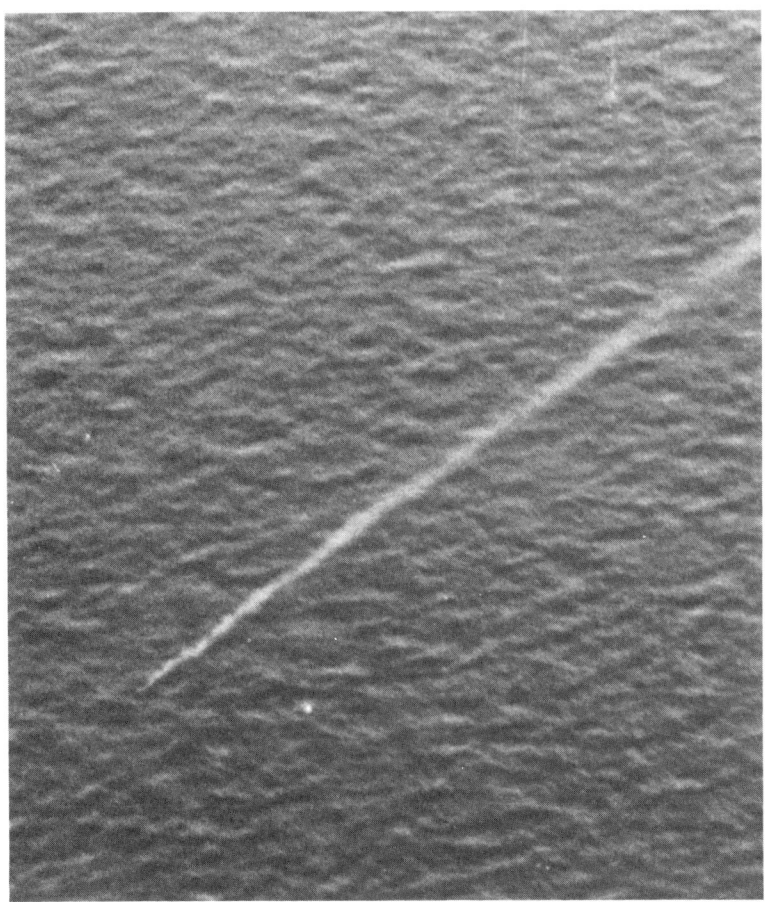

Ditching A/C.

S/Sgt. Walter H. Osika's story of 24 May 1944 mission to Berlin.

The mission to Berlin on 24 May 1944 was our 7th mission and our third to Berlin.

The beginning of the mission did not bode well of what was to follow, as the group had difficulty getting into its proper position in the bomber stream.

We were also apprehensive of the low altitude at which the bomb run was to be made over the city of Berlin, which was said to have 1,000 anti-aircraft guns protecting it. Besides we were assigned the unenviable position of 'Tail End Charlie' in the high box — the only place in the formation which was worse was purple heart corner,' Tail End Charlie in the low box. There is no one flying behind you to protect you from the fighters attacking the formation from the rear in either one of these positions.

We finally made it to the target in spite of all our fears, and had not as yet had a fighter attack, although 'bandits' had been reported in the area. However, all hell broke loose at the target, as we were hit by heavy flak over Berlin. We had just dropped our bombs and a burst of flak must have hit us squarely, as the plane shook violently and the next thing I knew we were diving downward.

I lost contact with the crew as the explosion had cut the interphone system and there I was in the tail of the airplane not knowing what was happening. I reasoned that something bad was wrong so I grabbed my chest chute, plugged into my walk-around oxygen bottle and headed for the waist position. When I got to the waist, everyone seemed to be all right but were all looking out the window. I looked out and saw that we had lost both engines on the right side of the airplane and the propellers were wind-milling. The door through the radio room into the bomb bay was open and I could see the engineer, T/Sgt. Virgil D. Naylor, trying to revive the pilot Lt. Harry W. Stafford who had lost his oxygen supply in the explosion. The co-pilot had his hands full trying to fly the airplane, feathering the propellers on the damaged engines and attending to all the things that two pilots usually performed in an emergency.

Well, the pilot was revived and they got every thing under control as well as possible under the existing conditions. We had lost the formation in the melee and were floundering around out there away from any protection and some enemy fighters spotted us. Fortunately we had lost enough altitude so we were not far from the clouds and when we saw the fighters we headed for the protection of the clouds.

We continued losing altitude and when we came to the vicinity of Helgoland we were hit by flak and the third engine was put out of commission. The pilot asked us if we should try to get to Sweden or get as close to England as possible, ditch, and hope to be picked up by Air Sea Rescue. We all wanted to continue on and get as close to home as possible.

Knowing that ditching was our lot, we threw out all the guns and ammunition, flak suits, some of the radio equipment, and anything else we could find that was loose that would lighten our load, stretch our glide, and get us as close to land as was possible. We also started work on dropping the ball turret, which turned out to be easier than we expected as one of the men had brought along some wrenches.

During all this time the radio operator, T/Sgt. Virgil R. Hook, kept sending a 'mayday' signal to inform Air Sea Rescue of our position.

We then planned our seating arrangement in the radio room for all but the pilot and co-pilot, for ditching. About 15 minutes before we were to ditch we jettisoned the overhead hatch in the radio room, threw out the remainder of the radio equipment, and took our ditching positions. We all sat down with our backs against the front bulkhead between the radio room and the bomb bay, facing the rear of the plane, with four men on either side of the now closed door into the bomb bay. We all placed our clasped hands behind our heads and leaned forward to absorb the shock of the airplane hitting the water at close to 100 miles an hour.

When we hit the water, and hit the water we did, the incoming water 'flushed' us up and almost out of the hatch. We came tumbling back down into the radio room which was now about half full of water. We had inflated our 'Mae Wests,' and it was not difficult for us to get out of the hatch again. We crawled and swam out on the wings, five on either side, inflated our dingies and carried them to the end of the wings, holding on to the line 'for dear life,' until each man had first jumped into the water and then crawled up into the dingy. We did this to prevent any part of the dingy from being punctured by sharp flak holes in the airplane.

I really do not remember much about getting in the raft for apparently I had a mild case of shock and when I jumped in the water I did not try to swim toward the raft, but being supported by the 'Mae West' started floating away from the raft. I did not know how to swim and in the shocked condition needed some help from my crewmates who jumped into the water and pulled me back to the raft. The crew pushed the rafts away from the airplane for it soon sank. Sometime later we raised the radio antennae, by a kite tethered by a wire. We all took turns at cranking the generator, the electricity from which powers the radio, which automatically sends out a continuous 's-o-s' signal.

Lucky for us, it was almost summer and the days were long and fairly warm. It did not get dark until late and then got light again about 0300 hours. The sea was fairly calm with only medium sized swells that did not cause us much discomfort. We saw planes pass our position in the distance and each time we shot flares but to no avail. Finally, in late afternoon of the second day, we were spotted and a PBY, which flew over us and sent a signal by Aldis lamp asking if we wanted the portable boat dropped to us. We decided we would stay in our rafts, which we had tied together so we would not get separated from one another. The PBY told us there would be a PT boat from the Air Sea Rescue coming in about an hour.

In about one-half hour the weather changed for the worse and big swells started coming in. We began to wish we had told the PBY to drop the boat. The PBY had been circling us and soon signaled they must leave us but not to be concerned as the PT boat was nearing our position and would soon be here.

Well, the PT boat arrived as we had been told it would; however, we had a difficult time boarding the boat because of the big swells. We learned that a 60 m.p.h. gale was approaching us and we would have a rough trip to land. We finally arrived at Great Yarmouth Naval Base and were glad to be back on land. We had been picked up in the 'nick of time.'

A strange aspect of the mission was that S/Sgt. Reginal W. Buxton was not a regular member of the crew and had bumped our regular left waist gunner as this was his 25th and final mission and afterwards could go back to the States. What a finish for a final mission of a combat tour!

After spending two weeks in a Red Cross rest home at Pangbourne, in the south of England, we resumed our flying on the 12th of June 1944, my birthday, as a lead crew.

Mission No. 52
27 May 1944
Target — Ludwigshafen/Mannheim marshalling yards (M/Y)

Crew of B17G, No. 42-38055

1st Pilot	2nd Lt.	Roger W. Birkman
Co-Pilot	2nd Lt.	Alexander Kucherenko
Nav.	2nd Lt.	Michael N. Stanko
Bomb.	2nd Lt.	James M. Cochran
Engr.	T/Sgt.	Raymond Koch
Radio Op.	T/Sgt.	Andrew Kafka
LW Gun.	S/Sgt.	John L. Toney
RW Gun.	S/Sgt.	James C. Jones
B. Turret	S/Sgt.	John Buechel
Tail Gun.	S/Sgt.	Errol Bailey

457th Bomb Group Mission Narrative

Six combat wings of the 1st division were dispatched today to bomb the marshalling yards in the twin cities of Ludwigshafen-Mannheim on the banks of the Rhine River. Other yards in this part of Germany were also attacked.

The 457th BG, as lead of the 94th CBW, led the 8th Air Force in the procession to these targets. Thirty-six aircraft formed the lead and low boxes of the wing. Col. Luper led, in the PFF plane, while Major J. McGavock Dickinson/Lt. Malcolm E. Johnson led the low box. Take off was at 0829 hours and after assembly the wing proceeded to Beachy Head, assumed the lead position, and set course southeast for La Treport and the flak-free course north of Paris to southern Germany. The climb to bombing altitude of 25,000 feet

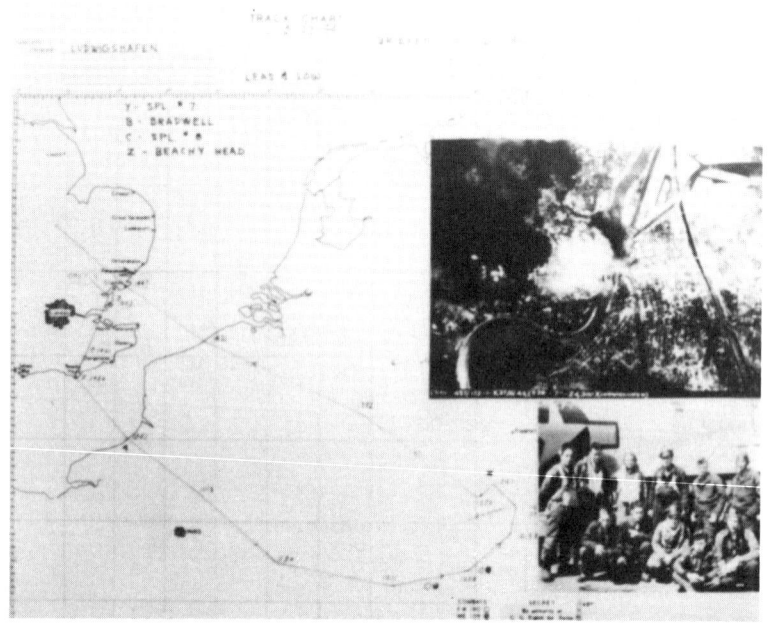

Track Chart, Mission No. 52, 27 May 1944

was made on this leg of the mission. There were no clouds to obscure the ground.

At 1220 hours, immediately after passing Epinal, 50-60 Me-109's suddenly came in head on at the group in a mass-saturation attack. The fighters had not been seen before the attack. Four of our B-17's were damaged in the attack. Lt. Artie J. Whitlow, flying in the No. 5 position in the high squadron of the lead box, was hit in the right wing during the attack, a part of the wing being blown off. Also No. 3 engine was seen to be on fire. The plane spiraled down to the right, which turned into a spin. Four chutes were seen to emerge from the plane before it crashed and blew up in a wooded area. After the first mass attack the German fighters split up and again attacked the formation in sets of two's and four's. The 457th boxes tightened their formation, as the high box had been loose. These attacks continued for twenty- five minutes. Three more a/c were shot up during the attacks. Lt. Roger W. Birkman, Lt. William E. Dee and Lt. Summerville were knocked out of the formation. The first two joined together for defense and headed for home. However, five minutes later Lt. Birkman's plane did a 180-degree turn and headed for Switzerland; an engine was on fire and he was losing altitude. Some time later Lt. Dee was joined by Lt. Summerville. Lt. Dee seemed to be in difficulty and suddenly turned to the left and was last seen at about 12,000 feet altitude, in some flak bursts, and appeared to be losing altitude very fast. Lt. Summerville made it back to base although he had fires in three engines, losing two entirely, with the propellor breaking completely off on one engine and in doing so broke the tips off of the adjoining propellor.

In the meantime two escorting United States P-51 groups engaged an equal number of German fighters, disrupting their attacks on the bombers, and drove them off. The P-51's destroyed 33 of the German fighters that day. Five B-17's were lost from the high box and 25 chutes were seen in the air at one time, including four black German fighter pilot chutes. The German attack broke off at 1245 hours thus ending the first large-scale German fighter attack experienced by the 457th BG in 52 missions.

The enemy object of disrupting the approach to the target succeeded, however, as when the turn was made to the I.P. at 1252 hours, the low box did not take its required interval and came forward abreast of the lead box. The low box was allowed to bomb first, while Col. Luper took the lead and high boxes on a 360-degree turn and to the rear of the following four wings.

The low box continued on their bombing run and the bombardier dropped his bombs at 1259 hours from 24,000 feet. He had not 'killed his rate' properly and his bombs fell short of the MPI one mile, into a park on the river bank and around one end of a dock area.

When the lead box approached Ludwigshafen the second time, the target area was covered by several columns of smoke rising several thousand feet into the air. Lt. John Blachley could not see his target and dropped his bombs into the center of the city. The bombs hit the worker's district just west of the I. G. Farbenindustrie Plant, with a few bursts falling on the plant.

The low box had bombed 14 minutes earlier. It joined another wing and flew home. The lead and high boxes flew home together. Fighter cover was good enroute but no enemy fighters were airbourne to make attacks. Flak from the 150 anti-aircraft guns located around Ludwigshafen was intense but dispersed and inaccurate. Thirteen planes received flak damage. The group received credit for destroying one enemy fighter and damaging five others. They landed at 1540 hours having lost three airplanes.

S/Sgt. John L. Toney's story of the 27 May 1944 mission to Ludwigshafen.

We were on a mission to Ludwigshafen, Germany, on 27 May 1944 and some time after we had flown near the town of Epinal, France, were attacked by a large number, possibly 50 or more, German fighters, mostly Me-109's. They came at us from the front at first, and 20mm cannon fire cut the oil line on our No. 1 engine. The propeller was wind-milling and could not be feathered so we were forced to leave the formation. Lt. Birkman pulled the airplane up in a stall and the wind-milling propellor stopped turning.

By this time we had descended to about 10,000 feet because of the damaged engine and the other engines were not performing well. Scattered anti-aircraft guns were shooting at us, and a piece of flak hit our No. 2 engine and set it on fire. When Lt. Birkman saw that the fire was out of control, he gave the signal for us to bail out. Being the oldest member of the crew I helped some of the others get ready to bail out. Lt. Birkman saw that I had not jumped and he stayed at the controls until I jumped. I fell about a mile before I opened my chute, hoping I would not attract the attention of anyone on the ground. Just before I reached the ground I noticed that one of our crew had landed in a tree. Some of us landed in a barley field just across the road from a Gestapo Headquarters (I found out later). How lucky can you be!

I quickly rolled up my parachute and hid it. Then I noticed a woman working in a field next to where I had landed. I went to the woman to get some directions, which I was told later was a risky thing to do, as some of the people with relatives in German prisons might turn in allied airmen in exchange for their relatives. We did not speak the same language but she indicated that the 'bosch' were very close to where my crewmate had landed in the tree. She urged me to go in the opposite direction and, although I didn't like to abandon my friend, I decided that nothing would be gained by both of us falling into German hands.

A man and his young friend had seen our parachutes open and where we had landed, so they came to my aid immediately. They directed me to get down on my hands and knees and crawl along the hedge-rows for what seemed to me to be for miles, before they indicated it was safe for me to stand up. At one place a loud argument took place between my benefactors and some German soldiers who were searching for the downed American flyers. I remained very quiet and later learned that the German soldiers had

Fire in an airplane can panic the crew.

threatened to shoot my new-found friends, until they had deceptively convinced the soldiers they had not seen any American flyers.

The German soldiers had barely left the area when I received directions to continue crawling on my way. I marveled that these people showed so little regard for their own lives, to help some one they had not seen before. But this was only the beginning of the episode! They brought me food and civilian clothing and later that evening took me to the town of Moerbeke, where I was introduced to the De Windts, who hid me in their home at extreme risk to their lives, for a considerable period of time.

I was taken by the French Underground to the town of St. Nikolas, where I stayed briefly with a family by the náme of Smets and then moved to the home of a family by the name of Van Kerchoves. Lt. Birkman was later brought to the Smets, where he stayed until the arrival of the American troops and was liberated.

While I was at the Van Kerchoves', Lt. Kucherenko, the co-pilot, was also brought to the house to stay. We stayed at the Van Kerchoves for a few weeks and when we heard the Allies had moved into southern Belgium we mistakenly reasoned we should leave our safe haven and try to reach our troops. One day we waited until both members of the family — husband and wife — were away from the house and we hit the road. We had realized the extreme danger we were to our hosts by keeping us in their homes, but also we did not realize the concern for our lives felt by this gracious family. When the Van Kerchoves returned home to find we were not at the house and found the note we had left telling them of our plans, they were frantic and tried desperately to find us.

We walked until it was agony to lift one foot in front of the other and then, through sheer luck, happily met up with other members of the underground. They took us to the home of Louis DeRom in Termonde, where we stayed a few weeks before being taken by car to Brussels. Fuel for the car had been stolen from the Germans. On our trip, at a military roadblock, we were stopped and our driver was questioned about his passengers in the back seat, who of course were Lt. Kucherinko and I. While we were shaking in our boots, the driver was blithly 'lying in his teeth' as to our identity. We had fake identification papers which apparently were adequate to the fuzzy-faced young German military policeman.

We arrived in Brussels and stayed at the home of a Belgian soldier who had previously escaped from a German prison. We were later moved on from there when they thought it was safe and taken by bicycle and train to a camp in the Ardennes forest.

After a time a group of American Rangers came to our camp and we were liberated. The 'Stars and Stripes' never looked so good to me as it did that day. We were taken to the bivouac of the Army Rangers and strangely enough I recognized a fellow officer of my bother Col. Robert L. Toney, who I had met while visiting my brother in southern England prior to the Allied invasion of the continent. The Fifth Armoured Division, of which my brother was the Inspector General, was stationed nearby and I was taken by jeep to see my brother. He was relieved to see me alive after being informed I had been MIA since 27 May. We rode together in his jeep as the troops advanced to Luxemburg, and then took a mail truck to Paris.

In Paris we were checked, given military uniforms, and sent back to England, through prisoner of war channels, and eventually back to Glatton from whence we had come. When I arrived at Glatton I made it a point to visit the men in the parachute shop and tell them I had no complaints about their work!

I was fortunate to catch a ride in a DC-4 which was returning to the United States and did not have to suffer through a long ocean trip.

I have since found out that five of the crew were hidden by the Belgium underground and five were captured by the Germans and made POW's for the duration. All returned safely to the United States after the war.

Following his return to the United States S/Sgt. John L. Toney wrote to the members of the Belgium Underground who had hid him from the Germans, and thanked them for their unselfish aid in returning Allied flyers to their bases following their being casualties of the air war over Europe. The following are excerpts from the answer he received from one of the families.

12 July 1945

Dear Johnny:

Many thanks indeed for your most welcome letter. We have been so worried about you both that it was a great relief to us to know at last that you were safely landed, after all the troubles you took, the fantasy to take.

After liberation there was an official inquiry about you, by an officer of the R.A.F., and we were repeatedly told that you had been caught and shot by the Jerrys. There should have been altogether 5 American airmen in your case.

We have long ago forgiven you for your wild escape on that Sunday afternoon. We have never understood why we were so foolish to leave you alone for so many hours. It was quite a suprise and upsetting not to find you anymore in the place. My wife went upstairs and found the two notes you had left and started crying, then she turned around as if getting mad. I got out the bicycle and toured the whole town without finding you. What grieved us most was that all roads to St. Nicholas were blocked by black men who were searching for spies. The Chief Constable was informed in case one of his men had laid hands on you, you would have been put in a safe place.

                                signed
                            L. Van Korchove

As have many American airmen, John L. Toney has, since World War II, visited many of the people who befriended him during the war.

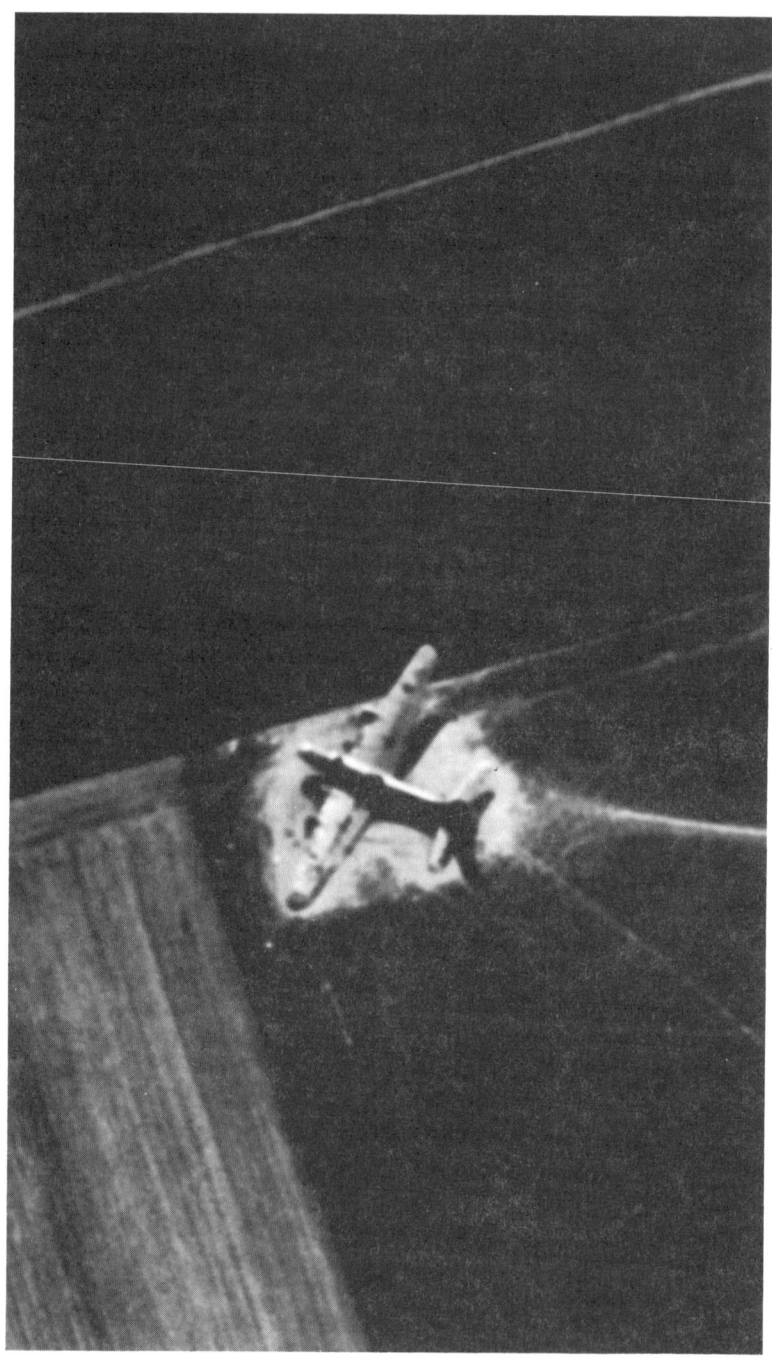

Downed B-17 in Germany.

Mission No. 53
28 May 1944
Target — Dessau Junker Aircraft jet engine factory

Crew of the B17G, No. 42-31520

1st Pilot	2nd Lt.	Clyde B. Knipfer
Co-Pilot	2nd Lt.	Richard H. Bruha
Nav.	2nd Lt.	George R. Dardinski
Bomb.	2nd Lt.	Stanley V. Gray
Engr.	T/Sgt.	Stephen T. Voit
Radio Op.	T/Sgt.	Nicholas F. Bendino
LW Gun.	S/Sgt.	Percy Walt
B. Turret	S/Sgt.	Nicholas D. Furrie
Tail Gun.	S/Sgt.	Joshua Goldstein

Lt. Clyde B. Knipfer's A/C No. 42-31520.

Lt. Clyde B. Knipfer's story of the 28 May 1944 mission to Dessau, Germany.

What turned out to be our last mission of a tour of duty in the 457th Bomb Group, in the 8th Air Force, based in England, was the mission to Dessau, Germany, to bomb the Junkers jet engine plant.

We had the unenviable assignment of flying back there in the low flight of the low squadron, 'purple heart corner,' where to keep your position in the formation you were either 'pouring the coal' to her and hanging on your props or almost dropping the flaps to keep from over running the element leader!

The mission had been relatively uneventful until we reached the I. P., had turned on course and opened the bomb bay doors. But things sure changed in a hurry! A big bunch — and I mean a bunch — of German fighters, 60 or 70 of them, seemed to appear from nowhere! There had not been any reports of 'bogies' before, but here they came all lined up coming at us from head on! They made a pass through the formation with cannons blazing! I guess I had never seen so many fighters before.

Well, we got hit by 20mm cannon shells which set engines No. 1 and No. 2 on fire. I peeled away from the formation and tried to put out the fires, but to no avail. The fires continued to burn and I saw no alternative but to abandon the 'old girl' and take our chances on the ground.

I hit the bail-out bell and all the crew parachuted to the ground, where all were picked up by the German military and incarcerated for the duration.

Mission No. 66
14 June 1944
Target — Paris/La Bourget A/F

Crew of B17G, No. Unknown

1st Pilot	2nd Lt.	William F. Rogers
Co-Pilot	2nd Lt.	Stanley J. Wolczanski
Nav.	2nd Lt.	Wilbert J. Collard
Toggle.	T/Sgt.	Milton E. Bunch
Engr.	T/Sgt.	Joshua D. Lane, Jr.
Radio Op.	T/Sgt.	John Chumas
RW Gun.	S/Sgt.	David H. Quick
B. Turret	S/Sgt.	Ray Jones
Tail Gun.	Sgt.	Orion H. Shumway

457th Bomb Group Mission Narrative

The enemy had committed over 300 of his single engine fighters to back up his front lines. Reconnaissance revealed their principal bases to be the larger airdromes around Paris, France. They had to be neutralized, so today over 1500 heavy bombers were dispatched against 11 bases in France and 4 in Belgium.

The 457th BG furnished the entire 94th 'E' CBW, composed of 36 a/c, to attack the Villaroche airfield located 20 miles southeast of Paris and 5 miles north of Melun. Lt. Col. Cobb/Lt. Malcolm E. Johnson led the CBW.

In addition, 12 plane high boxes were supplied to the 'B' and 'D' CBW's, two of a force of 4 CBW's assigned to attack La Bourget airdrome in the northeastern suburbs of Paris. Major J. McGavock Dickinson led the 'B' box and Major Fred Spencer led the 'D' box.

Fifty-seven of the proposed 60 a/c took off at 1420 hours without difficulty and assembled in their various wings.

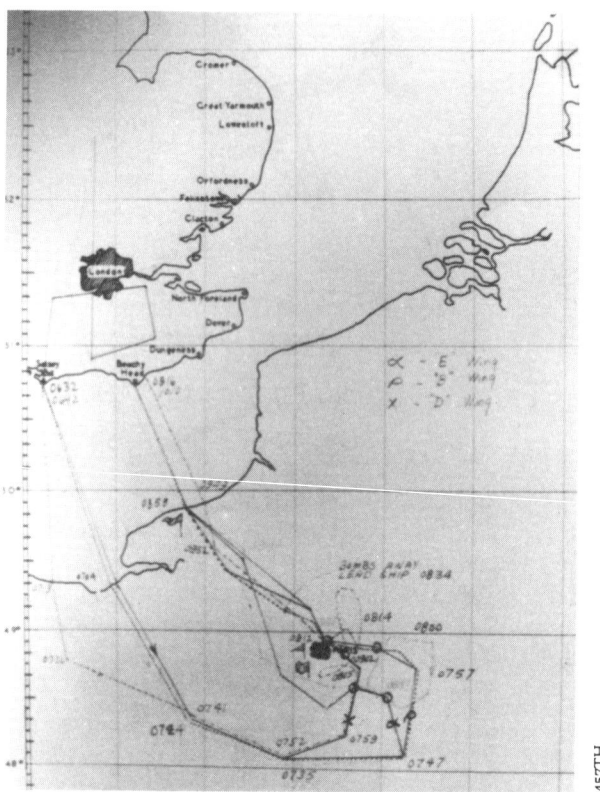

Track Chart, Mission No. 66, 14 June 1944

The 94th 'B' CBW, third in the division of 14 CBW's, preceded the other 457th BG planes to the target area. The flight, without incident, followed the briefed course from Selsey Bill across the invasion beach into the Paris area from the south. Bombing intervals were taken and a turn toward La Bourget was made about 4 miles south of the I.P. A hard 'S' was made to place the formation behind the preceding wings. As the formation drew near the target, the enemy flak, bursting in the formation, became increasingly accurate. Committed to the bomb run, the formation took no evasive action. Thirty seconds from the BRL, there was a burst of flak directly under the tail of the lead ship. The camera doors flopped and the bombardier in the deputy lead plane thought it was the bombs being released. He dropped his bombs and the rest of the formation followed suit. Lt. William F. Rogers, on his 29th mission, was hit by flak, dropped out of the formation, and was not seen again. L. Charles R. Blackwell, on his 28th mission, was also hit by flak in one engine and left the formation. Three chutes were seen near Lt. Blackwell's plane. Lt. James LaPaze had a wing punctured and gasoline was seen streaming out of the hole. Lt. LaPaze remained with the formation until they reached the English Channel and there the crew bailed out. Four men and two bodies were picked up by the Air Sea Rescue. The lead plane dropped its bombs on Gisors M/Y on the way home.

Major Spencer, with the 'D' box, approached Paris twenty minutes after the 'B' wing. On nearing the I.P. the wing leader took the formation on a 360 to the left, probably because the target appeared to be covered by clouds. The same cover existed the next time around, so he assembled the boxes in a wing formation and continued north looking for a target of opportunity. At Soissons a left turn was made to Campeigne and then back south toward Paris/La Bourget. The target was now visible so the boxes again took bombing interval for a bomb run. Lt. Frank Pearman, lead bombardier, sighted by triangulation as the MPI was obscured by clouds. He dropped at 0911 hours from 23,000 feet. His MPI was only 481 feet northwest of the assigned but the pattern was spread out. Hits were scored on 5 small hangers. Very little or no flak was thrown up at the box. The formation did encounter flak at Dieppe on the return trip home, which damaged three planes.

The 94th 'A' wing, 13th in the division formation, after an uneventful flight approached the I.P. in trail and started the bomb run. For some unknown reason the lead ship abandoned the run and started a 360 to the right. Probably it was because a turn had been made too soon before the I.P. and the target could not be picked up through the 3-5/10 clouds. Thirty five minutes elapsed before the very large 360 was completed and the I.P. crossed the second time. Half way around the 360, 10 to 15 single engine fighters made a head-on pass through all three boxes which were all in trail.

The deputy lead plane, flown by Lt. Gibbons, was hit by cannon fire, setting the plane on fire and knocking out an engine. Lt. Gibbons hit the bail-out bell and jumped out the open bomb bay. The fire was located in the flares behind the pilots seats and was extinguished by the engineer. The rest of the crew remained in the plane because the intercom in the rear of the plane was not working and the crew in the front of the plane could not get the escape hatch in the crawlway open. When the engineer put out the fire, Capt. Raymond Syptak resumed control of the airplane and brought the airplane home.

The enemy fighters had kept up their attacks on the bombers until the I.P. was reached at 0851 hours. Eight minutes later the lead ship, Col. Cobb/Lt. Johnson, was hit by either flak or fighters and it zoomed up through the high squadron, then dove down to the right apparently under control. Two chutes were seen. Somewhere along the flight path, Lt. Roy W. Allen, the third plane in the lead squadron, disappeared as a result of enemy fighter attacks. Now there were no more planes left in the lead element. Lt. Benny Flowers came down from the high squadron and assumed leadership but it was too late to sight and drop the bombs. The bombs were returned to the base.

The low box, one minute to the rear, suffered no losses but found the meagre flak at the target quite accurate. Lt. Irwin Rosen, after having difficulty in picking up the well camouflaged target, dropped his bombs but hit 1890 feet from his MPI, although on the field.

Lt. Jones, coming in next with only seven planes in the high box, four having aborted, had the same problems. His pattern fell 3330 feet southwest of the assigned MPI. All three boxes swung to the south of Paris and flew home without further incident. The last plane landed at 1145 hours.

T/Sgt. Milton E Bunch's story of the 14 June 1944 mission to La Bourget/Paris A/F.

On 14 June 1944 at approximately 0330 hours I was called to fly with Lt. William F. Rogers as a substitute bombardier.

Our target was the La Bourget A/F in Paris, France. The lead bombardier could not identify the MPI through the partially overcast sky and the Air Commander called for a 360 and the formation swung away from the target to make another bomb run. This gave the anti-aircraft defense another chance to shoot at us and this time they hit us and knocked out our number 4 engine. Also a big hole was shot in our right wing, piercing the gasoline tank and the resulting fire melted the engine mount of the number 3 engine, dropping the engine off the airplane.

The pilot rang the bail-out bell but the airplane was still gliding along, so I crawled back through the hatchway and saw that Lt. Rogers was trying to tie the control column so the airplane would continue its glide, so he could jump too. It was then I found out that he and I were the only ones left in the plane. Well, I jumped out the hatch door, pulled my rip cord and while floating down in my parachute, watched that airplane circle me! I thought it was going to run into me but it didn't.

I hit the ground and two French ladies and a man came running

Mission No. 66

T/Sgt. Milton E. Bunch standing at the left rear. Others unknown.

up to me. They told me to run and hide so the Germans could not capture me. I pointed down to my left ankle, which was badly sprained when I hit the ground. They helped me walk, mostly carried me, over to a small nearby village.

In about 15 minutes there were about 150 Frenchmen all around me trying to decide what to do with me. We had been instructed to do what ever they told us to do, if we fell into the hands of the French underground. In a few minutes they took me to a blacksmith shop where some girls brought me some breakfast of eggs and pork chops. After I had eaten the food they took me up in the hay loft and massaged my sore leg and ankle with alcohol. They took turns massaging the leg for a couple of hours, one at a time. I responded to this treatment very well.

After two or three hours I was taken from the blacksmith shop to a hedgerow where I was told to crawl across an uncut hay field to the other side, where a member of the French underground would meet me.

Late in the afternoon a Frenchman from the underground came over to me and told me that they would notify my people that I was in their hands and was all right (I later found out that the information did not get to the right people). When darkness came they took me by automobile about twenty miles to a house where a dinner had already been prepared for me. They showed me a letter typed in English, which asked how many other crew members parachuted from the plane from which I had jumped. I told them all I knew.

After I had eaten, they took me to a location about twenty miles north of Paris, which was a big house in which lived an old couple. I stayed there only overnight, for the next day I was given civilian clothes and my uniform was stuffed between the weather boarding of the house. The old lady of the house had brought me hot water every hour in which I soaked my sore ankle.

Later that day the pilot of the plane, Lt. Rogers, was brought to the house by members of the underground. I had told them where to look for the pilot but I wouldn't know him if I saw him. It was dark at 0330 hours, and I had not looked at him enough to recognize him again.

We were taken to the hay loft in a nearby barn where we stayed for about three weeks. The Frenchmen would bring us food in a basket each day. We were given mostly bread, cheese, and wine. We never were given any water to drink.

One night the French underground members got drunk and shot some German soldiers and as a precaution we were moved from the hay loft to a nearby woods. They loaded a cart with pots and pans and headed for a woods. There were eight of us, the two of us and six French underground police. We went right down the road, passing by some German soldiers. They took us all to be French. We finally arrived at a field in the middle of which was a small woods, where we stayed for a time. The only thing we could find to eat were rabbits, but they were good rabbits, especially when you do not have anything else to eat. We set snares at night, and when we caught one would either fry or barbeque it.

While we were there in the woods it began to rain and it rained for a day and all the next night. We were taken to a nearby cow stable to get in out of the weather. The next day Lt. Rogers said, "Let's work our way to the coast." I was ready for anything but this sitting around, so that night we slipped out of the stable and started walking toward the west.

The next morning we came to a little town and there was a bridge about 100 yards long over a stream, between us and the town. On each end of the bridge were German soldiers with machine guns, guarding the bridge. We sat down in the trees and watched to see if the soldiers were checking passes. When we saw several people walk by them without being checked, we walked down the road and across the bridge, right by the German soldiers!

There were so many German soldiers in the little town we had to turn sideways to walk down the street. We walked through the town and just beyond it took a road that seemed to go to the north. A little distance beyond the town we sat down to rest by the side of the road. A German convoy came by and one German thought there was something fishy about our appearance. The officer wanted to get the two American fly-boys but the others in the convoy were urging him to keep on going.

Later that afternoon we walked about 100 yards off the road to find somewhere to sleep in the hay for the night. We walked up close to a house, but when a man came out on the back porch dressed like a king — white shirt and everything — to pour out a pan of dishwater, the pilot pulled me back by the arm and said, "Something's wrong. French people don't dress like that."

We walked over to another house about 100 yards away from the first house and told the people we were Americans. They were shaking with fear. They told us that the first house we had gone to was Gestapo Headquarters. They let us stay in the hay barn all night, although we were not more than 100 yards from the Gestapo.

The French people got us up in the morning before daylight, so that we could get out of there. Before we could leave, however, a Gestapo agent came out of a garage on his motorcycle, so we hid in the chicken house until daylight and then we started walking again.

Late in the afternoon we asked a Frenchman, who was riding a bicycle, where we could get something to eat and a place to sleep. He told us there was a big farm house just a short distance on down the road and they would provide for us there.

We walked up to the house and saw about 15 men working around the property. We told the man who was standing nearby, and apparently the owner of the farm, that we were Americans. He told everyone to keep working and when he gave the signal we were to run over to the house and just go in, and not stop to knock. We slept in that big, two-story house that night and every night for about another two and one-half weeks.

The next day the owner of the farm sent one of his men to bring the local priest to the farm. We had walked for two days and nights and our feet were blistered. The priest had been a captain in the Red Cross and knew how to treat the blisters. He came and instructed the lady of the house to prepare a foot bath and in short order took care of our problem. In a week's time our feet were all healed.

We remained in our assigned room most of our stay on the farm and apparently no one except the owner knew we were still there. The priest would come each Sunday and eat dinner with the family and bring with him his male secretary, who could speak English. There were two dining rooms in the house and the priest and the

Flak!

family would eat in one room and we, Rogers and I, would eat with the priest's secretary.

One day at lunch the priest told us that he had heard that the American army was coming. He was so tickled that he jumped out the dining room window, got on his bicycle, and yelled that he would see us in the afternoon.

Late that afternoon the lady of the house told us to go up to the attic to hide. She said that the Germans were coming. We didn't go hide, as we thought the priest had found the Americans and sure enough he had! We looked out and there were two Sherman tanks and a jeep coming across the field. Can you imagine, having two tanks and a jeep coming to liberate you?

When the American soldiers arrived at the house, two of them came into the house carrying Thompson sub-machine guns. They didn't know if they were stepping into a trap or not. Rogers and I were standing at the top of the stairs when they came in and they looked at us so suspiciously, I wasn't sure they were Americans or not. Then the Sargeant said, "You boys got any I.D.?" We said, "Yes sir," and ran down the stairs and showed them our dog tags and medical records.

The soldiers took us out and told us to get inside the tank. We asked the soldiers if they had any cigarettes, which they did. We gave the Frenchmen the cigarettes which the soldiers gave us, in appreciation for their hospitality.

We climbed into the tank and they started down the road. When we came to the main road the captain in charge of the tanks told the tank gunners to load their cannon, as there were two German tanks cornered on up the road. The soldiers were part of Gen. Patton's 5th Army and we were the first Air Force men they had picked up in their drive across France.

I told the captain we would just as soon not get involved in the fight and he grinned and said, "I guess I know what you mean." The captain then told two of his men to take us, in the jeep, back to their headquarters and get us out of danger.

Within fifteen minutes we arrived at their headquarters. The commander was surprised to see us and wanted to know why we were there. We told our story to several people before we were through. The next day we started working our way back to Normandy. We caught rides with several different American trucks and jeeps which were going or way, until we arrived at General Eisenhower's Headquarters. I took a bath in Eisenhower's shower and they gave us some army infantry uniforms. We were taken back to a rear area airbase, where we caught a ride on a C-47 for England.

There was a terrible storm blowing and the ride was pretty rocky but we made it back to England. We were then taken to the 457th base at Glatton. Having been gone for approximately three months, most of the people we had known had either completed their tour of duty or had been shot down and we knew very few people.

As with all airmen who had walked out of enemy territory, we were sent back to the United States for duty either in another theatre of war or to reassignment in the United States.

Mission No. 66
14 June 1944
Target — Paris/La Bourget A/F

Crew of B17G, No. Unknown

1st Pilot	2nd Lt.	Roy W. Allen
Co-Pilot	2nd Lt.	Verne H. Lewis
Nav.	2nd Lt.	Joseph C. Brusse
Bomb.	2nd Lt.	Lawrence Anderson
Engr.	T/Sgt.	Ray E. Plum
Radio Op.	T/Sgt.	William C. Goldsborough
LW Gun.	Sgt.	Leonard S. Renson
B. Turret	S/Sgt.	Ernest L. Smith
Tail Gun.	Sgt.	Gordon Long

Lt. Roy W. Allen's comments about being shot down on 14 June 1944.

We were shot down on the 14 June 1944 mission to La Bourget A/F outside of Paris by enemy fighters. We were flying the number three position in the lead squadron and were making a big 360 because the first time over the target the bombardier could not locate his MPI because of the 5/10ths cloud cover. The flak over the target had been, you might say, 'rougher than a cobb!' Then about half way around the 360, 10 to 15 enemy fighters hit us. We had two engines knocked out and we were on fire, so I hit the bail-out button and we all bailed out. We all made it to the ground except the bombardier Lt. Larry Anderson, who was shot in the air as he descended in his parachute.

My fate was to live with the French underground for about six weeks with civilian identification papers. However, the Gestapo caught up with me and, since I had no military identification, they sent me to Buchenwald Concentration Camp as a spy and saboteur for 15 weeks. They finally relented and accepted the fact that I was an American and sent me to Stalg Luft III for the duration. I later learned that, other than Anderson, all the rest of the crew were captured and sent to the various Stalags.

This was the second mission on which we had been shot out of the formation by fighters. On the 28th of May, just two weeks previously, on my sixth mission, we went to Dessau to hit the Junkers A/C plant. We were hit by fighters in the target area, which knocked out two of our engines. We dropped out of the formation and headed for the cloud bank to escape the enemy fighters. We were losing altitude and came out of the clouds just north of Hanover at about 5500 feet. We were pursued by flak all the way to Wilhelmshaven Bay and the North Sea but managed to get through it all without serious injury to the crew or damage to the airplane.

We prepared for ditching by throwing out all the guns, the ball turret and anything else that would come loose. The crew assembled in the radio room ready for ditching but the engines held up and we reached home base. We lowered the landing gear but only one came down. So I made a one wheel landing and fortunately no one was hurt.

Mission No. 66
14 June 1944
Target — Paris/La Bourget A/F

Crew of B17G, No. Unknown

1st Pilot	2nd Lt.	Charles R. Blackwell
Co-Pilot	2nd Lt.	Theodore R. Baskette
Nav.	2nd Lt.	Irving H. Byers
Bomb.	2nd Lt.	Verne M. Boone
Engr.	T/Sgt.	Thomas W. Howard
Radio Op.	T/Sgt.	Edward Nabozny
RW Gun.	S/Sgt.	Francis W. McCall
B. Turret	S/Sgt.	Thomas G. Leahy
Tail Gun	Sgt.	Sylvester C. Kuraszkiewicz

1st Lt. Charles R. Blackwell

Lt. Charles R. Blackwell's story of the 14 June 1944 mission to Paris/La Bourget A/F.

The mission to bomb La Bourget airfield in Paris, France, was my 29th mission and the crews 28th mission. I had flown a mission as co-pilot with Lt. Alfred Fischer before I had flown a mission as 1st pilot with my own crew. The mission was an orientation mission designed to acquaint me with combat flying. It was not just a routine mission but the first mission flown by the 457th BG to Berlin on 3 March 1944. Quite a beginning!

On the mission to Paris, I'm not quite sure why but the Air Commander chose to circle the target and come in upwind to La Bourget A/F. We had a very strong headwind and our ground speed on the bomb run was only 80 knots. The flak was intense and accurate and we were 'clobbered' by flak.

Our plane was hit by a burst of flak which knocked out three engines, only one of which were we able to feather. Flak cut gasoline lines and the flight deck was awash with gasoline! I don't know why the gasoline did not catch on fire, but with two engines running away it really gave me a weird feeling. In spite of the danger from fire we rode the plane down to about three thousand feet into a cloud layer. There I set the autopilot, rang the bail-out bell, and we all 'hit the silk.'

I landed in a tree and it took me some time to 'shinny' down and to also pull the chute down. Some French people found me before the Germans did and I stayed with a group of Free French for some time. Those French underground people would really get 'frisky' at night — blowing up bridges, and shooting 'krauts.' One day they learned that some 'kraut' soldiers were coming around looking for shot-down American flyers. We had been living in an old barn and we hid in a nearby ditch. The French gave me two hand grenades and an old double barrel shotgun. Thank goodness the 'krauts' did not find us. Nothing happened, but I decided to travel west with another downed flyer, a Polish pilot who had been flying with the R.A.F.

We had been given civilian clothing and we walked west for two days toward the American lines. One night we slept in the haymow of an old barn. In the morning a 'Frenchie' with a bunch of cherries in his hand came to the barn and motioned for us to follow him. He took us to the small town of Blonville. Then he introduced us to a woman by the name of Mme. Jane Vaillant, who took us into her house and hid us for five weeks until we were liberated by the American soldiers.

Bail out! Airplane on fire.

Mission No. 66
14 June 1944
Target — Paris/La Bourget A/F.

Crew of B17G, No. Unknown

1st Pilot	2nd Lt.	James La Paze	
Co-Pilot	F/O	Louis W. McGranahan	KIA
Nav.	F/O	Keith W. Morgan	KIA
Toggl.	S/Sgt.	Chester V. Hudec	KIA
Engr.	T/Sgt.	Henry L. Baker	KIA
Radio Op.	T/Sgt.	Charles Rogers	
LW Gun.	S/Sgt.	Oscar C. Hightower	KIA
B. Turret	S/Sgt.	Elmer Velicer	
Tail Gun.	S/Sgt.	Delbert Brookheart	

Lt. James LaPaze's story of the 14 June 1944 Mission to Paris/La Bourget A/F.

We were a replacement crew in the 457th BG and not one of the original members. On the mission to Paris, France, our position in the formation was on the extreme right side. The formation was coming over the target for the second time after having made a 360. The flak was as accurate as any I had ever seen and a shell exploded right underneath us and flipped the airplane over. I recovered and when we leveled out, I could see airplanes all over the sky in any position you could imagine. Fires, explosions, parachutes, we had them that day like you never saw before. When I looked ahead to the lead plane, there were no airplanes in formation between us. I heard all kinds of chatter on the intercom and I learned from it, that we had two badly wounded men on board. The ball turret gunner was wounded in the foot and the chin turret gunner was wounded in the leg. We had also taken hits in the left

2nd Lt. James La Paze

wing, while on the right wing both engines were on fire. We feathered both propellors and hit the CO_2 fire extinguisher and the fires went out on both of the engines.

We turned to the west, heading for the English Channel. We got part way to the channel and the engines caught on fire again. Although we tried diving the ship and everything else we could think of, we were unable to put out the fire. By the time we got out over the water the whole wing was on fire and smoke was filling the cockpit. We were now afraid she was going to blow up so I told Sgt. Henry Baker, the engineer, to get the wounded out of the ship, then come back and tell me when every one was out and we would jump. As it turned out that was a good decision as not long after we jumped, the airplane blew up and all the pieces fell into the water. We were at 18,000 feet when we jumped and the plane blew up before it hit the water. Had we tried to ditch the bird, we would have all bought the farm.

Sgt. Delbert Brookheart, the tail gunner, and Elmer Velicer, the wounded ball turret gunner, were both picked up Air Sea Rescue. Charles Rogers, the radio operator, and I were picked up by a British mine sweeper and later transferred to an Air Sea Rescue boat and returned to England. This all happened about half-way between Dover and the Pas-de-Calais.

Mission No. 71
20 June 1944
Target — Hamburg oil refinery

Crew of B17G, No. Unknown

1st Pilot	2nd Lt.	William B. Bomar	
Co-Pilot	2nd Lt.	Jack A. Lade	
Nav.	2nd Lt.	Charles Curione	
Bomb.	2nd Lt.	Robin E. Hill	
Engr.	T/Sgt.	Henry Gilbert	
Radio Op.	T/Sgt.	Edmund Klein	
LW Gun.	S/Sgt.	Erwin Tengler	KIA
RW Gun.	S/Sgt.	William H. Kane	KIA
B. Turret	S/Sgt.	Albert Leeming	
Tail Gun.	S/Sgt.	Richard A. Bohl	

Track Chart Mission, No. 71, 20 June 144

457th Bomb Group Mission Narrative

Weather having prevented the destruction of the crude oil refineries at Hamburg two days ago, it was necessary to make a return trip to these targets. Today, with the weather forecast with a slight wind from the east, promises visual bombing conditions. The two 18-ship boxes furnished by the 457th BG were assigned to the same combat wing, 94th CBW with only one of eight refineries as its target. This was the Europaische Tehklager-U-transport A.G., the largest in Germany with a capacity of 250,000 tons a year. In addition it had a storage capacity for a half million tons and was located on the western end of the dock area of the Elbe River.

The planes began taking off at 0446 hours with Major Hoffman A/C of the lead box and leading the wing. Major Smith was A/C of the low box. The route out from south of the Danish peninsula was the same as two days previously. The bomb run had to be shifted to the east because of the wind direction and the huge fires expected from the first bombs. Over England and most of the North Sea there was an undercast which cleared at the Danish coast, to become clear over Germany. The formation flew north of and around Lubek before turning toward the I.P. There the boxes swung in trail and turned smoothly toward Hamburg. Major Smith, was in the low box a few hundred feet behind the lead box, so Lt. Dino H. Tonelli could sight and drop his bombs before those of the lead box hit the target area. As the formation approached the target three huge fires were visible in the refineries, sending smoke up to 15,000 feet. Flak bursts blackened the sky ahead at flight level.

The lead team in the lead ship of the low box (Capt. Edward Dozier, Pilot; 1st Lt. Roland O. Byers, Lead Navigator; 1st Lt. Dino H. Tonelli, Bombardier, and Capt. William F. Smith, Air Commander) were operating under considerable handicap, as equipment in the airplane was not functioning correctly. In spite of this difficulty, however, Lt. Tonelli laid his bombs from 25,000 feet squarely on the MPI, the center of the refinery.

A large explosion sent flames thousands of feet into the air. Black smoke boiled into the air many thousands of feet in only a few seconds. Storage tanks were hit in addition to the boiler houses, distillation and cracking plant. Flak was bursting all around the formation and Lt. William B. Bomar's plane had its tail shot off and it went into a spin, exploding at 5,000 feet. Three to six chutes were seen.

As the last of the nine wings pulled away from Hamburg, every one of the eight refineries was left a burning and smoking ruin. This was one of the most successful raids of the war. The next day, as our planes flew 30 miles north of Hamburg en route to Berlin, smoke was still boiling up through the clouds at 15,000 feet.

After leaving Hamburg the lead and low boxes effected rally but the 401st BG never joined in the high box position. The let down was accomplished over the North Sea and the formation returned to Glatton between 1145 and 1245 hours. Eighteen planes were damaged by flak.

Major William B. Bomar's story of the 20 June 1944 mission to Hamburg, Germany.

I graduated from aviation cadets on October 1, 1943, at Stuttgart, Arkansas. From there I went to Sebring, Florida for B-17 transition. This was my first choice of airplanes. On completing the transition, I was transferred to Drew Field and was assigned to a crew.

At this point not one of the crew, other than myself, had ever been in a B-17. For the next three months it was my job to see that every man learned their job, as it applied to our crew.

At the termination of the training period at Drew Field, we were transferred, as a crew, to Hunter Field, Savannah, Georgia. There we received a brand new B-17G No. 42-102873. We checked over the airplane thoroughly. I signed a receipt for the aircraft and associated equipment.

As a 'seasoned' crew, I had about 250 hours of flying time and the crew had about 20 hours in a B-17. We departed for Great Britain as a single aircraft. Our first stop was Bangor, Maine, where we remained for several days awaiting favorable weather. Our next leg, to Goose Bay, Labrador, was to include a fuel management and consumption check. We were to fly at a specified altitude, I think about 8,000 feet, at an indicated airspeed of 150 MPH. Several hours into the flight, having made all of our calculations, a B-24 passed very close on our right. They must have been doing the same as us, but at about 160 MPH. We waved and continued on. After some discussion within our airplane, we decided to see just how the plane would fly at 170 MPH. Happily, we all waved as we passed the B-24. Soon the B-24 'swooped' past us again, probably making about 180 MPH. In amazement we again acknowledged their presence by waving. The fat lady had not yet begin to sing! We continued this game and saw 300 plus on our airspeed indicator. Upon our descent at Goose Bay, while in the pattern, the B-24 overtook us.

Once again we waited for a favorable weather forecast for our flight to Iceland. Weather forecasting was questionable, at best. We arrived at Iceland in a snow storm and somehow landed, without incident, well below the minimums. The next two legs, to Ireland and to Peterborough, England, were uneventful.

Upon arrival at Peterborough and reporting to the 748th Squadron, 457th Bomb Group, I was relieved of the new B-17G. We were given the oldest, battle-weary B-17 in the group. Several days of transition and orientation followed. I had completed four missions and it was on the fifth mission, on 20 June 1944, that we failed to make it back to base.

With one exception the original crew members were on the mission to Hamburg. Henry Gilbert was sick that day and I do not recall the replacement's name. I have since learned that 1257 heavy bombers flew on the mission and that 50 bombers and 7 fighters were lost on that day, however, we were the only crew lost from the 457th BG.

Since we were a new crew we had been assigned the unenviable position of low man in the low squadron, good old 'Tail-end Charlie.' I believe our altitude was about 25,000 feet. Our target was an oil refinery in Hamburg, Germany. It was well defended and the flak was very heavy. While on the bomb run, with the bomb bay doors open, we were hit by a burst of flak. I believe we were hit in the right wing, near the fuselage. The explosion knocked out the two right engines and the intercom, and locked the controls. The right fuel tanks were ablaze. At that point, no one on the aircraft was injured. Jack Lade, the co-pilot, was the first to reach the nose hatch door. In the rush and confusion, he spilled his chest chute, and he gathered it all up in his arms. He was blocking the exit. We pushed him out and followed him. We saw the engineer in his open chute but we never did see him again.

Unknown to me at the time, the two waist gunners and the ball turret gunner had decided not to jump. Their decision had been made prior to our departure on the mission. The radio operator, who knew of their decision, waved to them as he passed them on the way out to jump. They died in the following explosion.

Very soon after I exited the airplane, I saw it explode. The tail gunner was unable to make the several feet forward to reach the waist door, because of the spin. He was still in his position when the airplane exploded. Following a brief 'blackout,' the next thing he recalls he was in the harness of an opened parachute, uninjured, and falling earthward. He discovered his flying suit was missing;

Refinery bombed at Hamburg

however, he was wearing the heated blue suit, worn under the outer clothing.

Since I was at altitude with little oxygen when I jumped, I decided to free-fall to a more liveable altitude. I learned that I was able to turn myself down and then face up, turning over as one would in bed. This surprised me. When facing down, I realized that I was falling into an area of massive fire and destruction that we had just delivered. I made the decision to open my chute hoping I would drift away from the city and its awesome fires. I did not feel the shock when the chute opened. It was quiet and my hands were very cold. I reached into the front leg pocket of my flying suit, found my gloves and put them on. For a while, it seemed that I was going up instead of down. At the time I realized that I was descending, I heard a slight whistling noise and saw a hole about the size of a hat in the canopy of my parachute. The people on the ground were shooting at me! I began to swing back and forth as one would in a park swing, hoping to make myself an elusive target. Two more holes appeared in the canopy, but still uninjured I drifted over a flak gun emplacement at 40 or 50 feet. As I reached the top of my final swing and began the reverse direction, I abruptly struck the ground.

I was not aware of it at the time but the shock resulted in the fracture of a vertebrae. As I attempted to get to my feet, I was surrounded by 8 or 10 soldiers from the nearby gun emplacement. They barked an order at me, in a language I had never heard before. I unbuckled my chute harness and stood up, only to be knocked to the ground. I was totally frustrated. My reception committee then took turns beating me. At one point I was knocked into a waist-deep pond of water. They motioned for me to come out. I shook my head 'no.' One or more of them raised their rifles and I came out, only to be knocked down again. In what seemed to be an eternity, I was 'rescued' by the NCO of the squad. I sat beside a foot path while they rounded up several other American airmen.

Two of us, on foot, were taken by a soldier on a bicycle to a nearby village. Along the way, several civilians attempted to separate us from our custodian. They wanted to kill us. The guard had to resort to drawing his pistol to discourage their attempts. He was very serious about his charge to protect us, for which I was appreciative.

We ended up at a police station, apparently for interrogation. While awaiting whatever fate was to come, a German Luftwaffe pilot gave me a cigarette. I was at the police station for about one and one-half days. There were several sessions of interrogation. Several of us were then loaded on a flat bed truck and given a short tour of the destruction area. Civilians threw sticks and stones at us along the way. Later we were loaded on a train and taken to Frankfurt to a prison.

When I was shot down, I had with me a list of my crew members, their serial numbers, rank, and crew positions. That information was taken from me, but no other information was garnered from me. During my last interrogation session, conducted by a German officer speaking perfect English, I was told, "Since you refuse to tell us anything, I will tell you what we know about you." He told me where I had gone to high school, my wife's name, my aircraft number, group and squadron numbers, date and place I graduated from pilot training, my route of flight from the United States to England, and more.

I was taken to the United States officer's prison camp — Stalag Luft III — at Sagan. I was photographed and issued a metal identification plate, No. 6202, and assigned to the center compound. The compound was 'home' to about 2,000 American officers, including my navigator and bombardier. The length of my stay in this 'less than comfortable' location seemed endless. I lost sight of time. I managed to keep occupied with day to day chores, such as preparation of what little food was provided us. Reading and studying books from a quite adequate library, courtesy of the YMCA, helped pass the time. Some of my compatriots, who had musical talents, put together an orchestra, using instruments provided by the Red Cross. The Red Cross was able to get some food to us. I believe our survival was attributable to that organization. I was incarcerated at Stalag Luft III for seven months before being marched south, when our camp was evacuated in the face of the advancing Russians. I never did receive any packages sent to me through Red Cross channels. Long after I was safely back with my family, the postman regularly delivered the packages, filled with things that would have been so precious had I received them while in prison.

The march through Germany, since well publicized, was a true test of survival. We were subjected to the coldest of winter weather, with minimum rations and exhausting conditions. We were marched, crowded into freight cars, and ended up in Mooseburg, a place near Munich, Stalag 7A. It was the place at which Patton arrived and liberated us all.

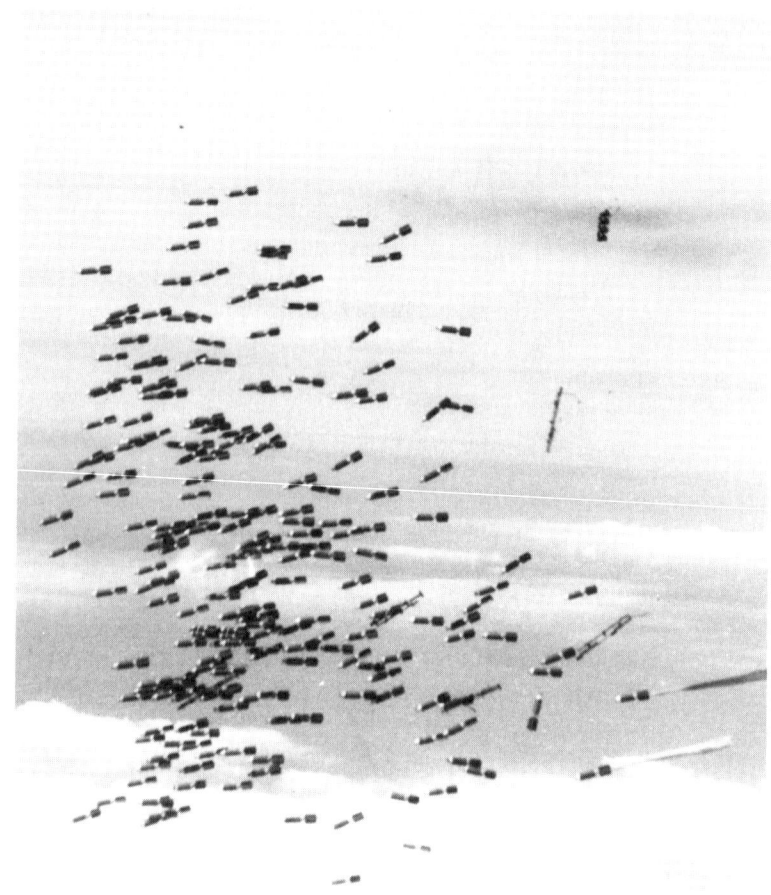

Cluster of incendiaries!

Mission No. 73
21 June 1944

Target — Berlin

Crew of B-17G, No. Unknown

1st Pilot	2nd Lt.	Hershel Wilson	KIA
Co-Pilot	2nd Lt.	Bailey J. Gaudiner	
Nav.	2nd Lt.	Chester Perkins	KIA
Bomb.	2nd Lt.	Joe Srout	KIA
Engr.	T/Sgt.	Joe Shenkin	
Radio Op.	T/Sgt.	Frank Garzia	KIA
LW Gun.	S/Sgt.	Frank X. Heekin	
B. Turret	S/Sgt.	Edward Attleton	KIA
Tail Gun.	S/Sgt.	George Vassiloupolous	

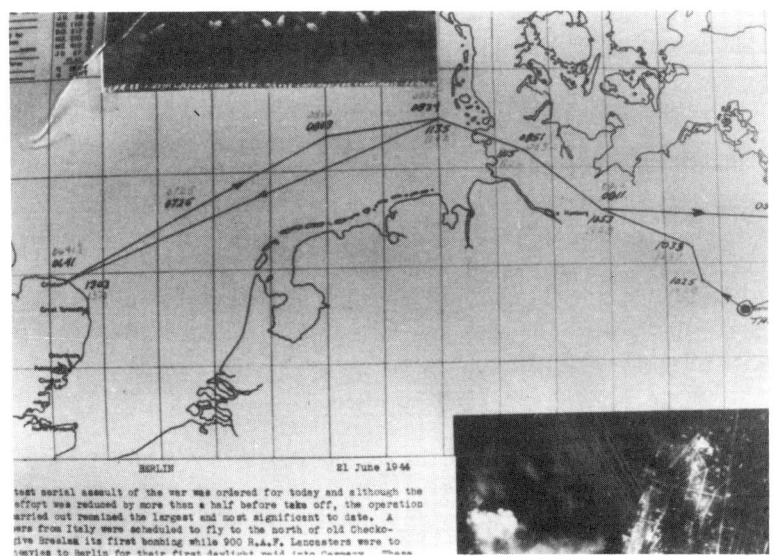

Track Chart, Mission No. 73, 21 June 1944

457th Bomb Group Mission Narrative

The greatest aerial assault of the war was ordered today and, although the scale of the effort was reduced by more than half before take off, the operation as actually carried out remained the largest and most significant to date. A thousand bombers from the 15 Air Force were scheduled to fly to the north of old Czechoslovakia to give Breslau its first bombing, while 900 R.A.F. Lancasters were to follow U.S. heavies to Berlin for their first daylight raid into Germany. These two operations were scrubbed.

In the first deep penetration since 'D'-Day the 457th BG dispatched 42 aircraft as part of the 'second force' of 500 heavies to bomb the center of Berlin, while 677 heavies went to bomb aero engine factories in the suburbs. In addition 163 B-17's were dispatched to the Ruhland synthetic oil factory southeast of Berlin and then to continue on to Russia.

The 457th BG composed the entire 94th 'B' CBW except for 12 planes in the high box. Three a/c aborted from the lead box, reducing its strength to 15 a/c. Major Leroy Watson led the wing in a PFF plane, while Capt. Hoelzer led the low box and Major Fred A. Spencer led the high box until he was forced to abort. Take off began at 0447 hours and, after assembly over Cottsmore buncher, the formation, fourth in the division line, proceeded over the same route as had the two previous missions to Hamburg. The old direct route to Berlin along the 52 degree and 33" parallel was abandoned some time ago for this flak-free route.

The North Sea was completely covered by clouds which, however, broke to 2-4/10ths as the formation penetrated the enemy coast at the base of the Danish peninsula. Smoke was still boiling up above the clouds at 15,000 feet from yesterday's bombing of Hamburg. The formation encountered no flak or fighters as it flew southeast and then east on a feint to Stettin before turning down on a circuitous route to the east of Berlin. On this leg, Lt. Robert Krumm, on his 29th mission, developed engine trouble, jettisoned his bombs, and left the formation. He landed the a/c in Sweden and was interned.

Major Watson gave the order for PFF bombing so the planes turned on the I.P. in wing formation. About half way down the bomb run he descended 2,000 feet because dense condensation trails covered the sky over Berlin at 27,000 feet. Also it was decided to bomb visually as the cloud cover was only 2-4/10ths. Lt. Tonelli, hurriedly made corrections in the bomb sight and selected the marshalling yard in the Horst Wesel district of Berlin, two miles east of the Friederickstrasse, as his aiming point. The assigned MPI in the center of the city was obscured by smoke. Tonelli dropped the bombs at 1019 hours from 25,500 feet and was followed by the other two boxes of the wing. The wing formation was very confused at the time. At least six distinct bomb patterns were made over a very large area. However, damage was made to the yards and to built-up areas.

Anti-aircraft fire was less intense than on previous missions because 100 of the 450 guns had been removed, yet it was intense enough to damage 24 of the 36 returning planes and cause the loss of another. Lt. Wilson, flying his first mission as a plane commander, was hit, caught fire, and blew up seven minutes after leaving Berlin.

The return trip was flown without incident. The let down over the North Sea was accomplished and the planes landed between 1320 and 1430 hours.

Fifty of the 1200 bombers attacking were lost in the largest deep penetration of the war to date.

S/Sgt. Francis X. Heekin's story of the 21 June 1944 mission to Berlin.

The number of men on the crew had been changed and I flew as the waist gunner for both sides of the ship. My first mission was on 21 June 1944 and we were one of the 1500 B-17's to bomb Berlin. We delivered the bombs as ordered and, just on the outskirts of Berlin, we received a direct hit by a burst of flak, in the front of the airplane. The concussion knocked me down and when I got up, I could see that one engine was knocked out and another was on fire. The pilot rang the bail-out bell, but no one heard it as the intercom had been damaged by the explosion. The tail gunner came forward, took off his oxygen mask, and asked what had happened. I pointed to the front of the ship and he, the tail gunner George Vassiloupolous, said, "What are we waiting for?" He kicked open the waist door and dove out. I helped the ball turret gunner put on his harness and chute and then we both jumped out the waist door, with me taking my first and only parachute jump! As I was floating down I chuckled to myself and thought, "Well, you asked for it and now you sure got it." I had lost my flying boots when the parachute jerked open and I had not brought my shoes with me, but fortunately the field in which I landed was soft dirt and I did not hurt my feet. I was immediately surrounded by German civilians, who covered me with a rifle and a revolver.

After they searched me for weapons, and didn't find any, one of the men struck me across the back with the butt of the rifle just to vent his pent-up frustrations on someone. They turned me over to the military, who put me in a detention room with about twenty other prisoners. Some time later, two other American airmen and I were taken by truck to a cemetery, where we were given shovels and told to start digging our graves! When the graves were completed, a truck arrived and the bodies of three American airmen were unloaded, two of which one of the other American airmen identified. I climbed up on the truck and looked at the dog tags of the other body and found it to be the body of T/Sgt. Frank Garzia, the radio operator on our crew. Garzia had been married at Delhart, Texas, while we were in training, and was the new father of a three-month old son he had never seen. Garzia was swollen up three times his normal size, which may have meant his parachute had not opened or he had been beaten to death by the German civilians.

I was taken to Berlin where I was placed on a train bound for Frankfurt. There, I was subjected to intense questioning. When they decided I was not going to tell them anything, they told me all that had happened to my crew. They told me that five members of the crew had died and only three, including me, were prisoners. Just how they knew who the members of my crew were was a mystery to me, as I had only given them my own name, rank and serial number.

Next, I was placed on a train through Berlin, where we laid over for fourteen hours. Then we were placed in a freight car full of captured P.O.W.'s and it turned out we were part of a whole trainload of captured prisoners. Anyway, we headed northeast and on 1 July we were unloaded at Gros Tichow, the town where Stalag Luft No. 4 is located. Stalag Luft No. 4 turned out to be a well-equipped prison camp, as prison camps go. For meals the usual menu was a cup of ersatz coffee for breakfast; at lunch, a plate of thin soup; at dinner, 3 raw potatoes to boil and 8 ounces of black bread. We usually saved part of the bread to eat during the day. This meagre fare was supplemented with Red Cross food packages, which we were provided once each week. This later turned out to be one-half of a Red Cross food package, as they had more prisoners than they had food packages.

I lost about 15 pounds of weight during my stay at Stalag Luft No. 4, but the camp was relatively comfortable and I was not mistreated. We had plenty of soap and water and could bathe as needed. All in all I had no particular complaints up until the middle of January, at which time we were evacuated and forced to march,

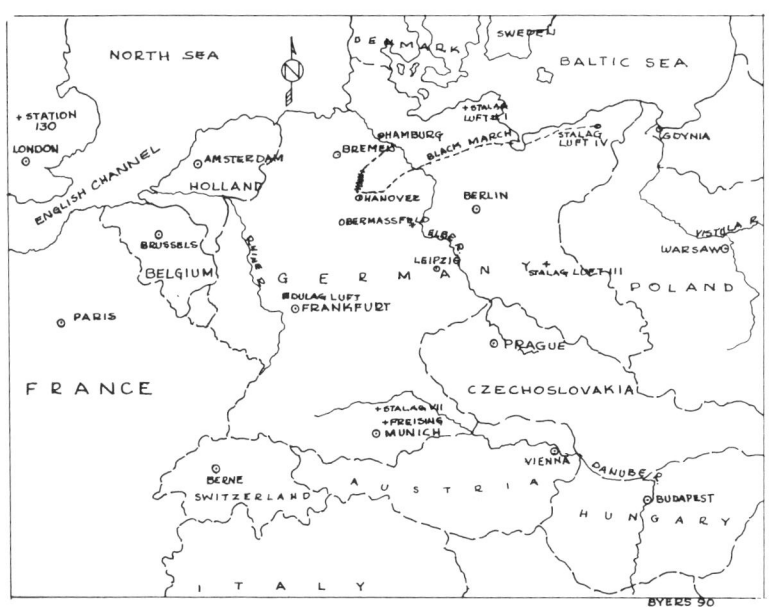

Black Hunger March

on foot, for 450 miles. We slept on the ground, in barns, or wherever the day ended. For food we were given 'ersatz' coffee morning and evening, and three boiled cold potatoes at night. The coffee was the only liquid we received and we were not able to wash at any time. We were all lousy and covered with vermin. The weather was very cold and many of the P.O.W's got pneumonia and died. Dysentary was prevalent and I was very sick for a week but continued to walk and made it to the end. We had an English doctor on the march and, while he had no medical supplies, he treated the dysentary for us by burning wood and making charcoal, which he had us eat.

The march started from Stalag Luft No. 4 on the 6th of February 1945, with about 1,500 men, and ended on 1 April 1945, at Stalag Luft No. 11B, located at Talinghostel, Germany. I do not know how many survived the march but many dropped out because of pneumonia, dysentary, and infections of many kinds, particularly of the feet. The route of the march was from Stalag Luft No. 4 west and south, because the Russians were advancing from the east. Talinghostel is located south and west of Berlin. We were at Stalag Luft No. 11B for only ten days as the English army was advancing from the west.

On evacuating Stalag Luft No. 11B on 1 April 1945, we began to march eastward and, as usual, without any provisions. Another prisoner by the name of Robinson and I decided to escape and we recruited two others to go with us. We had saved a few cold boiled potatoes, which were all the supplies we had. At the end of the first day's march at about 1700 hours, we were ordered to go into a barn for the night and were put under guard. Waiting until about 0100 hours, the four of us slipped by the dozing guards and met up with four others in the nearby woods. We walked at night and hid in bushes and ditches during the daytime. We thought we were traveling southwest toward the British lines but when we finally met some British soldiers, we found out we had been traveling to the southeast. While on the trip, one of the fellows poked into a straw stack with a stick and found five little wild pigs. We drew lots and I won the dubious honor of being the butcher. We pulled the little pigs out of the straw by the tail, cut their throats, cut out the viscera, and immediately fried two of them it in a small frying pan we had stolen before we made our break. Everyone agreed that was the best meal they had ever had in their life! We butchered the other three pigs, hung them in a tree, and ate them the next day.

We had been walking for seven days and we found a food wagon that had been abandoned by German civilians who had been caught in a fire fight between the English and German soldiers. In the wagon was sugar, sorghum, flour, and a large amount of different kinds of sausages. We made 'pigs' of ourselves at our first good meal in some time, which more or less knocked us out.

On the eighth day, two of the fellows became delirious from drinking contaminated water. They developed a temperature and were unable to go any farther. A fellow by the name of Jack Paris, from St. Louis, Missouri, and I were in better condition than the others. We decided that one of us should go over to a nearby road and try to locate members of the British army. We had been keeping off the roads during the day; however, we felt we would have to risk being captured again because of our sick friends. I walked down the road, meeting several German civilians, men, women, and children who were returning to their farms after having been run out by the fighting between the British and the Germans.

I must have been a terrible sight, weighing only about 140 pounds, with a heavy black beard and filthy dirty. I walked by the German civilians, who paid no attention whatsoever to me. Neither did I speak to them. Soon I saw two British Commandoes riding toward me in a 'Jeep.' I stood in the middle of the road and waved for them to stop, which they did. I told them my story and that I was an escaped American. They immediately turned the 'Jeep' around and took me to their commanding officer at their headquarters. I felt rather strange talking to those immaculately dressed British officers, with their highly polished boots. The British officer immediately ordered some tea, a small steak, cheese, and hard biscuits for me.

The British officer wanted me to go to the hospital but I insisted on returning to find my friends in the swamp, to which they finally consented. We climbed into a 'Jeep' and, accompanied by a 'half-track,' located the place along the road where I had first climbed out of the swamp. I now got in the 'half-track' and we splashed through the swamp to where I had left my friends. Two of the fellows were still delirious but Jack Paris was lucid and in as good shape as I. The two sick men were taken to a British field hospital, while Jack Paris and I accepted their hospitality for a week until we could find transportation back to England. I found the British to be in high spirits, chasing the Germans with orders to take no prisoners but to shoot any German who tried to surrender.

Back in England, I was hospitalized for two weeks and I guess my biggest thrill was to be deloused, have a hot bath, and, in clean pajamas, climb into bed on which were clean sheets and pillow cases. I was released from the hospital in about two weeks, having regained much of the 30 pounds which I had lost. I was given a ten-day furlough, which I spent in London.

I was sent to Liverpool, where I shipped out for the United States on the U.S. Navy-operated ship 'George Washington.' I was given a 30-day leave and returned home to Cincinnati, Ohio, for some very welcome rest and recuperation.

Lt. Edward Reppa's story of the mission on 21 June 1944 to Berlin.

I was flying the lead plane on this mission. The assembly and flight to Berlin was essentially 'text book.' We flew beyond Berlin and circled back to take advantage of the wind for the bomb run. The flak barrage over Berlin was imposing, to say the least. However, we penetrated the flak on our bombing run. Just as Lt. Irwin Rosen, the bombardier, dropped the bombs, everything seemed to happen all at once. We were hit by flak which knocked out engines number 2 and 3, both of our inboard engines. The bomb release light on the instrument panel kept flickering away, indicating the bombs had been dropped. In the explosion the top turret operator, T/Sgt. Eldon Krugg, had been hit by flak, as also had the ball turret operator.

When the radio operator checked the bomb bay to see if the bombs had dropped, he found them all on their shackles.

With two engines out, we were forced to leave the formation, the leadership of which had been taken over by the deputy lead ship. Lt. Rosen crawled back to the bomb bay carrying a 'walk around bottle' of oxygen, and 'toggled' out all of the bombs.

We turned on a course for home and, steadily losing altitude, continued to fly across Germany, staying below the bomber stream for protection. When we arrived at the coast and had flown far enough across the North Sea to minimize the chance for fighter attack, we jettisoned all our guns, flak suits, helmets, ammunition, and all other loose, expendable equipment to lighten the airplane, in hopes we would not be required to ditch the airplane in the cold North Sea.

We continued to slowly descend on our course toward England, maintaining a speed of 135 M.P.H., just fast enough to maintain flying speed. Both outboard engines were running smoothly and we were at about 150 miles from shore when some one 'yelled' over the intercom, "There is a fire in the bomb bay!" At that time I was not sure whether or not the radio operator had contacted Air Sea Rescue. We saw a group of B-17's above us and I ordered the radio operator to "Fire some red flares" (indicating we were in trouble and for them to hopefully contact Air Sea Rescue). As in all situations humorous things happen regardless of the seriousness of the occasion. Back came the radio operator with "Lt. Reppa, we threw out the flare gun and all the flares when you ordered us to lighten the ship."

Fortunately the reported fire in the bomb bay turned out to be just smoke from some shorting wires and was not serious.

We managed to continue our slow descent, the two inboard engines running smoothly. We arrived at Glatton, received priority for landing, made our pattern, and landed. Our right brake worked but the left did not and we ran off of the runway—shut off the engines and coasted to a stop. That mission was my last of the tour and, as I soon departed Glatton, I did not see any of my original crew until I arrived in San Diego in 1989—45 years later—when I talked with Eldon Krugg, the engineer, who was wounded in the arm that day.

Mission No. 79
29 June 1944
Target — Leipzig, Mitteldeutsche Motornwerke Aero-engine Plant

Crew of B-17G, No.42-37562

1st Pilot	2nd Lt. Albert Gumuslauskas
Co-Pilot	2nd Lt. William Neidhardt
Nav.	2nd Lt. Harry Will, Jr.
Toggle.	T/Sgt. Paul Beatty
Engr.	T/Sgt. Enos C. Bleacher
Radio Op.	T/Sgt. Anastasio R. McLeonardis
LW Gun.	S/Sgt. Charles Campbell
B. Turret	S/Sgt. Louis F. Beske
Tail Gun.	S/Sgt. Joy P. Stacy

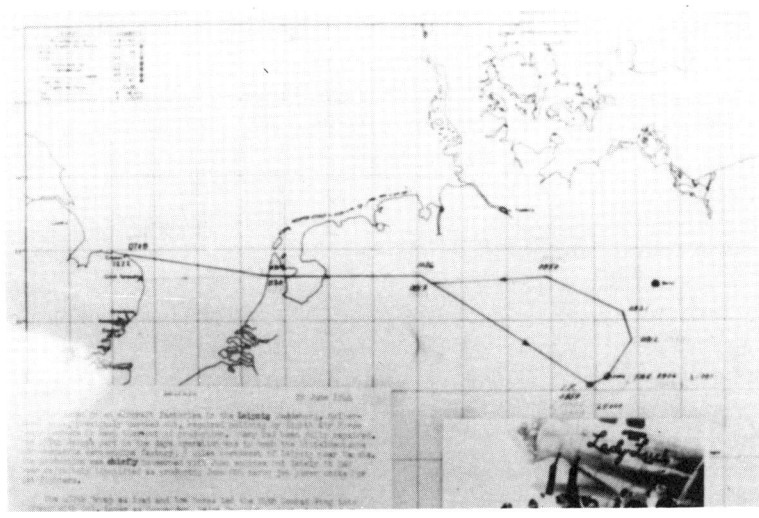

Track Chart, Mission No. 79, 29 June 1944

457th Bomb Group Mission Narrative

The dozen or so aircraft factories in the Leipzig. Maddeburg, Halberstadt area, previously knocked out, required policing by the 8th Air Force heavy bombers to keep them out of production. Many had been fully repaired. The 457th BG part in the day's operation was to bomb the Mitteldeutsche Motornwerke Aero-engine factory, 5 miles northeast of Leipzig near Talcha. Its production was chiefly concerned with Juno engines but lately had been definitely identified as producing Juno 004 turbo-jet power units for jet fighters.

The 457th as lead and low boxes led the 94th CBW into Germany. With Col. James Luper as commander. Major Peresich/Capt. Donald E. Lady led the low box.

Take off began at 0455 hour. The 7/10ths clouds at various levels and dense contrails, which caused 5 other wings to abandon their missions, also gave the 457th Group considerable trouble in effecting assembly. Points and altitudes were changed repeatedly. Although the missing squadron leaders were instructed to assemble with the wing over the North Sea, the entire low squadron of the low box and the high squadron of the lead box never found the formation, even though most of them flew to the Dutch coast.

Penetration was thus made with one squadron missing out of each box. Along the course to the target no enemy opposition appeared. The 10/10ths clouds over the North Sea had reduced to 7/10ths over Holland, to scattered low clouds over the target. At the I.P. the wing leader observed the clouds to be 10/10ths over the target and announced PFF bombing. The planes swung into a wing formation. Lt. Tonelli, bombardier in the lead box, was able to pick up the target through a thin smoke screen. The target area was only 2/10ths covered. Tonelli took over from the mickey operator and requested a 360 turn for a second and better run, with the groups in trail. The wing commander then led the wing on a 360 turn around Leipzig and back to the I.P. On this circle, six Me-110's, out of a force estimated to be 20, made one head- on pass at the lead box but damaged only one plane. Escorting P51's then drove them off.

On the second run the flak from the 100 guns tracked the formation accurately as it flew directly over the city. This time the target was covered with smoke from the bombing by the 41st 'A' wing. Lt. Tonelli dropped the bombs by triangulation; the strikes were not visible.

Lt. Walls, leading the low box, was not able to synchronize properly on the target due to the smoke, and held his bombs. However, four planes in the box let their bombs drop. Flak which had tracked the box all the way across the city scored a direct hit on Lt. Gumuslauskas' plane and it went down in a steep dive and blew up. Lt. Walls took the remaining eight planes over Wittenburg and dropped on the marshalling yards. Direct hits were made on two railway warehouses and six small buildings in an adjacent industrial area. Approximately 15 bombs fell into the choke point. The planes then rallied with the wing and the formation flew to the north of Magdeburg, Brunswick, and Hanover on the route home. The landing was made at 1345 hours, with 15 of the 22 planes damaged.

Lt. Harry E. Will's story of the 29 June 1944 mission to Leipzig

To set the stage for the 29 June 1944 mission to Leipzig, Germany, I have to start with the mission we flew to the Laon-Cauvron airfield 28 June 1944, since that was the beginning of our problems.

On 28 June 1944 we went to the briefing for the mission as usual and the G-2 told us the ceiling of 500 feet for take off would be burned off by the time we returned. If you were on that mission you will remember that when we got back to England the ceiling was still low and we all crunched into a P-51 fighter base. It was a close encounter of the worst kind and we almost collided with another B-17. We remained at the base for several hours and then decided to hedge-hop to our own field one at a time, which worked out satisfactorily. However, we were fed our dinner at 2100 hours and got to bed dead tired.

The CQ came to our hut between 2300 and 2400 hours and awakened the crew in the hut who were scheduled to fly but said nothing to the members of our crew. I was happy because I did not have to fly again that day. Shortly after I had gone back to sleep, the CQ came back and said that one of the pilots on another crew was sick and we were to fill in, on his crew, for the mission. We had a mixed crew—some of the enlisted men were from our crew and others from the other crew. As I remember we had three enlisted men who had never flown with us before.

We were late and I just barely made the navigators briefing and arrived at the airplane just at engine start time. The pilot, Lt. Albert Gumuslauskas, started the engines and taxied out onto the perimeter taxi strip. The taxi strip was under construction, with a ditch across it between us and the runway and our only access to the end of the runway was to cross the runway to the other side before the planes began their take off. Before we could cross the runway the first planes started to roll and we had to wait until all those ahead of us had taken off. I felt then that things were not going to go well on this mission. Al shut down the engines as did the others and I went to sleep—something I rarely did in the airplane. I woke up when the engines started again and we started to move. It was now daylight. I looked at my watch and saw it was close to the time that we should have joined the formation and gone on our way to Leipzig.

Al got around the taxi strip as fast as he could taxi in a B-17, turned onto the runway, and took off. There was no time to fly the three legs we normally flew to assemble. Rather, we headed straight for the coast departure point at Cromer. As we broke through the clouds we got there just in time to be the last plane in the low squadron, 'tail end Charlie.' We had never flown in that position before but, since we were filling in for a new crew, I guess we got their spot.

We crossed the North Sea and over the Zeider Zee, then passed by Dummer Lake to feint a course toward Berlin, then angled down to Leipzig to bomb the jet engine factory.

The clouds were 10/10ths all the way and the bombing was to be by PFF through the clouds. I was busy with crew checks, fixes, and entering information in the navigation log as we came up to the I.P. We opened the bomb bay doors and I moved up beside the chin turret gunner to be ready to salvo the bombs when the smoke bomb dropped from the lead ship. I noticed that a large hole in the clouds had opened up over the target area and it should be possible to bomb the target visually. The lead crew was not prepared for visual bombing and the next thing I knew we were turning off the bomb run to the east of Leipzig. We were making a 360 around the target to give the lead crew time to get set for visual bombing and for the boxes to take their positions in trail. One of the crew called on the intercom, "Navigator, where are we going?" I replied, "I think we are making a 360 around Leipzig so we can bomb visually." Then before he released his mike button, I heard some cursing from the crew member.

As we came around for the second run we had heavy and accurate flak as well as fighters attacking the formation. When we arrived at the I.P. I moved up beside the nose gunner again to drop the bombs. I had no sooner left my navigator's position than I heard a sound like someone breaking a plate glass window and felt a jolt to

B-17 on fire!

the whole airplane. The gunner and I both turned around to see a large hole over my desk where a 20mm shell had come through the side of the airplane. At that moment we didn't realize that the shell had lodged in the instrument panel and exploded, wounding both the pilot and the co-pilot. The co-pilot got a chest full of shrapnel and the pilot was hit in the neck. The nose of the airplane was a mess with papers, maps, and equipment strewn around. Almost immediately the engines started to rev up and we started down in a steep dive. I heard the pilot say, on the intercom, "Prepare to--------" and the intercom went dead. We dropped the bombs and the engineer came down in the hatch and said we were to bail out. I turned to the gunner, pulled the emergency release on his flak suit and it dropped to the floor. I then handed him his escape kit and turned toward the hatch to pull the red emergency cord which pulled the hinge pins—but the door didn't release, so I gave it a kick with my foot and it flew away. The nose gunner dove out the opening and I grabbed my chest pack, snapped it to my parachute harness and dropped out. I had also grabbed my GI shoes, which I held onto all the way to the ground. (They were taken away from me by the Germans.) I tumbled until I was down to what I thought was below 15,000 feet, where the oxygen supply is a little better, and I pulled the rip cord. That was the level of the cloud cover and where I was when the chute opened. It was a good thing that the intercom, oxygen, and heated suit connections were all break-away, for I had not disconnected any of them before I jumped. My hands were cold and hurting and, although I had intended to keep the 'D' ring, I dropped it because of the cold. It was very cold at that altitude even though it was summer below. I hit the ground harder than I thought I would but was thankful that I was on the ground and apparently not injured.

The engineer and the nose gunner were not so fortunate, for the nose gunner hit his hand on something, probably the bomb bay door, when he bailed out. The engineer was shot by German police through the neck with a small calibre bullet as he was being questioned on the ground. I met the engineer about ten days later and he had experienced partial loss of the use of his right hand but was recovering. He said he was unconscious for a time and when he regained consciousness he was in a hospital bed next to the co-pilot.

This was my thirteenth mission which lasted for ten months.

Mission No. 91
19 July 1944
Target — Augsburg Messerschmidt factory

Crew of B-17G, No. 42-97601

1st Pilot	2nd Lt. Noel A. Cunefare	
Co-Pilot	2nd Lt. Milton E. Durham	
Nav.	2nd Lt. Wesley C. Akins	
Bomb.	2nd Lt. Donald W. Barton	
Engr.	T/Sgt. Howard S. Drake	
Radio Op.	T/Sgt. Frank L. Nunn	
LW Gun.	S/Sgt. Ralph T. Hodson	
B. Turret	S/Sgt. Joseph W. Duvall	KIA
Tail Gun.	S/Sgt. John C. Sampson	

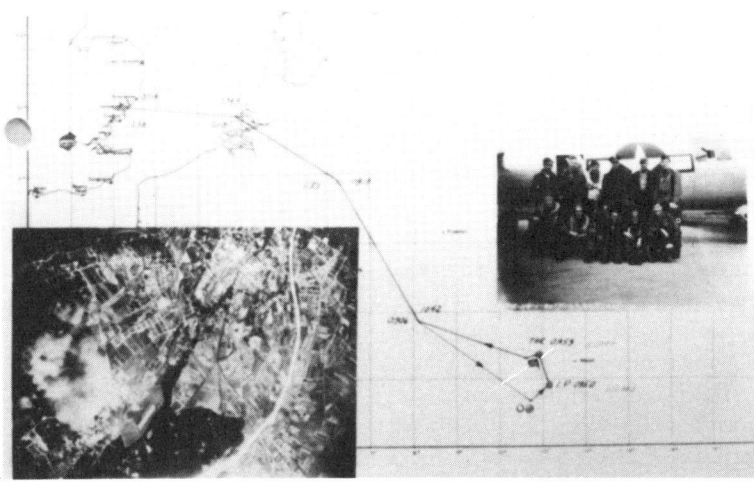

Track Chart, Mission No. 91, 19 July 1944

457th Bomb Group Mission Narrative

German jet propelled aircraft have definitely became a potential menace to American heavy bomber formations. Augsburg was the center of development for the Me 262 jet fighter with much activity in evidence at nearby Lechfeld, Leipheim, Laupheim, and other fields. Coordinated with other attacks on such targets were policing raids on the Schweinfurt ball bearing plants and the parent Messerschmidt plant at Augsburg. The 457th BG drew the latter as its target, furnishing 36 planes to form the entire 94th 'B' CBW as part of a force of 1242 Eighth Air Force heavies dispatched to southern Germany.

A new departure was made in the composition of boxes for deep penetration missions such as this one. For the first time the tactical 12-ship box was used on this type of mission. Col. Henry Wilson/Capt. Clarence E. Schuchmann led the three 12-ship boxes in the take off at 1454 hours with Capt. Jerome E. Godfrey in the deputy lead plane. The wing assembly was made without difficulty and Felixstowe was left behind at 0714 hours with the wing flying south in the division formation.

The continent was pierced at the same flak-free entrance over the Scheldt Islands but from that point there was a variance in the route used in the last four penetrations to the Munich area. The flight took the formation by Aachen and then across the Rhine River, through the Karlsruhe – Strasburg flak gap. The entire route was covered with 6-8/10ths cumulous clouds but they cleared to 3/10ths at the I.P.

Near Kempton, just before the turn to the I.P., the formation was attacked by approximately forty FW-190's and Me-109's coming from all directions but no saturation tactics were used. The Luftwaffe did not press their attacks and seemed inexperienced in the interception of heavy bomber formations. Only a few planes came in close to the bombers before peeling off. However, the deputy lead plane was hit and fell out of the formation. They were not seen again. The enemy fighter attacks continued all the way to Augsburg but we had no further losses.

The boxes had taken visual bombing interval at the I.P. and Lt. Dino Tonelli in the lead box and Lt. Irwin Rosen in the low box, after each making a smooth run, released their bombs at 1003 hours from 25,000 feet. Both hit in the hanger area on the east side of the field, which was the assigned area. The high box, coming in last had difficulty in the lead plane. The bomb bay doors would not open electrically and could not be cranked down in time to bomb.

Mission No. 91

The deputy was called to drop on a signal from the navigator of the lead plane. When the waist gunner of the deputy lead plane saw the bombs of a plane in the formation drop, he called "Bombs away." The navigator, thinking the call came from the bombardier, gave the signal with the Aldis Lamp. The formation dropped their bombs with the indices of the bomb sight still an inch apart. The bombs fell in open fields south of the target.

The three boxes rallied into a wing formation and proceeded on the return flight home. They split up again after effecting a let down over the North Sea and reached base at 1330 hours. Good weather enabled all of the 29 CBW's dispatched to bomb their targets visually. Destruction was extensive and was one of the more successful missions of the war.

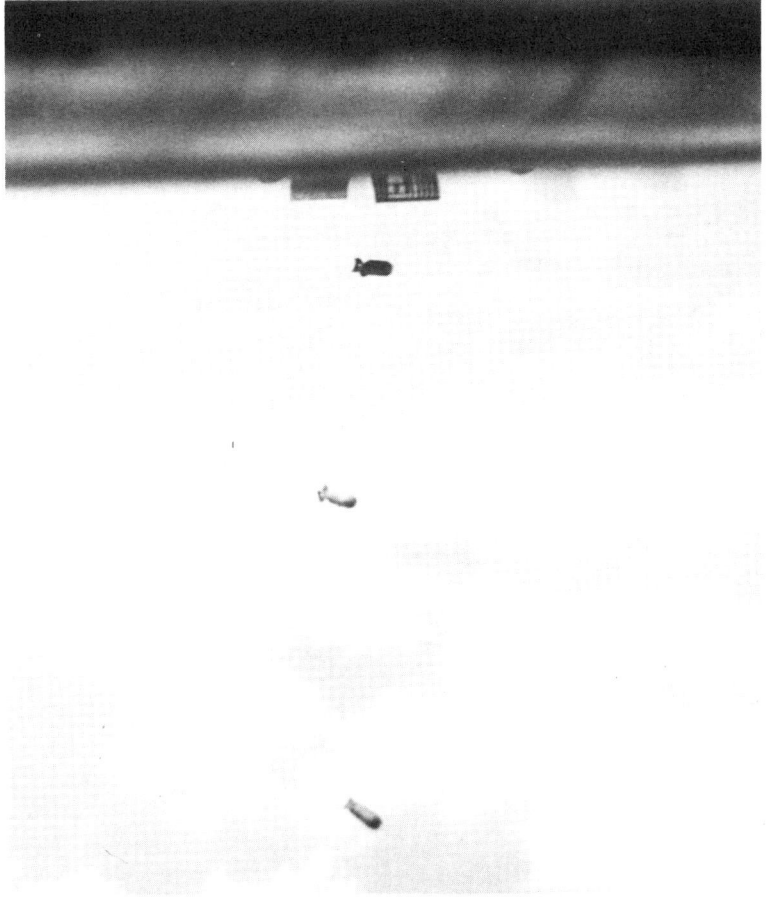

Bombing using 'toggle.'

Lt. Wes Akins' story of the 19 July 1944 mission to Augsburg, Germany.

The following is a description of what happened on 19 July 1944 along with the information given to me by Donald W. Barton, Howard S. Drake, and Ralph T. Hodson.

Immediately after turning at the I.P. for the target, a flight of about twelve FW-190 German fighter planes came at us from 12 o'clock, firing 20mm cannon. We were hit and I definitely remember that the number 3 engine was blown from its mount, as was the left half of the nose of the airplane. I was blown against the 'firewall' of the remaining portion of the nose section. I recall attempting to find an outlet for my oxygen hose. I suppose I failed to find the outlet as my only other recollection is that of engineer Howard Drake kneeling at the hatch escape door, with his popped chute in his arms. I suppose he did jump but I do not recall his doing so. Donald Barton recalled pilot Lt. Noel Cunefare calling me (navigator) for a heading to Switzerland. Either I was able to respond, or he turned to a south heading, toward Switzerland, as later Barton, Drake, Hodson, and I, all parachuted down and came down in the same general area, 20 miles from the Swiss border. I came down in the mountains 50 miles from Innsbruck, Austria. I have no recollection of jumping from the airplane. Either the oxygen at a lower elevation resuscitated me enough so that I had the presence of mind to pull my rip cord, or I was blown from the airplane and my chute opened from the explosion.

The German soldiers, who came up the mountain to get me when I landed, told me that an airplane had exploded in the sky not far from where I had landed.

According to Howard Drake, Cunefare had given him the signal to jump and he landed and was not injured. The others in the rear of the plane said the intercom was inoperative and that a fire engulfed the area of the radio room and the bomb bay. They knew they would not get a signal to jump, so all headed for the waist door exit.

Hodson and Barton were both injured and hospitalized. I was injured and was taken to a small hospital in Landec, where I stayed for ten days. When I was well enough to travel, I was taken to a Luftwaffe Lazeret on the northwest edge of Munich. I was transported to Stalag Luft No. 1 the last week of October 1944. When I arrived at Stalag Luft No. 1, I was reunited with Barton and we spent the remainder of our incarceration together, until we were liberated. Both Drake and Hodson were sent to a prison north of Danzig.

Mission No. 113
25 August 1944
Target — Peenemunde Electrolytic hydrogen peroxide plant building

Crew of B-17G, No. 42-9818
Pilot	2nd Lt.	Donald K. Goss
Co-Pilot	2nd Lt.	Phil B. Andreau
Nav.	2nd Lt.	Gerhardt Hoelzel
Toggle.	S/Sgt.	William H. Sokolowski
Engr.	S/Sgt.	Peter G. Stern
Radio Op.	S/Sgt.	Henry M. Githens
LW Gun.	S/Sgt.	John A. Roe, Jr.
Ball T.	S/Sgt.	Ruben L. Hernandez
Tail Gun.	Sgt.	Charles E. Gentile

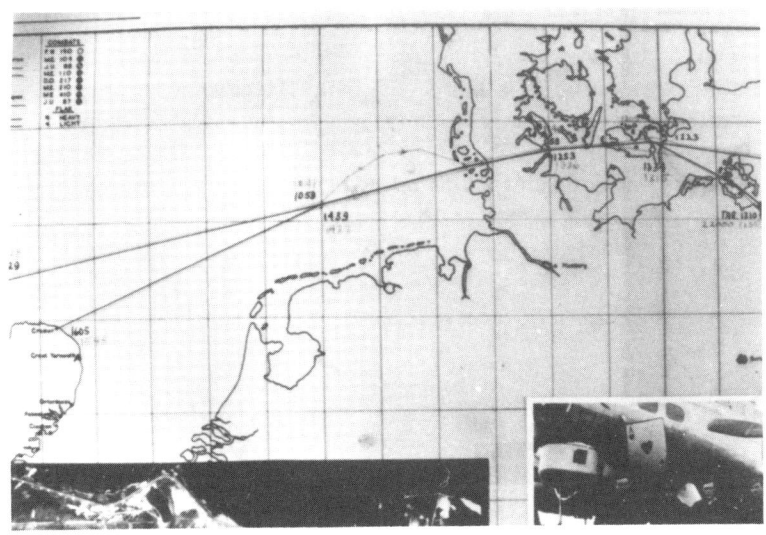

Track Chart, Mission No. 113, 25 August 1944

457th Bomb Group Mission Narrative

The heavy bomber effort of the 8th Air Force shifted today from central Germany to targets in northern Germany, along or near the Baltic Sea coast. Aircraft plants and oil refineries at Politz, Lubeck, Wismar, Anklan, Rechlin, and other points were targets. The 457th BG was assigned the Electrolytic hydrogen peroxide plant building at Peenemunde, on the shore of the Baltic Sea, already damaged during previous raids.

Col. Luper, flying with Capt. Dozier, led the three boxes in their take off at 0800 hours, to compose the 94th 'A' CBW, leading the 1st division in the flight across the North Sea to the target. Considerable difference between the briefed and actual winds, over the North Sea, caused the formation to gain 12 minutes time. The formation then led the division in a turn left of course and then 's'ed to prevent bunching up on the 10 CBW's of the 3rd division, flying ahead.

Considerable German shipping was seen after the Danish peninsula was crossed, as the flight eastward to the I.P. was continued. Heading into Peenemunde from the northeast, the target area was quickly picked up by the bombardiers in each of the three boxes. The 1,000 pound bombs were released at 1250 hours from 22,000 feet, those of the lead box, dropped by Capt. Henry P. Loades, falling slightly over the electrolytic H_2O_2 building, with possibly 5 hits. Those of the high box, dropped by Lt. Kenneth Taylor, hit the building squarely. Eight railway flak guns could be seen firing at the formation.

A few seconds after bombs away, the airplane piloted by Lt. Donald K. Goss was hit by flak in the left wing and blew off a large section of the wing. He peeled off from the formation and spun toward the ground. He was later reported to have crashed landed in Sweden.

The formation returned to base without attacks from German fighters and reached base at 1630 hours.

S/Sgt. John A. Roe, Jr.'s story of the 25 August 1944 mission to Peenemunde, Germany.

"I understand that you have not been properly briefed the past few days, so this time I am going to do the job myself." These words were spoken by a Major in the United States Army Air Force, in the briefing room of the 457th Bomb Group, in "Merry Old England' in the year 1944. Those words also started one of the most eventful days of my life. Prior to 25 August 1944, I had flown 31 combat missions as the tail gunner of a B-17 combat crew assigned to the 8th Air Force. I had flown missions to Berlin, Munich, Stuttgart and St. Lo, but the mission we flew on 25 August 1944 will always stand out in my memory as the most dramatic day of my life.

The briefing officer proceeded to brief us 'properly' for a period of time and portions of his briefing will always stand out in my memory. "You will meet very little fighter opposition and the flak will be light to moderate." I would remember his forecast of how the flak would be light, later that afternoon. We were then shown the map, illustrating the route across northern Germany to the target at Peenemunde. This meant we had a long trip ahead of us; however, much of it would be over water, the North Sea and the Baltic Sea. I glanced about the room and could see that most of the other crew members were trying to appear unconcerned but I had a good idea they too were thinking, as was I, that many of the men sitting here would not eat dinner that evening in a 457th BG mess hall. I had no way of knowing, however, that I would be among the missing.

When the briefing was over we gathered up our flying gear and were transported by truck to our assigned airplane. There was very little chatter as we rode through the pre-dawn fog and mist. One man did make an observation to the effect, "Light flak---- ha! ----the last time he said we could expect light flak, you could have ridden your bicycle across it!" Another man corroborated the first observation with "Yea, who does he think he is kiddin' anyway?" A third man joined in with "Boy, those jokers should go on one of these missions and get an eye full of that------no fighters------and light flak!------sometime, that they talk about all the time!" And so it went until we arrived at our plane.

We unloaded our gear and proceeded to preflight our 'flying fortress' for the mission ahead. Once aboard the airplane we checked our guns and the equipment in our crew position in the airplane and were ready for take off. The period of time between 'stations' and take off is usually filled with trivial talk, to keep the mind off of the danger they will face in the mission ahead.

While we were not one of the original crews in the group, many of which had completed a tour or were shot down, we had at this point in time flown more missions than any other operational crew in the 457th BG. We had been through many of these pre-take off sessions, during which we talked of past missions, of crewmen who were no longer with us, the possibility of this mission being 'scrubbed,' and the ever-present question of what we thought this mission would be like. There had been a mission to this same target on 18 July and we had heard that it was a comparatively easy mission, no fighters and very ineffective flak, with only one plane damaged. Today, however, just might be different. One never knew when the 'Hun' would send up his fighters to exact a toll on the invaders.

The waist gunner, radio operator, and I were in the radio room when we heard the pilot starting engine No. 1, as it coughed and came to life with a mighty roar. In rapid succession the other three engines joined No. 1 in a crescendo of sound and our 'fort' moved out of the revetment in the pre-dawn darkness and, with brakes squealing, wended its way to the end of the runway.

After an uneventful take off the squadron went through the job of forming into the usual bomber formation. As our plane was one of the lead planes we were among the first into position, slightly to the left and to the rear of the group leader. One by one the other planes eased into position to the rear, some higher and some lower than our own.

All the time we were forming we were making our way out of the south eastern coast and as soon as our formation was complete we started the long tedious trip across the North Sea. From my position in the tail I could look down upon the water, many thousands of feet below in the dawn's greyness. The water looked smooth from up here where I was sitting, but I was certain it was choppy and cold. The very thought of what might happen in case of engine failure or other mishap, which could lead to ditching in the cold, green water, made me shiver with apprehension. There was very little chatter over the intercom at this time of the morning, as there was always the chance of enemy fighters patrolling the North Sea and diving through our formation and catching one of us by surprise. We were, however, alert to the possibility and I settled back to scan the western sky.

Our North Sea crossing was uneventful and we crossed the Danish peninsula without experiencing any flak or fighters. We flew out over the Baltic Sea and continued over water to our I.P.

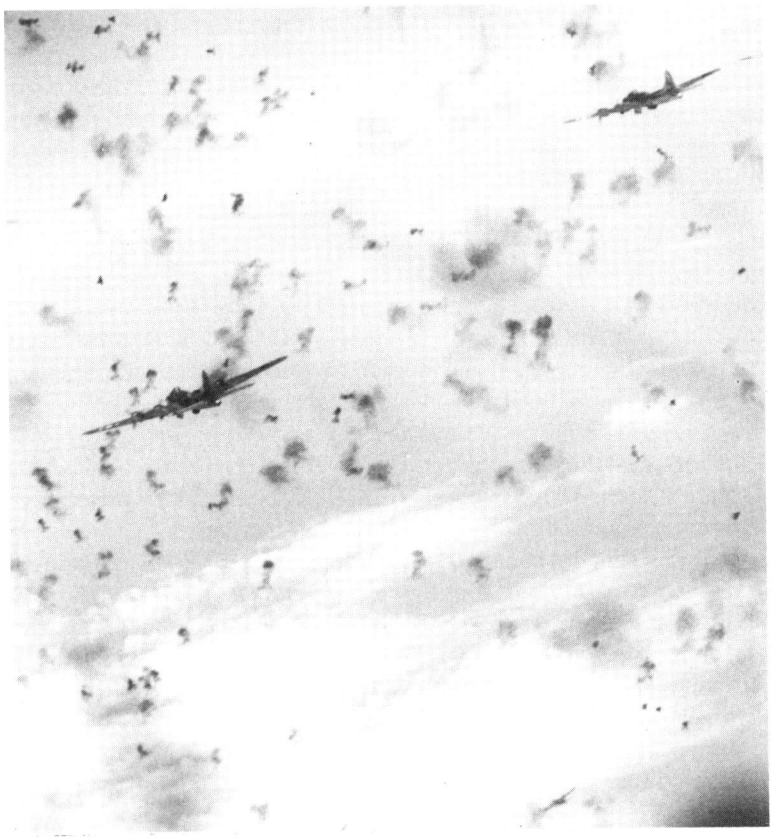

Intense and accurate flak!

which was a set of coordinates over water. It was close to noon when the coast of Germany was sighted to the south. The target was located on the coast and now came the time to be doubly alert, for once the planes reached the I.P. and was on the bomb run, they were 'sitting ducks' for fighters and flak.

I was hunched over my guns watching for 'bogies' when the most 'blood chilling' voice came over the intercom that I think I have ever heard. It wasn't a scream, just a statement of fact from the ball turret gunner! "My door came open." Although spoken in a low voice, it was a voice so filled with fear and terror it made the hair raise on the back of my neck and my blood turn cold. The door on the ball turret located underneath the belly of the plane had somehow come unlatched and 'Chuck' our ball turret operator was hanging out in space by his knees! He was completely outside the plane and no one could reach him to assist in any way to get him back in the turret. To make matters worse, the anti-aircraft batteries had began shooting at us and the sky was filled with bursting shells. Somehow the ball turret gunner, by sheer strength and determination managed to pull himself back into the turret and get his door closed before we reached the target.

As we reached the target area, every second that ticked by seemed like minutes. The light to moderate flak we were supposed to encounter had turned into 'intense,' the word used to describe the condition that existed when the 'Jerries' laid down a barrage that could be used for a highway. Somone remarked, "They must have moved more guns into Peenemunde for our benefit." I thought to myself, those intelligence guys should see some of this 'light flak!' they say we should not worry about!

That was the last clear thought I had for some time. The airplane seemed to leap upward, and the bombardier's voice called out over the intercom, "Bombs away." Just at that time there was a sound of tearing metal and the airplane shook just as if a giant hand had taken hold of it and shook it! The plane fell off to the right and began to spin downward! Almost immediately the sound of the bail out buzzer was actuated by the pilot. I moved with considerable difficulty from my position seated behind my guns, over to the little escape hatch immediately behind my position in the tail of the airplane.

I was numb. All I could think of was, "Surely this isn't happening to me?" I had read about such things but they always happened to someone else. The plane seemed to come out of the spin (I later learned that our pilot, a six foot, three inch, 220 pounder, had pulled it out of the spin by sheer strength). Although the bell to abandon ship had rung, I began to think there was a possibility that we would not have to bail out after all. I looked down at the floor in front of me and, "Good Lord!" My parachute had somehow caught on something and had spilled out of its pack and was laying on the floor at my feet!

Really frightened, I looked forward into the waist of the airplane and I saw nothing but confusion. I could not tell what was going on but several of the crew were grouped around the ball turret. Gathering the parachute up in my arms, I began to crawl around the tail wheel and into the waist section of the airplane. I knew there was a spare parachute in the spare parts bag we carried along for emergencies. When I got to the waist, 'Herky,' the waist gunner, was sitting on the emergency bag and I had to pull him off to get to the parachute. I found the spare chute and unclipped my chute and clipped the spare to my harness. I then looked around to see what was happening.

Mission No. 113

The sight that met my eyes almost made me crawl back into the tail. Our ball turret gunner was lying on the floor, bleeding in a dozen places. Our radio operator's hands were shot up and blood was dripping from both of them. 'Herky' was almost in a state of shock, which was short lived, however, as he got up from the bag and attended to the ball turret gunner. First of all we could see that his left arm was broken above the elbow, and 'Herky' tore some wooden strips off the side of the airplane and made some splints. He dusted some sulpha powder on the open wound in the arm, bandaged it, and then applied the splints. Chuck was in terrible pain and 'Herky' took the morphine surette out of the first aid kit and gave him a shot. Chuck kept trying to raise up and to point at his left leg. I looked down and saw that his pants leg was soaked in blood from his thigh to his foot. 'Herky' and I took the knife and split the pants leg down the side; the sight that met our eyes was enough to make a young intern sick. His leg was a mass of wounds, both large and small, from his thigh to his foot. 'Herky' bandaged the wounds starting at his thigh, and I started at his foot and we bandaged all the holes. A wound in his foot went completely through the arch in his foot. After wrapping Chuck's feet tightly with bandages, I turned my attention to the radio operator. His hands were still bleeding but not excessively. I looked at his hands and could see there were several small wounds in them but they had clotted and he was not losing a lot of blood. I wrapped his hands such that it looked like he was wearing a pair of mittens. (This turned out to be somewhat of an error, as he later needed help to free himself from his parachute.)

While we were consumed in medical work, we did not have much time to worry about the condition of the airplane. However, 'Pinky' the engineer came into the waist and told us that the pilot had headed the plane for Sweden and would try to land the airplane there. The plane was vibrating very badly and I was hoping we could make it that far. 'Pinky' told us that an anti-aircraft shell had exploded in the bomb bay and the structure supporting the wings was in very bad condition and could cause trouble in landing. I looked out the left waist window and was shocked at the size of the hole in the wing behind No. 2 engine. No wonder the wings were flapping! We made our wounded as comfortable as possible and settled down to see what developed.

We didn't have long to wait. I looked out the left waist window and saw a fighter plane, on the side of which was an emblem in the shape of a shield in which were three crowns, flying along beside us. I surmised it must be the ensignia of the Swedish Air Force. I had seen lots of German planes and it did not resemble any of their planes. Someone looked out the other window and saw another fighter there. The pilot of the fighter waved to me and I waved back. The plane gave me a feeling of security I had not felt for some time.

My feeling of security soon was to disappear as 'Pinky' came back to us and said the pilot was going to stall the airplane to see if it would withstand a landing. We braced ourselves, and after the stall, we felt the plane 'shudder.' The plane dropped, the wings flapped, and we could hear the violent stress to which the structure was strained. 'Pinky' came back into the waist with the message that we were to bail out at the signal, as the pilot did not feel that the airplane would withstand the stress of a landing and would probably break up. Again I had the feeling that this could not be happening to me. I was having a bad dream and I would awaken soon, in my bunk back at the base. But the emergency bell rang and I knew we still had work to do.

Sooke, the nose gunner, had joined us in the waist and he and I dragged Chuck to the waist door. After placing his good right hand on the D-ring of the parachute we pushed him out into space. I motioned for Sooke to go next, as he was a little closer to the door than I. However, he picked a fine time to be polite as he motioned for me to go out. I moved toward the door, and then the same thought hit me: this can't be me jumping out of a crippled airplane! I leaned forward and the slipstream held me suspended momentarily, so that I had time to look down at the ground beneath us. We were at about three thousand feet and the ground looked to be miles away. I could see people and vehicles moving around and they looked like tiny bugs.

I gave a little extra push and fell free into the blue sky. Ignoring all I had heard about counting to three and then pulling the rip cord, I pulled immediately after I had cleared the plane. The silk burst out of the pack and my downward plunge was slowed by a mighty jerk, as I floated freely in the sky. There was little sensation of falling, only one of being suspended in the air and swinging to and fro.

The wind seemed to be pushing me toward a farm I could see from my perch and I became almost frantic with the fear I would be slammed full force into the side of a barn. I was also drifting, at least it seemed so, sideways. I had heard that the parachute jumper should always land with the wind at his back and I reached up to the shroud lines to try to turn my chute. Having no idea what I should be doing, I pulled what I thought was sideways to correct my drift and only succeeded in letting some of the air out of the chute. Boy, what a scare that gave me. No more of that! I could envision myself plunging to earth and the parachute cascading down around me.

Those were the last thoughts I had while still in the air, for as I looked down I could see the ground rushing up to meet me and I bent my knees to absorb the shock of landing. ----Whoooosh----and I rolled forward to take a large part of the shock out of my landing.

As I stood up and unsnapped my parachute harness, I looked up a nearby hill and saw a stocky young Swede running toward me, with his hand outstretched, shouting, "Welcome to Sweden, welcome to Sweden." I breathed a prayer and thought to myself, "Buddy, you said a mouth full."

Nose compartment of B-17G.

A/C hit by German rocket.

Mission No. 123
17 September 1944
Target — Nijmegen Siegfried Line

Crew of B-17G, No. 42-97951

1st Pilot	1st Lt.	Douglass L. Grantham, Jr.
A/C	Major	George C. Hozier
Nav.Lead	Capt.	Patrick W. Henry
Nav.Mickey	1st Lt.	Robert E. Costello
Nav. DR	2nd Lt.	Howard P. Quinn
Bomb.	2nd Lt.	Robert O. Douglas
Engr.	T/Sgt.	William N. Suggs
Radio Op.	T/Sgt.	Buford R. Milner
LW Gun.	S/Sgt.	August E. Kujala
RW Gun.	S/Sgt.	Sophus C. Tucker
T.G.(Obs.)	F/O	Arthur Gennari

457th Bomb Group Mission Narrative

The historic mission flown by the 457th Bomb Group on this day was the tactical bombing of the Siegfried Line, prior to the Allied airbourne landings in Nijmegen, Holland. German tanks and guns had to be knocked out to make it possible for our armies to break the 'line' in an attempt to outflank the Nazi forces in the lowlands.

Four twelve-aircraft boxes were dispatched at 0630 hours with Major George C. Hozier as A/C. Simultaneously 420 a/c of the 3rd division took off to attack targets north and west of the 1st division. We were 'B' CBW and second in the division formation. After assembly at 13,000 feet on the Glatton buncher the group flew the briefed route over England. Between point 'B' and control point No. 1, a diversion of 30 minutes was ordered and the formation made a 180 degree turn in the direction of the base to lose time.

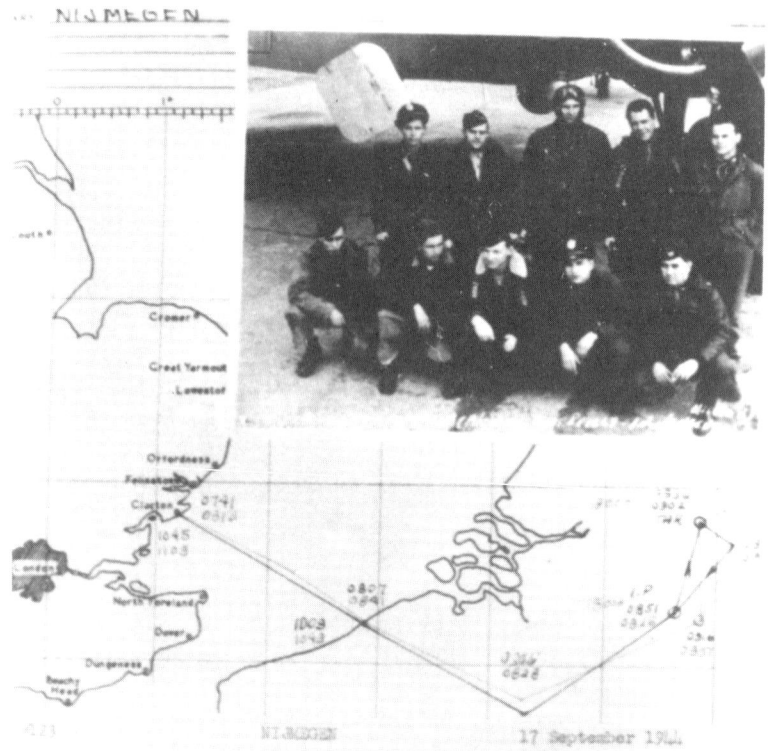

Track Chart, Mission No. 123, 17 Sept. 1944

The group then returned to course and followed in trail of the 94th 'A' CBW.

The Belgium coast was crossed at 0841 hours at a point near Brussels. The formation then headed northeast to the I.P. but swung right of course, in the vicinity of Weert, Holland, as the lead a/c No. 42-49751 was hit by flak. The deputy lead a/c was also hit; however, the deputy lead took over the lead and corrected the heading. Since it was necessary for the lead a/c to make a visual run, several check points were found and the bomb run made with very good results.

After bombs away, the formation turned right and returned to the point at which they had begun the run, almost due south of the target. The No. 3 and No. 4 boxes never did rally and proceeded to base individually. The let down was made over the English Channel and the group landed at 1120 hours.

Lt. Strosser landed plane No. 42-97190 in Belgium, having lost two engines and having another damaged. Beside losing one plane and crew, 5 other planes received major damage from flak.

Col. (Ret.) Douglas L. Grantham, Jr.'s story of the 17 September 1944, mission to Nijmegen, Holland.

The 8th Army Air Force flew a tactical mission in support of the First Airborne Army which was making parachute and glider landings of 20,000 men in the Netherlands. The heavy bombers attacked flak batteries and gun installations in the vicinity of the drop and were forced because of cloud cover to fly much lower than briefed.

The 457th BG, which was leading the 8th Air Force, encountered moderate but accurate flak at the target. The lead a/c, piloted by 1st Lt. Douglas L. Grantham, Jr., and with the A/C Major. George C. Hozier, was hit by a flak burst at the root of the right wing as the formation turned on the I.P. The flak burst set the a/c on fire and destroyed the flight control system, except for the elevator trim tab. The electrical system was also destroyed, thereby eliminating the use of the super-chargers (only 20 inches could be pulled) [Ed. this is an air pressure measurement.] The throttle quadrant was partially destroyed, and the pilot's window was broken, making it difficult to fly the a/c. I salvoed the bombs and attempted to sound the bail out bell but could not do so because of the loss of the electrical system.

The bomb bay was ablaze. The crew in the waist section of the airplane could not communicate with those in the front of the airplane and all bailed out.

I followed Major Hozier to the nose hatch escape door and after all others had bailed out, I too 'hit the silk.'

I have since learned that all members of the crew parachuted safely to the ground. Major Hozier sustained a cut on the head when he hit the bomb bay door as he jumped, and T/Sgt. Suggs broke his foot when he landed on the ground.

Nose art. A/C 42-9740, Lt. Robert I. Ellsworth's plane 'Oh Kay'

Lt. Robert Ellsworth shot down 28 September 1944.

Mission No. 128
28 September 1944
Target — Magdeburg, Germany
Krupp works machine shop

Crew of B-17G, No. 43-38181

Pilot	1st Lt.	Albert L. Sikkenga
Co-Pilot	2nd Lt.	Paul P. Reichert
Nav.	2nd Lt.	Angelo A. Archiopoli
Bomb.	2nd Lt.	Vivian C. McWhorter
Engr.	T/Sgt.	Charles T. Darnell
Radio Op.	T/Sgt.	Anthony Villane
LW Gun.	T/Sgt.	Robert S. Christofferson
B. Turret	S/Sgt.	Alton T. Eason
Tail Gun.	S/Sgt.	Stanley B. Hojnowski

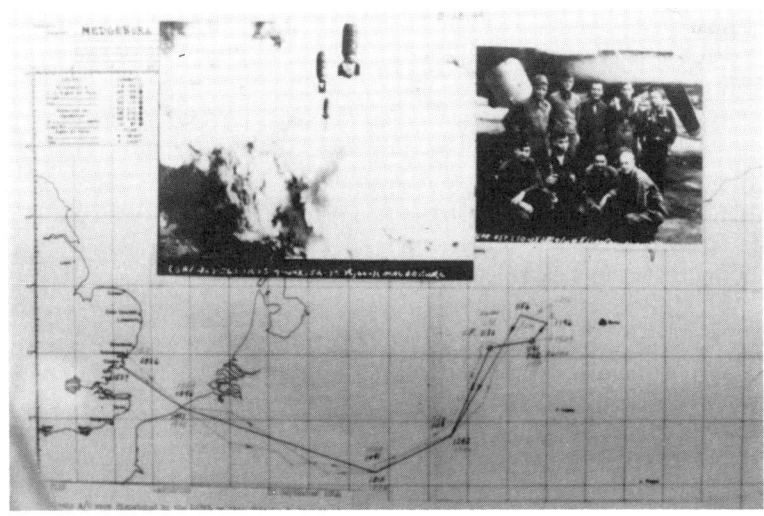

Track Chart, Mission No. 128, 28 Sept. 1944

457th Bomb Group Mission Narrative

What turned out to be one of the most disasterous missions of World War II for the 457th Bomb Group occurred on this mission to Magdeburg, Germany, as six crews were lost to fighter attacks. The crews are here identified by the number of the airplane and the name of the 1st pilot: A/c No. 43-38181 with 1st Lt. Albert L. Sikkenga as pilot; a/c No. 43-38026 with 2nd Lt. Charles J. Schultz as pilot; a/c No. 42-102948 with 2nd Lt. Keylon C. Clarke as pilot; a/c No. 42-97470 with 2nd Lt. Robert I. Ellsworth as pilot; and a/c No. 43-37834 with Fred J. Lockwald as pilot.

Thirty-six aircraft were dispatched by the 457th BG on this date to destroy the Krupp works machine shop in Magdeburg, Germany. The plant, employing 35,000 people, produced Mark IV tanks and flak guns. Eight groups of the 1st division were to attack the target ahead of the 457th BG, our group comprising the 94th 'C' CBW.

With Major Peresich as air commander, the ships took off at 0800 hours under hazy conditions and 1-2/10ths cumulous clouds. Because of the clouds the assembly was accomplished at 10,000 feet—2,000 feet higher than the briefed altitude. The formation departed the English coast at Clacton in its proper position in the division line-up.

Crossing the Belgium coast at 0954 hours the formation flew south of course and about 20 minutes later than the briefed time. The course over enemy territory was flown in trail of the wing leader. Northeast of Luxemburg the group turned left up to the I.P.

Just before reaching the I.P., the group was attacked by 25 to 50 Me 109's and FW 190's. The attack beginning at about 1146 hours, the majority of the attacking planes came at the formation from 4 to 9 o'clock low and directed at the rear of the formation. Most of the enemy aircraft approached to within 100 to 300 yards of the formation before pulling away in a pursuit curve. Our claims on this attack were 14 e/a destroyed, 4 probably destroyed, and 2 damaged. Five of our planes were shot down during the attack. One more B-17 went down to flak, at the target.

At 1158 the group released its bombs by PFF, as there was 8/10ths cloud cover at 15,000 feet at the target.

The formation experienced no trouble on the return flight to base and landed at 1540 hours.

Belly landing.

Lt. Angelo A. Archiopoli's story of the 28 September 1944 mission to Magdeburg, Germany.

I was originally the navigator on a crew of which Lt. James Vizanko was the pilot, Robert Cook the co-pilot, Tom Battley the bombardier, Joe Masters the radio operator, William Moore the engineer, Al Eason the waist gunner and Matty Prezbyz the ball turret gunner. I'm not sure of the name of the ninth man.

On 20 July 1944, we flew a mission to Leipzig. I believe it was our 10th or 11th mission. We sustained considerable damage to the airplane due to fighter attacks when a 20mm shell exploded at the root of the right wing, near the top turret. The engineer was not hurt due to the armor plate in the turret around his legs. Vizanko was wounded by shrapnel in the right leg and buttocks. However, we made it back to base with the formation that day. Our crew was 'set down' (did not fly) for a few days while Vizanko was in the hospital and the others in the crew were given leave. When Vizanko returned to duty, we flew two more missions; however, Vizanko had physical problems from the wounds and was returned to the United States for hospitalization. The crew was broken up and Sgt. Eason and I were assigned to Lt. Albert L. Sikkenga's crew.

On 28 September 1944 we were alerted and flew the mission to Magdeburg, Germany to bomb the Krupp iron works, which manufactured flak guns and Mark IV tanks. With a good bomb release we could strike a blow for both the foot soldiers and for ourselves.

After briefing we gathered our equipment and were taken to the flight line where our regular ship was located. We found that it was not ready for flight, as one engine had not been fixed after receiving damage on the previous days mission.

We collected our equipment and were taken by truck to another airplane. We found the plane to be a new, silver B-17G, which contrasted considerably with the camouflaged airplane we had been flying.

We were assigned to lead the high squadron and the 'shiney' airplane leading five camouflaged airplanes made us 'stick out like a sore thumb.' Although we really didn't like the situation, we had to go to war, regardless.

This was my 24th mission, and it was the 21st for Vivian C. McWhorter, the bombardier. 'Mac' was hoping to finish his tour of 30 missions by the middle of October as his wife was expecting their first child around that time. We often kidded 'Mac' about whether the baby would get there before he did! Al Sikkenga was flying a second tour; Paul Reichert, the co-pilot, was on his 16th mission, I believe.

We lined up for take off and got into the air without any problems. It was a nice sunny day in East Anglia, somewhat different than many of the days. We followed the briefed course in our assembly; however, the formation was strung out more than usual, probably because of the briefed indicated airspeed of 160 knots which differed from the 150 knots at which we usually flew.

As we passed by Kassel, Germany, we started a slow left turn to a northerly heading toward the I.P., to make the bomb run on the target at Magdeburg. We had just about completed the turn when we were jumped by German fighters coming at us from 6 o'clock, out of the sun. The fighters surprised us as there had not been any warning at all of 'bandits' in the area. We were hit by 20mm shells on their first pass through, which knocked us out of the formation. Engines No. 1 and No. 2 were on fire and the airplane was vibrating badly from a run-away propeller. The ship seemed to be out of control. The first German fighter I saw, I believe it was an FW 190, flew across in front of us followed closely by an American P-38 in 'hot pursuit.' About that time I felt Reichert, the co-pilot. tap me on the back and told me to bail out. He then tried unsuccessfully to open the escape hatch. I told him to go aft and tell the rest of the crew to bail out, as the intercom was not working.

I ripped off my flak suit, oxygen mask, and intercom wires, threw down my helmet, turned to McWhorter, and said, "Let's go." I grabbed the handle of the escape hatch, gave it a twist and it came off in my hand. I then gave the door a kick and it went flying away. I bailed out at about 24,000 feet and 'Mac' was right behind me. I must have lost consciousness from the lack of oxygen as the next

Lt. Albert L. Sikkenga's A/C No. 43-38181

thing I remember was the upward jerk of the parachute. I also felt my flying boots pull off my feet with the jerk. All I had on my feet were my GI wool socks. I also remember descending through a rain storm; which drenched me, as I dropped through the clouds. As I approached the ground I could see a crowd of people awaiting my arrival, I hit the ground in my stocking feet and fortunately did not break any bones. However, I felt pain in my back and neck from the impact. As I stood up I felt blood on my face and saw some blood on the jacket of my heated flight jacket. One German man approached me holding a shotgun which he held about six inches away from the end of my nose and it seemed that I was looking down a long tunnel. He gestured for me to raise my arms, with which I immediately complied. Luckily I had parachuted down into a soft farm field near the village of Bursuum, Germany.

I was taken to a nearby barn, as the rain was coming down very hard, and made to stand with my face against a wall while being covered by the shotgun. I heard noises from time to time and attempted to turn around to see what was taking place but was hit on the neck each time and told to face the wall. I did glimpse the bodies of two men but was unable to determine who they were or if they were dead or alive. Some time later a police officer arrived to take me to the local jail. He tied my hands behind my back, placed a rope around my neck and led me outside the barn, into the pouring rain. We walked over to a horse-drawn cart and there he tied me up to the back of the cart. I noticed a body lying on some hay in the cart but I did not recognize who it was. I gestured with my foot to the flying boots in the cart. The officer put the boots on the ground and I stepped into them. I did not know what to expect from the people, as I walked along behind the cart through the village. Some of the villagers did come outside their houses, in the rain, to throw stones at me as I walked by. The police officer was sitting on the seat of the cart, beside the driver, and did nothing to prevent the people from throwing the stones. I was placed in the jail along with two other American airmen, both of whom were wounded and who I did not know. I sat down against a wall next to one of the badly wounded men and he laid his head on my lap. I tried to find out his name but all he could say was that his name was 'Tony' and he was from New Jersey. Some time later the men were taken from the cell of the jail, I presume to a hospital, I do not know. Much later I was taken by two German soldiers to an unknown military installation, where I was placed in solitary confinement. I was later interrogated by a German colonel to whom I gave only my name, rank, and serial number. He threatened to shoot me as a spy since I was not wearing a full uniform. I had worn my heated flying suit and an o.d. shirt with my rank on the sleeves and had my wings pinned over my left shirt pocket. I did respond to some questions about baseball as I was an ardent baseball fan. He did not bother me again after that interrogation. The prison guard in the solitary confinement section spoke good English and he told me he had lived in Hoboken, New Jersey for thirty five years and he had returned to the 'Fatherland' to participate in a glorious victory. I told him that I hated to disallusion him but that the war would probably be over by the end of 1944. While I missed the date somewhat, the outcome was the same. On the 1st of October 1944 I was taken to a PW assignment camp at Wetzlar and from there I was sent to Stalag 1 in Barth, Pomerania, on the Baltic Sea. I arrived at Barth on the 6th of October 1944. At Stalag 1, I met members of a crew that I had trained with at Sioux City, Iowa, and I selected a bunk in their room. There were 20 men to a room, with 5 rows of 4 high, stacked bunks. There were some

Mission No. 128

inconveniences: shortage of food, 0200 hours surprise searches, not much heat, cold water showers, dysentary, occasional water shortages, and my loss of weight from 155 to 125 pounds while in the prison. We had no fat on us, just muscle. Weather permitting we engaged in some athletics, touch football, and softball. Equipment was provided by the International Red Cross, but walking the perimeter of the compound every day was our chief exercise.

While I was a PW, one of my greatest concerns was the fate of my crew members, as I had not seen or heard anything about any of them since we were shot down. I often thought about the members of the crew and one of them, Bob Cook the co-pilot, was a clean living fellow who did not smoke or drink but was a choc-o-holic. He and I would always trade our ration tickets each month: he, for the candy and I, for the cigarettes. Bob's locker was right next to mine in the hut and as we were flying a lead plane the co-pilot was replaced by the air commander in a lead ship so Bob was not flying on the day we were shot down. My parachute back-pack did not fit me well and on that day I had borrowed Bob's parachute because it seemed to fit me well. I often wondered what his, reaction was when he looked for his missing chute.

When the outcome of the war was no longer in doubt, on Monday 30 April 1945 the guards and administrators of Stalag 1 departed the camp and left us in charge. We were about 40 miles inside the Russian Zone and all the Germans wanted to be captured by the Allies rather than the Russians. When the guards departed we took over the camp, burned down the hated guard towers, and went into the nearby fields and slaughtered cattle for food. About all we did for about two weeks was to eat and sleep and wait for the Russians to come and 'liberate' us. The ranking officer of the camp was Colonel Zempke,

We left Barth on Sunday the 13th of May 1945, flying on B-17's early in the morning, to Laon, France. From there we were taken to Reims, France, and from there to Camp Lucky Strike, near La Harve, France, where we awaited transportation back to the U.S. of A.

When I returned home in June of 1945, I visited with Al Sikkenga's parents, Dr. and Mrs. Sikkenga of Orlando, Florida, at the old hotel Pennsylvania in Manhattan, New York. We had a very long talk and a nice visit. I learned that Al was an only son and subsequent to that I saw them again in 1959 when I visited them in Orlando.

Removing injured ball turret gunner from A/C No. 42-97455.

Mission No. 133
7 October 1944
Target — Politz, synthetic oil plant

Crew of B-17G, No. 44-38046

1st Pilot	Capt.	Alfred W. Fischer	KIA
A/C	Col.	James R. Luper	
Nav. Lead	Major	Norman A. Kriehn	
Nav. D.R.	1st Lt.	William J. Morrow	
Nav. PFF	1st Lt.	Frederick A. Asbell	
Bomb.	Capt.	Henry P. Loades	KIA
Engr.	T/Sgt.	John W. Koehler	KIA
Radio Op.	T/Sgt.	Ancil V. Shepherd	
LW Gun.	S/Sgt.	John J. Derling	
Tail Gun.	1st Lt.	Edward A. McNeal	
Grp. Surg.	Major	Gordon. H. Haggard	KIA

Col. James R. Luper, 457th B.G., C.O.

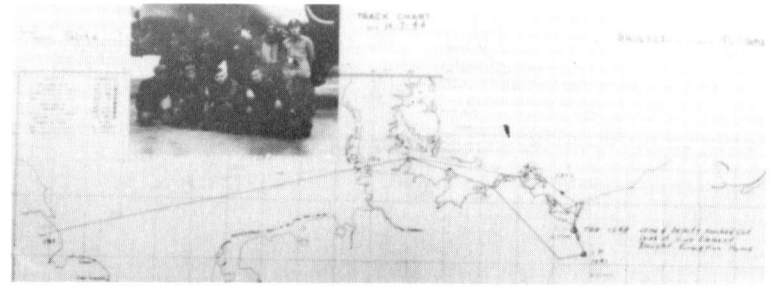

Track Chart, Mission No. 133, 7 October 1944

457th Bomb Group Mission Narrative

Although the synthetic oil plant at Politz, second largest of its kind in Germany, had been attacked several times this year, it was again the target for the 457th BG today. The MPI assigned was the distillation plant which had not sustained much damage. Thirty-six a/c made up the 94th "A" and 12 a/c to the composite "D" CBW's.

We were the first of four groups, including the 94th, over the target. Other forces were sent to attack oil plants in Brux, Ruhland, Merseburg, and Lutzkendorf.

Carrying 10x500 pound GP's, the planes took off at 0700 hours with Col. Luper in the lead. After assembling on the Glatton buncher at 5,000 feet, the group flew the route over England on time and on course and assumed its proper position in the division formation.

Because of winds the group was almost 5 minutes behind time in reaching the English coast. Once over enemy territory, however, the group was able to gain two minutes and arrived at the I. P. three minutes late.

The lead squadron made the turn at the I.P. on a heading of 329 degrees, magnetic. The visibility was good but the target was obscured by a smoke screen, so triangulation had to be used to locate the MPI.

The lead a/c made the majority of the 8-1/2 minute bomb run, but was hit by the intense flak just before reaching the BRL. The lead plane opened its bomb bay doors and then closed them without releasing the bombs, apparently as a signal to the deputy lead plane to take over the lead. The number 3 a/c in the lead flight was hit by fiak at about the same time as the lead plane and salvoed its bombs. Two other a/c in the lead squadron, believing this to be the bombs of the lead a/c, also dropped their bombs. The deputy lead a/c also experienced difficulty as it approached the BRL. They lost altitude rapidly and were seen to salvo their bombs. Then the remaining a/c in the lead squadron toggled their bombs. No sighting operation was performed.

The low squadron crossed the I.P. on course and found the same conditions existed over the target area. The bombardier killed his course on the corner of the elongated woods short of the target. The rate fell on the "X" formed by the confluence of two small rivers to the right of the target. A study of smoke bursts through the smoke screen indicated that the bombs dropped at 1238 hours from 24,800 feet fell just short of the MPI. The lead plane pilot, Capt. Vinton H. Mays, was killed by a piece of flak through his heart about one minute before the plane reached the BRL. Intense and accurate flak interfered with the bomb run but the bombs were released at 1258 hours from 26,000 feet on a magnetic heading of 332

Capt. Alfred W. Fischer, KIA on 7 October 1944.

degrees. A study of the bomb bursts showed that the target was missed to the left of the MPI.

The leader of the high flight, Lt. John F. Angier, took over the lead of the group and led it on the return to the base. The planes landed at 1620 hours with 5 aircraft missing, which were as here listed: a/c No. 44-38046 with Capt. Alfred W. Fischer as pilot and Col James R. Luper as A/C; a/c No. 42-97638 with 1st Lt. William H. Flannery as pilot; a/c No. 44-6469 with 2nd Lt. Vernon M. Moland as pilot, (with story hereafter); a/c 42-102905 with 2nd Lt. Clarence R. Jennings as pilot, (was interned in Sweden, with story hereafter); a/c No. 43-38529 with 1st Lt. Ernest T. Salzer as pilot (story of ditching hereafter).

Lt. William J. Morrow's story of the 7 October 1944 mission to Politz.

Concerning the mission to Politz on 7 October 1944, Major Norman Kriehn, the Group Navigator, apparently slated me to fly on the mission at the last minute, as I had not been alerted to fly on the following day's mission and had been assigned the duty of escorting the local girls back home from the enlisted men's dance. I returned from Peterborough at about 2400 hours and had no more than 'hit the old fart sack' and dropped off to sleep than I was awakened by the orderly, who was shaking me and saying, "Sir, you are scheduled to fly D.R. [Ed. dead reckoning navigation] in the lead plane with Col. Luper, on today's mission." Well, the mission was an on – off situation because of the weather. However, time was running out. The navigators briefing was held while the other crew members went out to the planes. I was taken to the airplane and, since we were the first to take off, the engines were running when I arrived. As soon as I swung up into the escape hatch, the pilot started to taxi. As a result, I had to complete all my plotting and paperwork during the assembly. I did not know who was on the crew, other than I had been told by the orderly that I was flying in the lead plane with Col. Luper as A/C. As soon as I crawled up into the nose, I saw that Major Norman Kriehn was there, along with Captain Henry Loades, both of whom I recognized (this ignorance concerning the rest of the crew caused me some difficulty later during the German interrogation).

Well, the group and wing formations were formed and we joined the bomber stream more or less as briefed. We were not attacked by fighters on our route to the I.P. We turned on our bomb run and Capt. Loades was working over the bomb sight when we were hit by some of the most accurate flak I have ever experienced. I did not have any specific duty to perform until the bombs were dropped and was sitting at the navigator's table, facing the rear of the airplane, unconsciously watching the navigation instruments with my right hand resting on the navigation desk, when a piece of flak came up through the bottom of the airplane, through the desk and the palm of my right hand (breaking bone and knuckle and cutting a couple of tendons). I recall holding my wrist with my left hand, looking out the window on the right side of the airplane, and seeing the oil bubbling from a hole in the cowling on engine No. 2. A fire developed in the nose hatchway, on which the fire extinguisher was used to no avail. There was another burst of flak and I could see the right wing was on fire. This all happened in a very short period of time—possibly less than a minute. I later learned that Asbell and Derling bailed out when the flames erupted in the bomb bay. Because of an electrical 'glitch' the bombs were not released at the target. When Al Fischer gave the order to bail out, I yanked off my flak suit, oxygen mask, and intercom wires and released the handle on the nose hatch. The rush of air from the open hatch revealed Col. Luper, who had come down in the hatchway to see what had caused the fire. He looked at me and saw I was ready to jump and he shook his head and said, "No." So I backed up into the nose, as did Kriehn and Loades, who were also getting ready to escape the blazing 'fireball' airplane (a play on words as the 457th Bomb Group was named, 'The Fireball Outfit'). Things became hazy after that, for I had not replaced my oxygen mask. However, I have since learned that Col. Luper went back up on the flight deck and talked to the crews that remained in the 457th formation.

 I recall a red glow out the right window, of feeling the ship fall off in a spin, of hearing the high pitched whine of a propellor running away, and then a terrific explosion! We had been flying at about 26,000 feet and by the time I recovered consciousness, I must have free fallen to about 8 or 9,000 feet. Then, when I realized I was falling through space. I opened my parachute at about 4,000 feet. I landed in the middle of Stettin Bay and luckily managed to free myself from the chute, which quickly sank. I heard another person land in the water about 50-75 yards away—I do not know who—I yelled and asked, "Are you O.K.?" and did not get an answer, but I did hear a lot of splashing around as he began a wild swimming stroke in my direction. In the meantime I had inflated my 'Mae West' and I rolled over on my back and tried to back-stroke in his direction. When I rolled over and looked again I could not see

What a well dressed airman wears: 'Flak suit,' oxygen mask, 'tin' helmet, heated suit and gloves, parachute.

anyone. Whether he could not get free from his chute, or couldn't get his 'Mae West' inflated, I do not know. I had thought it might be Capt. Loades, the bombardier, as I recalled seeing a 'Mae West' laying in the nose of the ship. (Upon arriving home after the war, I learned that Loades had been picked up, and had died a couple of days later, so it must have been someone else.)

I tried in vain to reach a channel buoy. After 20-30 minutes a couple of boats (mine sweepers) came down the bay and one of them picked me up. They treated me well, they bandaged my hand and brought me blankets and some hot tea. Shortly, I was taken below deck, where I removed my wet flying clothing in a heated room. After an hour or so we arrived at the Baltic Port of Swinemunda. I was taken to another boat where I met Col. Luper and Major Kriehn. They had been picked up by the other boat several hundred yards from where I had landed. My hand was redressed at the ship's infirmary and that evening we were taken to the naval (Kriegsmarine) hospital in Swinemunda. Col. Luper had a superficial cut on his forehead and a cut on his leg dressed. Major Kriehn was not cut, but had some bruises. They were taken to the local jail and the next day to Frankfurt. There they met Lt. Asbell and Sgt. Derling. Eventually, Col. Luper, Major Kriehn, and Lt. Asbell ended up at Stalag Luft III. I do not know where Sgt. Derling was sent.

My hand was x-rayed and put in a cast. After 10 days in the hospital I was sent to several different German hospitals. When my hand had healed to their satisfaction, I was sent to Dulag Luft near Frankfurt for interrogation as was most everyone else at one time or another. I was questioned about the other crew members and I could not name them, as I had arrived at the plane late and had never had a chance to find out who the other men were. The interrogators were skeptical of my answers, thinking that I might be a member of the OSS sent to spy on them. The reason they were skeptical, other than the fact I did not know the others, was that they did not have any information about me in their files.

On the second day of my interrogation, one officer walked out of the room and I noticed he had left a book on the table, probably intentionally. I picked it up and leafed through it, to find that it was a history of the 457th Bomb Group since its inception — where it had been formed and where it had gone through training — with the names of the people who comprised the group, including all the staff, squadron officers, and crews. It was very up to date and included many people that I knew. They were really not interested in what I knew about the group, but rather whether I was a bonafide aircrew member. I was then sent to Luft III on the 12th of January 1945. It was there I first learned about Asbell and Derling. They knew nothing of what happened to the others on the crew except for Sgt. Koehler, who had been killed in the explosion.

We were evacuated in front of the Russian from Luft III to Stalag 7, near Munich. While there, we were liberated on the 29th of April 1945. In a few days we were flown in C-47's to La Harve, France, where we caught a boat and sailed for the United States.

Mission No. 133
7 October 1944
Target — Politz, synthetic oil plant

Crew of B-17G, No. 43-38529

Pilot	1st Lt.	Ernest T. Salzer
Co-Pilot	2nd Lt.	Rex R. Monson
Nav.	2nd Lt.	Kenneth Post
Bomb.	1st Lt.	William H. Steffen
Engr.	T/Sgt.	Jack F. Scarborough
Radio Op.	T/Sgt.	Vincent A. Toth
LW Gun.	S/Sgt.	Richard F. Mitrenga
B. Turret	S/Sgt.	Benjamin W. Hamrick
Tail Gun.	S/Sgt.	Elbert D. Conger

Lt. Ernest T. Salzer and 'Mission Maid.'

1st Lt. Ernest T. Salzer's story of the 7 October mission to Politz, Germany

The story starts on the afternoon of 6 October 1944. I was asked to take the B-17G No. 43-38529 on a test flight. Regardless of the 'build' date, I took the airplane to be brand new. It was definitely newer, not painted, and less war weary than my regularly assigned aircraft, 'Mission Maid,' No. 42-38021.

Without a full load of fuel and bombs, she would not perform properly and hold altitude at normal cruise settings. I took her back and 'red lined' her. Guess what? I got her the next morning, 7 October 1944, on the mission to Politz!

With a full load of bombs and fuel she proved to more than equal her poor performance of the previous day, with an added feature – her main gear refused to retract electrically. Our engineer, Jack Scarborough, spent some time trying to get them up electrically and finally was forced to crank them up by hand.

We arrived at assembly with one wheel yet to be retracted, and some of the less alert tried to assemble on us rather than the group lead plane.

On the way to the target, fuel consumption was unacceptable and leaning out the engines produced higher than acceptable cylinder head temperatures. We pulled out of formation to conserve fuel and trailed the group to the target. At the target we joined the formation and bombed with the formation, then trailed the group toward our base.

When we left Politz, we estimated we had only 200/300 gallons of fuel remaining, just barely enough to make it home! We threw out everything but the guns, ammunition, and crew. When we passed Sweden we took a vote and the outcome was 8 to 1 for Sweden. Since the vote was only advisory, we continued towards home. Actually the vote was 9 to 1. I had a stowaway on board! One of the ground crew had decided he wanted to experience the rigour of combat.

West of the Frisian Islands, we threw all the guns and ammunition overboard and called the Air/Sea Rescue – I still remember the call signs – Vinegrove, We DF, t. As by now all tanks showed empty, we transferred whatever gasoline remaining in the inboard tanks to the outboard tanks. We found not one but two RAF corvettes, made a pattern on them, and ditched between the two.

One man fell off the airplane into the water – he always did the same thing during drill – and the rest climbed in the rafts and over to the ship. He was fished out, none the worse for wear.

Two other things of interest. First, already on the RAF ships was a Lancaster crew, shot down the night before with a 10,000 pound bomb aboard. Their aircraft, I was told, sank within 45 seconds.

Second, the commander of the naval base told me the next day that they found old No. 43-38529 still afloat the next morning and they tried to tow her to port, but found she behaved like a sea anchor. At least she was as consistent on water as was her performance in the air. He told me they had sunk her with a machine gun as a hazard to navigation. I privately thought that it was too bad that whoever had assigned her to me in that condition should have been on board with us.

Mission Maid, A/C No. 42-38021

Lt. Ernest T. Salzer's A/C 42-38021

Mission No. 133
7 October 1944
Target — Politz, synthetic oil plant

Crew of B-17G, No. 42-102905

1st Pilot	2nd Lt.	Clarence R. Jennings	
Co-Pilot	2nd Lt.	Richard R. Garland	
Nav.	2nd Lt.	Martin Schwartz	
Bomb.	2nd Lt.	Stewart W. Jakku	KIA
Engr.	T/Sgt.	Hardy S. Bell	
Radio Op.	T/Sgt.	Walter W. Karr	
LW Gun.	S/Sgt.	William N. Barth, Jr.	
B. Turret	S/Sgt.	Charles Sparnick	
Tail Gun.	S/Sgt.	John D. Wood	
Obs.	Capt.	Floyd A Cox (Intel. Officer)	KIA

Lt. Clarence R. Jenning's A/C No. 42-102905 which he flew to Sweden.

Lt. Richard R. Garland's story of the 7 October 1944 mission to Politz.

My crew and I had trained in the United States and we flew a B-17G to England, on orders dated the 9th of September 1944. We landed in Wales where we were relieved of the plane, to be taken to a depot for modification. We were assigned to the 457th Bomb Group, as a replacement crew for crews which had either been casualties or had completed their tour.

We boarded the train for Glatton, located in East Anglia, 60 miles north of London. We went through the usual orientation lectures, such as escape and evasion, radio procedure in the UK, operation of 'Gee,' formation flying, and other subjects peculiar to the European Theatre.

I had flown one mission before the 7 October 1944 to Politz. The mission was to Kassel and fortunately proved to be a 'milk run' (no enemy fighters and very little flak). On the 7 October 1944 mission, I was flying as a co-pilot with Lt. Clarence R. Jennings. I had not previously met any of the members of the crew before the flight. I was awakened at 0430 hours on that fateful morning, and taken to the briefing to fly with Lt. Jenning's crew. There is one thing about the briefing that remains indelibly impressed in my mind all these years. During the briefing, we were told that if we got into trouble during the mission, we had the alternative of flying to Sweden and there be interned for the duration of the war. We were briefed about the airfields located in the southern part of Sweden, which had runways on which the B-17 could land. After the briefing. I remember that Capt. Floyd A. Cox, an intelligence officer (S-2) came up to me, introduced himself, and said words that have rung in my ears for these 40-odd years. He said, "Lt. you are going to have me along as dead weight today." I have often thought how prophetic were those words.

We had a big breakfast that morning, and were then transported to the flight line where our airplane was located. Another thing of note that I remember was that while we were getting our equipment in position in the airplane, one of the signal flares accidentally ignited and caused a great commotion, something you were not expecting. But the crew, with the help of the maintenance ground crew, put out the fire with fire extinguishers.

We finished our preflight checks, started the engines and, at the signal, began our taxi onto the perimeter ramp on the way to our position in the line-up for take off. We made our take off and found our position in the sky, in the formation, without difficulty. As I recall, we were a few minutes late departing the Glatton buncher.

Another thing that impressed me about that day, and I have related it to many people, as when we were crossing the enemy coast I turned and looked back to observe the hundreds of airplanes in the 'bomber stream.' And I thought at the time of the tremendous ability of the United States to mount a 'war effort,' as this was my first chance to see the tremendous power of the Eighth Air Force.

The mission was flown pretty much as planned as we progressed across occupied Denmark, across the Baltic Sea, and into Germany proper. We did not encounter any opposition from Luftwaffe fighters on our flight course to the I.P. I recall that after turning northward toward the target, on our bomb run, we 'bucked' a very strong headwind and our speed to the target was very slow. We made our bomb run and as we neared the target we encountered very accurate, tracking flak that seemed to engulf the planes in the lead squadron. However it was only during the last seconds of the bomb run that our plane was actually hit by the flak. I was watching the planes in the lead squadron and I saw flak bursts hit Col. Luper's airplane. It appeared to be in trouble, then I saw three chutes appear near the waist door. Then the plane on our right wing appeared to be in trouble and was flying erratically. A few seconds later, a burst of flak exploded immediately in front of our airplane and the two engines on our right wing, No. 3 and No. 4, were knocked out. Also I noticed we had lost our oxygen supply

'Flak' hole in horizontal stabilizer on A/C 42-102905 made airplane 'skip across sky!'

and here we were at 26,000 feet without oxygen. We immediately lowered the nose of the airplane and descended as rapidly as possible. We also learned that a piece of the flak had critically wounded Lt. Stewart W. Jakku, causing him to prematurely toggle the bombs, thus lightening our load unexpectedly. With everything else happening all at once, I had not noticed the bombs dropping. I was later to learn that Lt. Martin Schwartz, navigator, had been injured and that Capt. Floyd A. Cox had been killed by the flak explosion that had knocked out two engines, our oxygen system, and the intercom.

I want to here give credit to the engineer T/Sgt. Hardy Bell, who crawled down into the nose and tried to give first aid to Lt. Jakku. I had been given the morphine surrettes and as soon as we had descended to 10,000 feet where the oxygen supply was adequate to sustain life and we had partial control of the plane, I too crawled down into the nose of the airplane and there found Capt. Cox dead and Lt. Jakku in a severe state of shock. Bell was cradling Jakku's head on his lap and trying to calm him. Lt. Schwartz had been wounded in the shoulder and he, too, was in a state of shock, but less so than Jakku. We administered morphine to Jakku, because he was the most seriously wounded of the two men. At the time I had left the flight deck and had crawled down into the nose, we had not been able to close the bomb bay doors. Neither had we been able to feather the the propellers on the two starboard engines, which were windmilling and causing a tremendous drag on the right side of the plane. We were having lots of trouble controlling the airplane because, we later found out, a large hole had been made in the left horizontal stabilizer by an anti- aircraft shell, which made the airplane 'skip across the sky.' Fortunately the shell had not exploded, or the airplane would probably have been more seriously damaged.

Further examination of the aircraft revealed that we had no hydraulic pressure and that both oil and gasoline were leaking from our right wing.

Lt. Jennings and I took stock of the condition of the airplane and the fact that we had severely wounded men aboard and decided that to help for our wounded men as soon as possible, we would head for Sweden.

I asked 'Marty' if he had a map of Sweden and if he could he give us a heading for an airfield in Sweden. Although badly wounded, he managed to come up with a map of Sweden and a heading for a landing field.

I looked around and found the bomb bay doors were still open, although the radio operator and the waist gunners had tried, without success, to manually crank them closed. I happened to glance out the right window and saw that the right wheel was partially lowered and I suggested to the men that possibly they were cranking on the wrong socket. My assumption was correct and the bomb bay doors were eventually closed. I found that the motor which lowered the wheels was still working and I retracted the wheel into the nacelle again. Closing the bomb bay doors helped to minimize the drag on the airplane and we flew toward Sweden on two engines without too much difficulty, if you ignored the 'skipping' and the 'crabbing' to the left. However, old No. 905 was still partially airworthy.

As we approached the southern coast of Sweden, we found it to be covered with clouds and I asked 'Marty' Schwartz if there were any airfields farther north large enough to land a B-17. We decided to try for a town, the name of which was printed as large on the map as that of Stockholm, by the name of Jonkoping. It was located at the south end of a large lake and would be easy to locate from the air. At about 1500 hours the clouds were almost negligable and we found the town for which we were searching. We descended and started circling the city in a counter-clockwise direction, always turning into our good engines. The airfield we found to be a very small grass field without paved runways, hardly large enough on which to land a B-17. The wind sock indicated the wind to be from the north and in a direction that required us to approach the field down a hill to get to the airport.

Recognizing that we must land without brakes, because we did not have any hydraulic fluid, I told Jennings that I had read about a way to slow down an airplane by using parachutes and thought this would be an appropriate place to try it. He agreed and I asked the gunners to break out the waist windows and to attach parachutes to the gun mounts. When they felt the wheels touch the ground they were to pop a parachute on each side of the airplane.

As we circled the field we fired red flares to indicate that we had wounded men on board that needed medical assistance. We did not have radio contact with the tower and could not explain our problems. As we circled the field we could see that hundreds of people had come to the field to see what must have been the first B-17 to land this far north in Sweden.

Jennings made an outstanding approach and landing. The wheels touched down and the men handling the parachutes did a tremendous job. They threw the chutes out just as the wheels touched the ground, and as luck would have it only the left chute billowed open. Although both Jennings and I were both standing on the left rudder pedal, trying to get the plane to follow the

Battle damage on A/C 42-102905.

perimeter of the field around to make as long a roll as possible, it was the one parachute that pulled the airplane around in a semicircle and brought us to a stop right in front of the hanger. We couldn't have done a better job even if we had had control of the airplane.

I had cut the switches as soon as we touched the ground to minimize the danger of fire from an electrical spark, in case we crashed.

The Swedish National Guard approached the airplane and indicated a concern for the gasoline which was leaking copiously out of the right wing. they put buckets under the leaks to preserve the precious fluid.

The National Guard showed they were in control of the situation by motioning for us to raise our hands above our heads as we climbed out of the airplane, where they searched us for weapons. One of the men indicated to me, by pointing and saying "kaput, kaput," that Capt. Cox was dead.

Surprisingly, as I was talking to the member of the Swedish military, I heard the unmistakable sound of a B-17 and turned to see another B-17 approaching the field. It circled the field and landed, and although the pilot had control of the plane—having hydraulic pressure—he could not stop the plane before he hit a ditch at the edge of the field. I do not recall the name of the group that the airplane came from, but the plane had the vertical stabilizer was painted red. [Ed. The 1st CBW—91st, 381st, and 398th groups had that identification.]

The ambulance crew loaded up 'Stew' Jakku and 'Marty' Schwartz into the ambulance and drove them to the hospital. There were no wounded men on the second B-17.

The other members of the two crews were taken by taxi cabs, two to a cab, along with their Swedish guard, to a restuarant in town where we were fed a beef stew dinner, which tasted very good. The time was now about 1700 hours and it was getting dark. We were taken to a hotel and I remember walking through a ballroom to reach our rooms. In the room were people in formal dress and some in military uniforms. Later that evening, a member of the United States Legation came to the hotel and spoke to us. He informed us of the ground rules of being interned in a neutral country. There were two internment camps in the area and we would probably be assigned to one of them. We would be required to wear civilian clothing and he did not know how long we would be interned. However, Count Bernedat, a man who was very influential in the Swedish government, was very pro-American and had intimated that interned Americans would be flown out of the country as soon as arrangements could be made. It turned out that we were interned for only two months. We were not restricted to the compound where we were quartered, and our internment was not a hardship by any means.

When it was determined that we were to be repatriated we were sent to a safe house near Stockholm, where we awaited the airplane that would fly us back to England. The airplane was a black, stripped down B-24, which arrived one night at about 0200 hours after we had been at the safe house for a couple of days.

As I was standing in line to board the airplane, I was handed the first mail I had received from my family during the time I was in Sweden. Upon reading the letters, I learned that I had been listed as killed in action and that a telegram from the War Department had been sent to my mother, listing me as such.

The contents of the telegram were:

Dated 12 October 1944

The Secretary of War desires to express his deep regret that your son 2nd Lt. Richard R. Garland was killed in action on 7 October 1944, over Sweden.
    Signed
    Adjutant General

The telegram did say that I was killed over Sweden and my mother refused to believe, correctly it turned out, the authenticity of the facts in the telegram. My mother later received a telephone call and then a letter from the Adjutant General that the telegram was indeed incorrect, that I was all right, and had returned to duty in a neutral country.

We returned to the 457th Bomb Group base at Glatton and from there returned to the United States for reassignment.

Left to right: Lt. Richard R. Garland, Swedish airman and Lt. Clarence R. Jennings.

Mission No. 133
7 October 1944
Target — Politz, synthetic oil plant

Crew of B-17G, No. 44-6469		
1st Pilot	2nd Lt.	Vernon M. Moland
Co-Pilot	2nd Lt.	Scott S. Millis, Jr.
Nav.	2nd Lt.	Leo J. Higgins
Bomb.	2nd Lt.	Arthur H. Jensen
Engr.	T/Sgt.	William D. Ackerson
Radio Op.	T/Sgt.	Cecil D. Woodruff
LW Gun.	S/Sgt.	Earl S. Howell
B.Turret	S/Sgt.	John R. Koziel
Tail Gun.	S/Sgt.	James A. Gunnels

Lt. Leo J. Higgins' story of the 7 October 1944 mission to Politz.

While curiosity may have killed the cat, it almost certainly saved my life. I was busy during the bomb run of the mission to Politz, as I was as far forward in the plane as I could get, hovering over the bombardier's shoulder trying to see the POW camp that was located near the I.P., when a burst of flak exploded and took out my regular position — including the navigators table, chair, floor and practically everything else in the nose of the airplane except 'Art' and me. I was saved by this desire to see a POW camp, which I was soon to see from the other side of the wire fence. Although my chute was full of holes and my oxygen hose was severed, I was uninjured except by the 3/8" armor plate on the floor of the aircraft which was torn loose by the explosion and hurled against my butt with such force as to inflict bad bruises and a circular wound on my left thigh, made by the hole with which the plate was bolted to the floor of the airplane.

Our aircraft was not immediately totally disabled, and we were able to remain airborne for about a half hour before engine and finally wing fires, forced us to bail out. Although other crew members were injured, they all survived the flight, bail-out and German POW camp.

Flying tight formation.

Mission No. 136
17 October 1944
Target — Cologne transportation facilities

Crew of B17G, No. 43-37606

1st Pilot	1st Lt.	Norman M. Chapman	
Co-Pilot	2nd Lt.	Raymond K. Mills, Jr.	KIA
Nav.	F/O	Kenneth H. Johnson	KIA
Bomb.	2nd Lt.	Oliver W. Wicks	KIA
Engr.	T/Sgt.	Marshall T. Windham	
Radio Op.	T/Sgt.	Robert T. Brady	
LW Gun.	S/Sgt.	James R. Dixon	
B. Turret	S/Sgt.	Carl M. Weibel	
Tail Gun.	S/Sgt.	Joseph M. Budich	

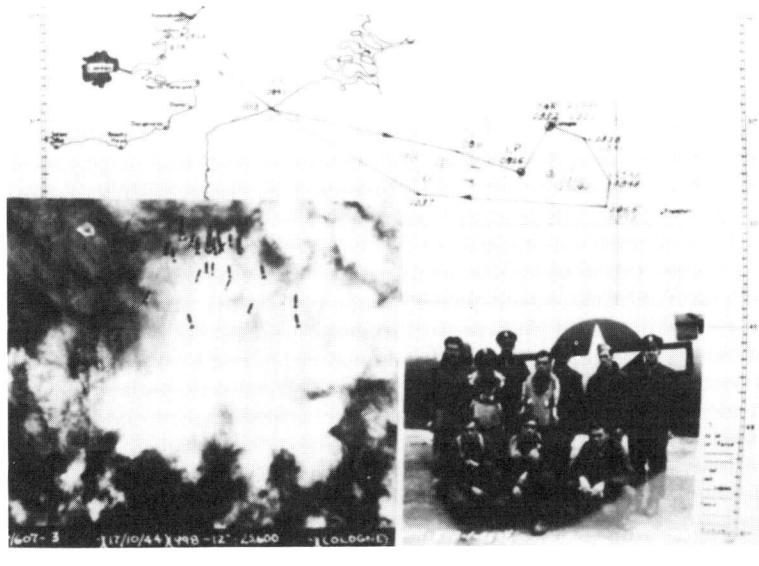

Track Chart, Mission No. 136, 17 Oct. 1944

457th Bomb Group Mission Narrative

In an all-out effort to knock out communication and transportation facilities in Cologne, all three divisions were sent up today to again attack this target.

With Major Wilbur D. Snow in the lead a/c, the 457th BG took off at 0620 hours, carrying 34x100 pound G.P.s and M17 I.B's. After assembly at 11,000 feet the group flew the route to the division assembly approximately as briefed. The group departed England at Clacton.

From control point No. 2 to the I.P. the group flew south of course in order to remain in division formation. The I.P. was overshot, however, in an attempt to attain the bombing altitude of 25,000 feet.

The lead squadron made the turn on the bomb run about 15 miles east of the briefed I.P. The target was covered by 10/10th clouds. At this point 'Jerry' began throwing up his welcome sign in the form of heavy and accurate flak. A/c No. 43-37606, piloted by Lt. Norman M. Chapman, was hit by flak, made a 180 degree turn, and left the formation.

The C-1 functioned normally but the PFF equipment went out of control 1/4 of the way down the bomb run. Bombs were released at 0933 1/2 hours abreast of other smoke markers.

The lead a/c of the low squadron performed its own sighting and dropped at 0934 hours. The high squadron dropped on the smoke markers of the lead squadron, since its PFF equipment was also inoperative.

The return route was flown north of course, in order to maintain division formation.

At 1220 hours, the planes landed. No further word was heard of Lt. Chapman's crew.

T/Sgt. Marshall T. Windham's story of the 17 October 1944 mission to Cologne, Germany.

The Eighth Air Force, 457th Bombardmant Group (Heavy), 750th Squadron, of which I was a member, was stationed at Glatton, England. On 17 October 1944, the crew of the B-17G 'Flying Fortress' named B.T.O. (Big Time Operator) was assigned to fly its third mission in four days. The target for the day was a marshalling yard in Cologne, the second largest city in Germany.

We knew the flak would be heavy but I was always one who believed nothing was going to happen to me it was going to happen to others.

This would be our last mission before we would go on a 'flak leave,' a vacation of a week, at a Red Cross-operated 'rest home.'

It was an ordinary day, everything progressed as usual—breakfast, briefing, etc...except for three changes. We had a new bombardier, Lt. Oliver Wicks. He would fly his first mission with our crew, replacing Lt. Jerold Hoelzel, who had been transferred to a lead crew. Hoelzel had been shot down 10 days earlier on the mission to Politz and was interned in Sweden.

Sgt. Stephen Lupo was a member of our original crew and had flown several missions with us but had been grounded because of ear trouble. He had been our waist gunner and was replaced by S/Sgt. Joseph M. Budich.

I, T/Sgt. Marshall T. Windham, was moved from the chin turret position in the nose of the plane to the engineer's position in the top turret, just behind the flight deck. I replaced T/Sgt. Joseph Schambri, who had been killed in an accident on the base. Little did I know at the time that fate had just taken a turn as to whether I would live or die in this great war.

Everything went routinely, as the take off and assembly were as briefed. We had a little engine trouble with No. 3, but nothing that would prevent us from continuing on the mission. We crossed the English Channel and gained altitude, went on oxygen at 10,000 feet, loaded and tested our guns, and climbed to about 29,000 feet. Everything had to be ready for any eventuality when we arrived over enemy territory. We watched for enemy fighters, dodged a little flak, and saw our 'little friends,' our own fighter escort, the P-38's P-47's, and P-51's. Then came the I. P. and the bomb run to the target on which evasive action from flak or fighters could not be taken. Ahead was a black wall of flak over the target, the marshalling yards in Cologne, that was being shot up at the groups which proceeded us to the target. During the five or so minutes before the BRL is reached, the lead airplane is in the hands of the bombardier, who is manipulating the controls of the bomb sight, which in turn flies the airplane because it is connected through the automatic pilot to the control surfaces of the airplane. While on the bomb run, 'the big bird' was really what you might call 'a sitting duck.'

The black wall is getting blacker and more intense as we get closer to the target! Then it happened!--*---*---We had two direct flak bursts, right under the ship — one under the cockpit and the other under No. 3 engine. The explosions seemed to lift the plane upward for twenty or thirty feet. Two engines on the right wing of the airplane and one on the left wing were knocked out. The pilot pulled the plane out of the formation and asked the bombardier to salvo the bombs, but he received no answer as the intercom connection to the nose of the airplane had been knocked out, so the pilot salvoed the bombs.

Just about all the instruments in the airplane had been knocked out along with the intercom to the nose. Lt. Chapman was doing a great job of keeping the wounded bird level. He checked on everyone's condition in the back of the plane and although everyone was shaken, they were all 'ok.'

We were fast losing altitude and Chapman, not knowing when the plane might blow up or catch on fire, ordered the crew to bail out. He said he would "try to fly the plane in a gradual glide and try to make it out of enemy territory," which was only about 60 or 70 mile to the west in Belgium or to the vicinity of Aachen, Germany.

Having no desire to bail out in enemy territory, the crew all expressed the opinion to remain in the plane with Chapman. By this time, we had lost enough altitude to take off our oxygen masks and Chapman agreed that the crew could go with him. He said, "Throw out everything that is loose to lighten the plane and stretch the gliding distance."

I came down out of the turret, stood behind the flight deck and asked Lt. Chapman, "Is there was anything I can do to help?" Before Chapman answered, I noticed that Lt. Mills had not moved and his head was slumped over. I put my hand on his shoulder to check on him and I guess I knew that he was dead. At the same time, Lt. Chapman looked at me and said, "Lt. Mills is dead." He also said, "Go down in the nose and see how things are down there."

I had noticed that Chapman was having a hard time keeping the plane airborne. When we broke away from the group, it wasn't long before we were in heavy cloud cover. With the instruments knocked out, he was flying by the seat of his pants. I could tell

T/Sgt. Marshall T. Windham

when he was diving a little too steeply because I would feel light on my feet. Likewise, when he pulled up too sharply, I would feel heavy footed. In spite of the problems, however, he was doing a fine job. I had great faith in him, for we had a good crew. The men in back were busy throwing out everything that was loose and were trying to drop the ball turret.

It was when I reached the nose section that the full impact of our situation really hit me. There were many holes in the plane, some of which were huge, and I wondered if it was possible to continue to stay airborne. F/O Kenneth Johnson, our navigator, was still sitting at the navigator's table. His head was almost completely gone! I believe that a piece of the propeller from No. 3 engine came through the side of the airplane and hit him.

Lt. Wicks was still in his position, forward in the nose. I made my way to him, past the large holes in the ship, and asked him, " How are you?" He said, "I was hit in the knee and in the side," and he showed me, but it was hard to tell how badly he was wounded through the flying suit.

This was when I realized that, except for the events leading up to the mission, it would have been me manning the nose gun turret, for I had flown all our previous missions in that position.

I went back to the flight deck and informed Lt. Chapman of the situation, and that Wicks wanted to ride the plane down. Chapman thought it would be better for Wicks to bail out, and told me, "Go back down and throw him out."

I went back down in the nose section and talked to Lt. Wicks but could not convince him to bail out. I could not throw him out either, as his chute had been riddled with flak and was full of holes. Again I went back and told Lt. Chapman the situation and he said, "If you can move Lt. Wicks to the rear of the plane, in a safer position, it will be all right for him to remain in the plane."

Back down in the nose I crawled again. Each time I crawled around all those holes in the plane, with the wind howling through at 100 mile per hour, I had the feeling that I would fall through or the nose would break off from my added weight. I reached Lt. Wicks again and explained that we had to find a safer place to secure him for a crash landing. As we struggled, my pulling and his trying to crawl and slide along, I could tell he was suffering a great deal of pain; however, he never said so or complained. We finally reached the small area behind the top turret where he could lie

S/Sgt. James R. Dixon. Flak hole in ball turret.

F/O Kenneth H. Johnson   S/Sgt Stephen Lupo

down and there I secured him to the best of my ability.

All this time, Jimmy Dixon, Carl Weibel, Joe Budich, and Robert Brady were working desperately to drop the ball turret to lighten the load, in hopes that we might get a little more distance out of old B.T.O. But it was all in vain...there was just not enough time.

I had returned to my position and had just asked Lt. Chapman if there was anything else I could do, when we broke out below the clouds in a fairly steep dive. I could see that we were coming awfully close to the ground, even through the rain and fog and resulting poor visibility. Chapman then told me, "Get every one into the radio room, in ditching/crash position." As fast as the ground was coming up, he didn't have to tell me twice! I crossed the catwalk in the bomb bay and into the radio room as fast as I could and yelled at the men working on the ball turret to come into the radio room. We all got into position and didn't have long to wait. Those few moments felt like an eternity however! I still recall the eerie quiet after Lt. Chapman cut the power on the one engine, and the tense feeling of expectation...of a crash! Then I felt only a series of small bounces and very little noise, ------then a slide ------ that seemed it would never stop! I kept waiting for a tremendous crash! Subconsciously, I just knew that a long slide would end in a crash! Finally the slide ended and we came to a stop, but there was no crash! Chappy, as we sometimes called him, had done a great job. As far as I was concerned he should have been awarded the Distinguished Flying Cross! We had stopped just a few feet from some trees and a hedgerow.

I shouted for the crew to get out of the airplane in case there was a fire or an explosion. It didn't take them long to evacuate the plane. I met Lt. Chapman helping Lt. Wicks out of the plane, as I went forward to get him.

It was quiet and peaceful and we were sure we had made it out of enemy territory. Lt Chapman located the first aid kit and dressed Lt. Wicks wounds, as the limited supply of bandages would permit. Lt. Wicks' was still in a lot of pain but would not take the shot of morphine he was offered.

We talked about where we had landed and Lt. Chapman told Carl Weibel and me to scout around and see if we could determine our location. Carl and I walked toward a hill beyond a line of trees from which we could see the surrounding countryside. We had no idea which compass direction we were walking as it was drizzling and hazey and you couldn't see much more than a quarter of a mile ahead of you. We had gone possibly 200-300 yards up the side of the hill and were at the edge of a woods but as we looked back we could still see 'old B.T.O.' However, we saw there were more people around the airplane than just the crew. We decided they were soldiers and they seemed to be helping our crew.

There were some 'fox holes' on the side of the hill and we crawled into one and watched the soldiers for a while. The 'fox holes' appeared not to have been used for some time, indicating that the war had already passed by here. From what we could determine, the soldiers did not seem to be belligerent, although we still could not make out their nationality. By this time, however, some of the soldiers left the crash site and were walking up the hill toward our position. They were still about 250 yards away and we were still uncertain as to what country they were from. Scared, still shaken, and not wanting to be separated from the rest of the crew, Carl and I talked the situation over and I guess, wanting to believe they were friendly and not the enemy, decided to join them. How wrong we were! For us the war was over!

The soldiers had taken us about 100 yards when the Allies must have seen what was happening and tried to save us by shooting artillary shells over our heads, to cut the Germans off. But it was too late!

I'll never forget the scream of those shells! When the first shell or two came overhead the Germans 'hit the dirt' and we just stood there while the shells passed over our heads and exploded 30 or 40 yards beyond us. It didn't take us long though to learn that when the next shells came over, we 'ate dirt' just as did the German soldiers. Then the Allies quit firing. We had landed in 'no man's land,' between the the Germans and the Allies. Just a few hundred

T/Sgt. Robert T. Brady

1st Lt. Norman M. Chapman

yards and we would have made it back to American-held soil.

The German soldiers took us across the field to a barn located at the edge of a woods, about one mile from the crash site. Lt. Wicks walked with our help, one man on either side of him. We could tell that he was in great pain, but he did not murmur a sound. After we arrived at the barn they took Wicks away, they did not say to where, but we assumed to a hospital. This was the last time we ever saw him. Evidently he died, for later, after we were liberated, Lt. Chapman and Sgt. Weibel received letters of inquiry asking about Lt. Wick's physical condition the last time they saw him. Any of the others on the crew who survived have never found out as to what happened to him.

We were taken to Frankfurt, to Dulag Luft, the interrogation center, where we officially became 'Prisoners of War.' Really, this was a big relief, for up to then we could have been shot as spies, or killed trying to escape and listed as 'Killed in Action.' As POW's we had to be accounted for, according to the 'Geneva Convention.'

At Frankfurt, we saw the last of Lt. Chapman for some time. He was sent to Stalag Luft 17B and we were sent to Stalag Luft IV, northeast of Berlin on the Baltic Sea, where we stayed for three months. We hoped we might be liberated by the Russians, because for two weeks we could hear the war going on to the east of us.

When it became apparent the Russians would probably overrun the camp, we were moved. They moved us in 8x40 boxcars, some 3,000 of us, and we were the lucky ones. Some 6,000 others walked endlessly, until the war was over.

We were locked in the boxcars for 8 days and nights! We had very little food, mostly Red Cross packages we had brought with us. For water we drank melted snow.

The members of our crew all reached Stalag Luft IV at about the same time and rode the same train to Stalag Luft I at Barth, where we were liberated by the Russians. The Air Force flew us to Camp Lucky Strike, near La Harve, France. From there we were put on the U.S.S. Hermitage, on which we sailed back to New York City.

We had flown over New York City and the 'Statue of Liberty' on our way overseas, but she never looked so beautiful as when we returned.

I reached San Antonio, Texas on 23 June 1945, my birthday! A 22-year-old veteran. There I met my wife-to-be, Mary Rosalie Zavesky. We now live in Columbus, Texas, and have five children, Donna, Marshall T., Jr., Rhonda, Polly, and Amy, and also eight grandchildren.

We are still trying to locate Brady and Lupo; however, the rest of us get together once each year and reminisce about that time in our lives we hope and pray our children and their children will never have to experience.

2nd Lt. Raymond K. Mills, JR. (KIA)

Mission No. 139
25 October 1944
Target- Hamburg oil refinery

Crew of B-17G, No. 42-97899

Pilot	1st Lt.	J. Francis Angier	
Co-Pilot	2nd Lt.	Samuel E. Cashman	
Nav.	2nd Lt.	Samuel A. Plestine	KIA
Bomb.	F/O	Robert J. Maitland	
Engr.	T/Sgt.	Howard H. Lang	KIA
Radio Op.	T/Sgt.	William M. Thomas	
LW Gun.	S/Sgt.	Charles D. Osborn	
B. Turret	S/Sgt.	Edwin C. Vantine	
Tail Gun.	S/Sgt.	Maynard E. Judson	KIA

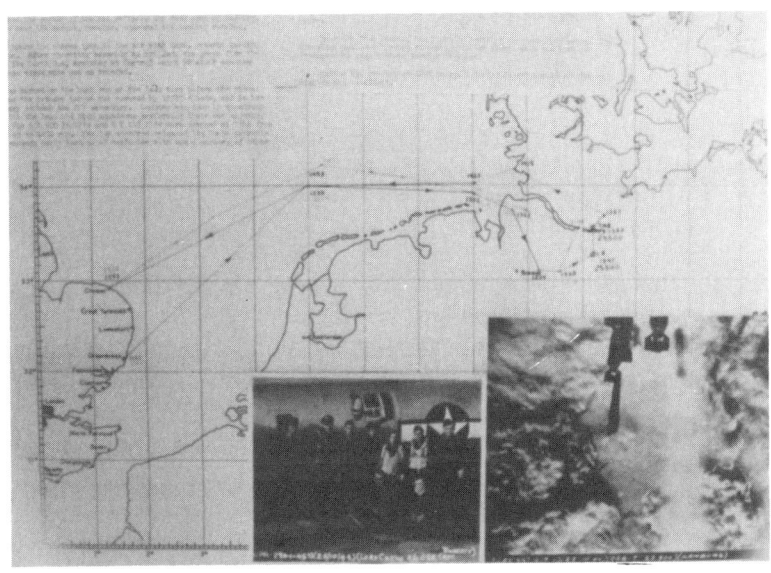

Track Chart, Mission No. 139, 25 Oct. 1944

457th Bomb Group Mission Narrative

Comprising the 94th 'B' wing and second over the target, the 457th today attacked the center of the oil refinery and dock area at Hamburg. 10/10ths clouds over the target area, however, obscured the results.

At 0930 hours the planes took to the air with Capt. William K. Doherty leading the formation. After executing the assembly as briefed, the group flew the course over the North Sea, arriving at control point No. 2 eight minutes early, because winds were not as briefed.

The group turned on the bomb run on the last turn before the visual I.P., because the primary target was covered by 10/10ths clouds and it became necessary to bomb the PFF secondary target. Bombing was performed by squadrons in trail, with the lead and high squadrons doing their own sighting preparations. The 6x500 pound GP's and 6x17 IB's were dropped at 1344 hours from 25,500 feet on an AFCE run. The low squadron dropped its bombs early because of confusion with smoke markers from other groups.

Flak near Dorum took the toll of one ship, that piloted by Lt. J. Francis Angier. The plane was hit at 1315 hours at 26,000 feet and was seen to break up. Two to four chutes were reported to have emerged from the airplane. The flak at the target was inaccurate but heavy.

The formation let down through a hole in the clouds over the Wash and proceeded to base without further incident. The group landed at 1600 hours and the fighter cover was reported as excellent.

Lt. J. Francis Angier's story of the 25 October 1944 mission to Hamburg, Germany.

On the 24th of October 1944, I went off DNIF [duty not involving flying] and back on flight status after 10 days of recuperation from a piece of shrapnel in the upper arm — a memento of the mission to Cologne on the 14th of October. Relaxing and writing letters until almost midnight, I had just decided to get some rest for an early morning practice mission that Capt. Dozier had spoken to me about when a 'jeep' pulled up and a very polite little sergeant said, "You are on alert to fly tomorrow's mission, if you feel up to it." This was not the usual procedure but I appreciated the concern for my physical condition.

Breakfast, as I remember it, was terrible, worse than awful! The

'Debris falling with me.'

powdered eggs and catsup had a slight petroleum taste but I was never one to complain. Ask Richard Fitzhugh, one of my Quonset-hut mates. I did bring the subject up to the 'cook' and in the same light-hearted manner, he promised me pancakes and real Vermont maple syrup 'next time.' There was not to be a 'next time' for me, at Glatton.

After getting my gear ready and removing some of my crew members from the schedule (one of them, Sgt. Tunstall, had flown 84 missions!), I went to briefing and met my replacements. It looked like a fairly routine mission, a strike at the Port of Hamburg.

Aircraft No. 42-97951, assigned to me at Langley Field, Virginia, had 16 hours ferry time on it and 4 hours shake-down when we left for the U.K. via Gander, Newfoundland, to Holy Head, Wales. It was a beautiful radar-equipped pathfinder plane, with all the latest gadgets installed. My navigator-bombardier-radar operator, Lt. Earl Beyeler, checked out the performance of the equipment and the flying qualities with me and we were as pleased as if we had a lifetime title to No. 951. However, once we arrived overseas, everyone else wanted it as well and I was nearly court marshalled for refusing to give it up at each base where I landed. It did end up at Polebrook and I did fly some missions from there but it wasn't assigned to the 457th BG until early August. Meanwhile, my crew and I flew various other planes and tragically, on 17 September 1944, No. 951 was shot down over Holland with Major Hozier, who was leading the 457th BG on a maximum effort. Ironically, I had argued to fly with Hozier on that mission in No. 951, to the point that I believe that Col. Luper stepped in and, in effect, grounded me for the day. Forty-eight crews took part in the invasion of Holland and I had to 'stand down.'

The aircraft assigned to us on 25 October 1944 was No. 42-97899. I conducted the pre-flight inspection with my engineer, T/Sgt. Howard H. Lang, and the ground crewchief, as well as the communications and armament people, until we were satisfied with the condition of the plane. It was in excellent shape and we climbed into the plane, ready to carry the war to the Nazi! We took off, climbed to assembly altitude, and assembled in our assigned position in the formation as the leader of the high squadron.

As we approached the island of Helgoland, just north of the German coast, we turned to the right according to the briefed route that would take us along the east side of the Weser River estuary. We saw the usual flak coming up from Helgoland, letting us know they were awake, but it was too far away to bother us. Our penetration of enemy territory was through reported light defenses and over a cloud cover of a 30 to 40 mile area and, according to the weather forecast, at 2200 feet. This cloud cover obscured the coastline and when I observed the first anti-aircraft fire from the mainland, it appeared to be about 8 to 10 miles ahead and dead level with the groups flying in front of us but consideraably to the right of our flight path. Another four burst of heavy calibre fire appeared dead ahead of our aircraft and, as I was flying to the right and somewhat higher than the lead squadron, led by Capt. Bill Doherty, I moved slightly to the left to avoid any subsequent fire. Meanwhile, we were conducting an oxygen check. I had told my crew there was flak at our level at 12 o'clock. "Check your flak suits and oxygen and acknowledge, please." Just as the tail gunner, S/Sgt. Maynard E. Judson, acknowledged, three bursts of flak appeared immediately in front of us and the fourth struck us between the No. 3 and No. 4 engines, blowing a large hole in the leading edge of the right wing and the inboard engine. A small fire with a peculiar blue-green flame started in the No. 4 engine and we expended our fire extinguisher on that fire, with very little effect. We found we had no control of either of the two starboard engines, with No. 4 'revving' past the redline and No. 3 shaking very violently in the engine supports. The engineer called out, "The whole right wing is on fire." And indeed, the fuel tanks were burning so intensely we could see, inside the hole, the internal structure of the wing glowing red. Engine No. 3 was bending down and the vibration soon tore it loose from the mounts. Realizing there was no way I could save the airplane, I called the deputy leader and asked him to move the squadron above and to the left of us, so that any of the crew bailing out would avoid striking any of the planes in the squadron as they bailed out. I had just hit the bail-out bell and told the crew to bail out, as No. 3 engine fell away. Pieces of the metal from the engine struck S/Sgt. Osborn, cutting his face, as he bailed out the waist door.

Hoping that everyone had left the airplane, I started to turn out of the formation but the maneuver turned into a roll and then we started to spiral, due to engine No. 4 running wild and uncontrollable. I had absolutely no control of the airplane and was attempting to get out of my seat when the airplane 'zoomed' into a steep climb. When it reached a vertical nose-up attitude, all power stopped abruptly,------the plane started falling tail first---then it exploded,----violently! Approximately two and one-half minutes had elapsed since we were hit by the burst of flak.

I lost consciousness from the concussion, but I had the sensation of being ejected out the right side of the cockpit and felt the abrupt transition from the intense heat of the flight deck to the extreme cold on the outside of the airplane. I came to my senses at about 20,000 feet and my immediate concern was the condition of my parachute, anticipating that it had caught on fire, or had been damaged in the explosion. I reached back and examined the back pack and was greatly relieved that, although my leather A-2 jacket and my flight suit were badly torn, the chute seemed to be intact. I was bleeding some from several cuts and I could hear absolutely nothing.

I was falling 'like a log' on my back without spinning or tumbling and as I looked about, I could see both coasts of Denmark on my left and the Zeider Zee and the Friesian Islands on my right. Because the plane had no forward motion when it exploded, the debris was falling with me and around me. The bright yellow, 8 man life raft had inflated and was slowly, tumbling down, about a mile above me. Seat cushions and other odd pieces were below that level and some compact pieces of the plane had passed me. The tail section of the plane was falling erratically about 2-3,000 feet above me. My greatest concern was the left wing, with both engines and the bomb bay still attached to it. I could see the bombs which had not been armed were still in the bomb bay, completely exposed and they formed a pivot around which the wing was spinning quite rapidly, much like a maple seed spirals down on its own wing. The control cables, with the bell cranks still attached were whirling around outside the circle transcribed by the wing and created an obstacle for my parachute of about 100 to 200 feet in diameter. There were also other pieces of the plane which could damage my parachute if I were to open it, although the main part of the right wing was falling about a half mile or more away and was still burning, leaving a trail of dark, oily smoke. Remembering that we had been briefed that the cloud layer was at 2,000 feet, I decided to roll over and look at it to help judge my height and determine how much time I had remaining to safely open my chute. Up to this point I had had nearly complete control, but in turning over there was some unpleasant tumbling and I had difficulty breathing in the wind rushing past. I was, however, able to see the cloud layer and felt that I had a little more time to give the spinning wing a chance to drift to one side or the other, so that my parachute could pass through without becoming intangled in the cables. Somehow I had managed to monitor the time and had mistakenly calculated that my time to reach the ground was at about 3-1/2 minutes but it actually took less than 3 minutes. The wing was at this time less than 200 feet above me and suddenly I passed through the cloud layer and I could see tree branches and a dark brown landscape. I pulled the ripcord with the feeling it was too late, but it opened and I struck the ground almost immediately. Although it was instantaneous, I felt the sequence of events as I struck the ground feet first with tremendous force. My shoulders struck my knees, dislocating both shoulders. My face hit the ground, causing a severe and permanent neck injury. The jolt of the impact did considerable damage to all of my joints and caused some internal injuries.

The wing with the bomb bay still attached landed about 200 feet away and was burning quite intensely as fuel from the tanks drained down out of the wing. Other debris was falling on the three-acre clearing in a woods, where trees had been cut and left laying on the ground.

The impact stunned me for a time but the heat from the fire and the realization that the bombs could go off when they became hot enough motivated me into the painful process of getting out of my parachute harness with two dislocated shoulders. Somehow, I crawled out and was sliding and rolling toward a little wood road nearby, when I saw a body lying in a small space between parts of the wreckage. It was engineer Howard Lang and he had not opened his chute, possibly due to injuries from shrapnel, or quite likely not having cleared the plane when it exploded. After identifying Lang, I continued my awkward travel away from the burning aircraft and,

Formation on bomb run, with smoke bomb drop indicators.

upon reaching the road completely exhausted, I pushed myself, with my feet, across the roadway into a shallow ditch on the other side. The bombs went off perhaps 10 minutes later, uprooting and knocking over trees. I was unable to breathe for a time, as the blast pushed and rolled me through the underbrush. I also experienced excruciating pain in my legs and stomach. As I slowly recovered from this second explosion of the day, my hearing returned in my right ear, although I was experiencing a severe headache and considerable distress from my other injuries. Two boys, about sixteen years of age, were making their way toward me, one with blond and the other with black hair. The blond boy reached me first and tried to shake hands with me. By this time my shoulders, elbows, and knees were badly swollen and were very painful. Shaking hands was not what I needed at this time. "I'm a Dutchman," he said in English. I knew we were not in Holland, but I asked him anyway, "Is this Holland?" The black-haired boy answered, "Nein, das ist Deutschland!"

On a hill, about 3/4 of a mile away, was a hospital, a convalescent home for burn victims from Hamburg. There was an inspection party there that day and some of them had watched the pieces of the airplane falling into the wood through the overcast. They had not seen my parachute as it had opened at about tree top level and, from experience, they had learned not to approach shot-down bombers until the bombs exploded or they were fairly certain there were no bombs aboard the airplane.

The party of about twenty people started down the hill after the bombs had gone off. The first people to reach me called me names and yanked me to a sitting position in the road and kicked me several times and, when they had knocked me over, stomped on me. An old man with a club struck me in the nose just as some of the military arrived and drove off the civilians. I do not remember the trip up the hill to the hospital but I do remember my arrival there.

The Burgomeister punched me in the face and rifled my pockets, as they searched me. They left me in the switchboard office, where 4 or 5 girls were working, while the guards looked in at me every few minutes. One girl cleaned the blood from my face and another girl gave me tea. Then an officer came in and returned my billfold and rosary the burgomeister had filched. Two medics finally put my shoulders back in place, after a struggle and a great amount of pain. This was followed by a profunctory interrogation by an officer who explained how we were shot down and how accurate the new gun battery was. It could pick up a single aircraft or a lead plane and track it while the rest of the planes showed up as static on their screen.

They told me my crew members came down about 20 miles away and were brought to the hospital, where they arrived in a huge open car about dusk. They had been picked up by farmers, one of whom had two sons in a prison camp in the United States, so they were well treated and not badly injured.

I knew that Lang was dead and the German officer told me the tail gunner's body (Sgt. Judson) was removed from the tail section, which had landed in the trees several minutes after the main part of the wreckage had landed. They said he had apparently been killed by shrapnel. The fate of Lt. Plestine, the navigator, was unclear, but one of the guards asked me if he was the one with the "ring," saying he had been killed. Plestine had always worn a Jewish ring, in spite of repeated warnings as to what might happen if he was captured. Later comments by guards led me to believe he was killed by civilians, a few miles away from the crash site. Had the military not intervened, I'm certain I would not have survived, if they had continued to beat me. My condition left me too weak that evening to give my crew a 'pep talk' on surviving what lay ahead of them. Some of them had been with me for nearly a year and I had love and admiration for all of them, and fervently wished their fate could have been avoided and their families spared the anguish they were about to experience. Nevertheless, all those who had survived the explosion also survived the prison camps, even though the enlisted men worked under inhumane conditions and endured a march in winter under much worse hardships than the rest of us. But those are other stories which remain to be told.

TRAP!
2 November 1944
Mission: Merseburg/Luena oil refinery

The biggest air battle of World War II between the United States Air Force and the German, Luftwaffe in a limited area, occurred on 2 November 1944!

For almost a month prior to this date, the Luftwaffe fighters had not intercepted the American heavy bombers in any large numbers and intelligence reports predicted it was only a matter of time, before the steady build-up of German fighters would make its presence known.

The increase in fighter strength had occurred gradually at interceptor bases throughout Germany, following the decision made some time earlier to withdraw their steadily diminishing fighter forces from France and other occupied countries back into the German homeland, to protect the heavy war material industries. This fighter plane build-up had occurred in spite of the concentration of bombing effort by the United States 8th Air Force and British Royal Air Force on the German aircraft manufacturing industry.

By decentralizing to 'Shadow Plants,' its fighter manufacturing industry, the ingenious 'Touton' had actually increased his fighter manufacturing capability to the point they were building more planes than they had before the strategic bombing campaign by the United States and Great Britain.

The evaluation of intelligence information by the Allies indicated that Germany was reducing its bomber construction and concentrating on fighter production, following the German failure to bring England to its knees by bombing. This fact brought about by the 'dogged defense' put up by the pilots of the two British fighters the 'Spitfire' and the 'Hurricane' — who chased the 'Bloody Hun' from the air space over England.

The Allied recognition of this change in German aircraft manufacturing emphasis brought about the aerial mission of 17 August 1943, to bomb the Messerschmidt aircraft plant at Regansburg and the ball bearing plant at Schweinfurt, by the bombers of the 8th Air Force. It brought about the 9 October 1943 mission to attack the Focke Wulf aircraft plant at Marienburg and a sub-assembly plant at Anklam.

However, the winter months of 1943-44, November through January, brought respite to the 'Hun,' for because of foul weather in England the heavy bombers of the 8th Air Force and the Royal Air Force were grounded much of the time.

Then came 'Big Week,' 20-26th of February 1944. The skies cleared over England and over Europe and the now reinforced 8th Air Force, including the 457th Bomb Group and other new bomb groups, took to the skies to 'hit the Hun in his homeland.' In defense of his homeland, the 'Hun' scrambled every fighter plane for which they could find a pilot: single engine Me-109's, and FW-190's, and twin engine Me-110's, Me-210's, and Ju-88's, firing 20mm cannon, lobbing rockets, suicide ramming, and any way at all to fend off the attacking Americans.

The deadly aggregate of casualties by the 8th Air Force was 158 heavy bombers and 38 fighters. But the Luftwaffe had not escaped unscathed, for the estimated loss to the 'Hun' was nearly 600 fighters! This did not include the losses to industrial facilities from the bombing attacks on Lippstadt, Oschersleben, Schweinfurt, Regansburg, and Furth.

The clear weather of February had opened the door and the heavy bombers, now with long range fighter support (principally the P-51), slashed a path through the German aircraft industry, placing the Luftwaffe in such an untenable position their planes were withdrawn into the interior of Germany and for a time used to protect their heavy industry and oil refineries, industries which could not be decentralized.

The withdrawal of the Luftwaffe into the interior of Germany made possible, without greater losses, the invasion (Overlord) of the continent of Europe, on 6 June 1944, by the Allies. What planes the Luftwaffe retained in France were so widely dispersed they were ineffective in preventing or deterring the landings of the Allies on the beaches of Normandy.

After most of the tactical responsibilities in support of the United States ground forces was turned over to the B-26's, A-20's, and P-47's of the Ninth Air Force, from bases in France, the 8th Air Force was assigned as targets the German oil industry, which fueled the German Wehrmacht, as well as the Luftwaffe.

Mission No. 143

Smoke from fires at Merseburg.

During the summer of 1944, the 8th Air Force repeatedly attacked refineries at Hamburg, Merseburg/Luena, Brux, Politz, Magdeburg, Ostermoor, Misburg, Lutzkendorf, Montbartiers, Nienburg, Gelsenkirchen, Wesel, Harburg, and Battrop.

The month of October 1944 was stormy, both in England and on the continent of Europe. Of the bombing missions that were dispatched, most bombed by instruments, PFF---radar, which at best was more harassment than effective. The German pilot was not schooled in instrument flying in the clouds and generally remained on the ground and did not venture above the clouds, knowing the accuracy of PFF bombing to be ineffective against German industry.

The 2 November 1944 mission to bomb the Merseburg/Luena refinery by the 457th Bomb Group was part of a concerted effort of over 1,000 8th Air Force bombers to bomb oil refineries and marshalling yards at Castrop-Rauxel, Sterkrade, and Bielefield/Schielesche.

The route to the target was unusually direct, with no attempt to feint and confuse the Luftwaffe as to the ultimate target. Some observers have classed the mission as a 'trap,' an attempt to lure the Luftwaffe into the air with 1,000 heavy bombers as the 'bait'! There were 720 United States fighters mostly P-51's waiting to 'pounce on' and decimate the 'Hun.' The planners of the mission would not know, only speculate that today the Luftwaffe would scramble more fighters than it had ever sent up to intercept the bombers in a limited area before! They were presumably launched to protect the oil refinery at Merseburg/Luena. The now rejuvinated Luftwaffe waited with 'baited breath' for the droning armada of unsuspecting American bombers, pregnant with bombs, to approach the I.P.

Mission No. 143
2 November 1944
Target — Merseburg/Luena refinery

Crew of B-17G, No. 43-37556

1st Pilot	1st Lt.	William A. Dawson
A/C	Capt.	John B. Wallace
Nav.(Lead)	1st Lt.	Jerome Silverman
Nav.(D.R.)	1st Lt.	George B. Korb
Bomb.	2nd Lt.	Frank O. Pappenfuss
Engr.	T/Sgt.	John R. Roster
Radio Op.	T/Sgt.	Charles E. Lindquist
LW Gun.	S/Sgt.	Joseph M. Geller
B.Turret	S/Sgt.	George C. Hardin
T.G.(Obs.)	2nd Lt.	Charles W. Ford

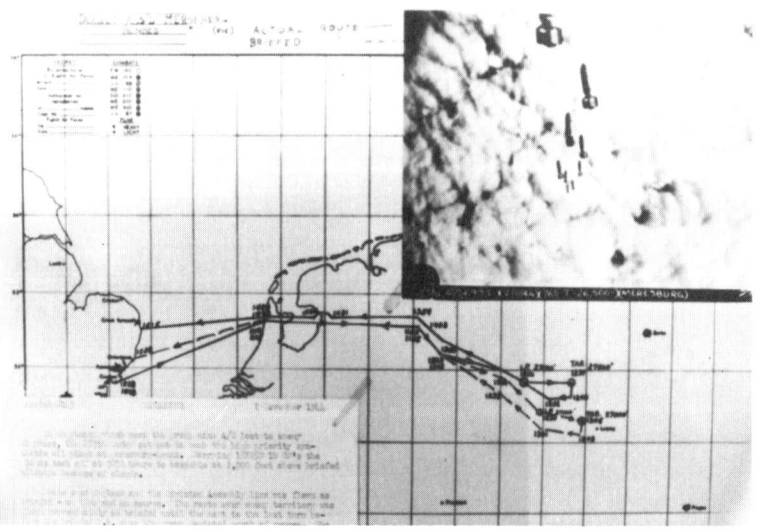

Track Chart, Mission No. 143, 2 Nov. 1944

457th Bomb Group Mission Narrative

In an attack which cost the group nine aircraft, lost to enemy fighters, the 457th BG set out today to bomb the high priority synthetic oil plant at Merseburg/Luena. Carrying 18x250 pound GP's the planes took off at 0830 hours to assemble at 2,000 feet above briefed altitude because of clouds.

The route over England and division assembly was flown as briefed—on time and on course. The route over enemy territory was flown approximately as briefed until the next to last turn before the briefed I.P., when the group deviated north of course. An I.P. was reached 30-35 miles north of briefed.

10/10ths cloud coverage made it necessary to bomb using PFF and the bombs were released at 1231 hours in the vicinity of Bernberg, approximately 35 miles north of Merseburg. The AFCE run was made parallel to and left of the other groups of the division. About fifteen minutes after 'bombs away,' the formation was attacked by about 40 enemy fighters—mostly FW190's. The Luftwaffe attacked the low squadron in closely spaced waves of 10 abreast. They pressed the attacks to within 100 yards and broke away in all directions. They were reforming for a second rear attack when P-51's upset their plans. Seven B-17's had been shot down out of the lead squadron. Two more, one each, were shot down out of the high and lead squadrons, respectively.

After the attack the return route was flown in division formation and 10-15 miles north of course. Over the English Channel it was necessary to deviate further north of course in order to let down through an opening in the clouds. A normal let down was made and the planes landed at the base at 1545 hours.

Because of the loss of a large number of planes, a hearing was called by Col. Rogner. The findings of the hearing were that a malfunctioning PFF set in the lead ship had caused an incorrect calculation, for the time of the turn at the I. P., for the target.

1st Lt. Jerome Silverman's story of the 2 November 1944 mission to Merseburg, Germany.

I was assigned to the 751st Squadron, 457th Bomb Group, of the 8th Air Force and stationed at Glatton, England during World War II. I was an original member of the 457th BG, as one of the 36 crews of the Hutchinson Provisional Group, which completed the flying complement of the 457th Group at Wendover, Utah, in

1st Lt. Jerome Silverman

December 1943. I had completed one combat tour with the 457th BG and was flying a second tour, as a lead navigator, when I was shot down at Merseburg on 2 November 1944.

The pilot of the plane in which I was flying was 1st Lt. William A. Dawson and, as we were a lead plane of the squadron, the co-pilot's seat was occupied by the air commander (a/c), Capt. John B. Wallace. The regular crew co-pilot rode as the tail gunner to report to the a/c the condition of the formation behind the lead ship, so he could 'police' the formation.

1st Lt. George Korb was the D.R. navigator, and 2nd Lt. Frank Pappenfuss was the lead bombardier. We did not have radar in the ship we were flying, and the 751st Squadron was leading the low squadron of the 36 plane group formation.

I remember that Major Eugene Peresich was flying as a/c of the group formation and that 1st Lt. Roland O. Byers (author) was flying as lead navigator of the group lead ship. Byers was also flying a second tour.

As we taxied from the hardstand, Lt. Jerry Page, a 751st Squadron navigator, was standing by the hardstand waving us off, with a rather grim look on his face. Maybe he knew something we didn't?

I have no recollection of the briefing, the take off, the assembly, or the route to the I.P. I recall very well, however, that I watched the lead squadron make a turn, 5 minutes before the time we had estimated for the turn on the I. P. I called the pilot to call the lead box and tell them, "Check your navigation." I knew we had to break radio silence to do so; however, we were going in one direction and the rest of the 8th Air Force was heading in another.

Well the group continued on the incorrect heading and we dropped our bombs on the wrong target. I knew that we were no place near Merseburg and only 'God' and some farmers knew what we had bombed. If we did any good at all that day, for our side, we must have caused the Nazi's to have a temporary shortage of milk.

Well, after bombs away, we broke to the right and chased the rest of the 8th Air Force, but we never quite made it. We must have been flying a heading of something like 270 or 280 degrees and were heading for England, when Lt. Ford, the tail gunner called out fighters to the rear! 30 or 40 or more! At first we hoped they were friendly. I was up in the nose of the airplane and couldn't see anything and the Luftwaffe didn't fly 'finger formations.' I couldn't figure out how the people in back could believe them to be 'little friends.' The 'bandits' came at us like a 'gaggle of geese'—flocks of them! I knew for sure they were not friendly when we started seeing white 'cottonballs' exploding all around us! We were bounced from the rear and I couldn't see much until they split-s'd down and away in front of us. I did see a FW-190 stall out, dead ahead of us, right at our level and of course Pappenfuss, our bombardier and nose gun operator, and I suppose every one else who could draw a 'bead' on him, must have all 'cut loose' all at the same time. For one of his wings were sawed off, right in front of us! He fell away just before we collided with him! By that time we, up in front, saw more of the fighters and at one point there was quite a 'shudder' telegraphed through the airplane. I thought it was caused by a direct hit by a cannon shell, for there was no flak about at the time. We were still flying level and on course when the a/c ordered all to abandon ship! I opened the escape hatch and sat with my legs dangling down and looked toward the clouds below us. At this point, Pappinfuss suggested that I untie the shoe lace with which I supported my oxygen hose, before I hung myself. I thought it was a good idea, so I did. I also remember thinking how far it was down to the clouds and I said, "Oh, crap," and I climbed back in the plane and hooked up the intercom. I asked the pilot, "Just what is wrong with this plane?" Whoever answered said, "We were on fire and that FW-190 collided with us and hit the wing right behind the No. 2 engine." Now I'm not from Missouri, but I had to be shown and besides, this airplane was the only transportation I had to get back to England and I had a date in a day or two in Scotland. So I made a personal inspection. This may sound dumb, but more than one crewmember bailed out and then others in the crew extinguished a fire and made it back to friendly environs. Well, I saw the gaping triangular hole in the wing, next to the navigator desk, and I could see wisps of liquid, gasoline streaming out of the wing that was flaming farther back like a blow torch! Then I crawled back toward the bomb bay and looked through the open radio room door into a blazing inferno. I was convinced! So I crawled back into the hatchway and prepared to bail out. I've seen plenty of guys go down in chutes, so it had to be OK. Besides, this plane isn't going to make it back to England anyway! So, I pushed myself out into the cold, hostile environment at 27,500 feet. Now back at Maxwell Field, Alabama, I blacked out from anoxia in the pressure chamber at about 24,000 feet in about 25 seconds, so I didn't plan to pull the rip-cord right away. I counted to ten to let myself fall for quite a distance and then pulled the rip-cord. I waited — and waited — and nothing happened! So I pulled again and this time the ring and wire both came out and the chute popped open. After checking the family jewels and my G.I. shoes, I was struck by the sudden silence. I was absolutely quiet — like I was on the ground with the bombers flying away. Then, there was a new sound of engines — fighter engines — but I couldn't see anything. About that time I penetrated the layer of clouds which was below me and I located the fighters, three or four of them in a big 'Luftberry,' nose to tail, going round and round in a big circle, and I was in the center with three or four other chutes in sight. I thought the Germans were firing at the chutes and spilling them, but not so! I saw an Me-109 circling, followed by a P-51, and the front edge of the wing of the P-51 was sparkling — firing .50 cal. bullets at the Me-109. There was another layer of clouds below me and I prayed to reach that layer of clouds, which I soon did! Upon breaking through the clouds I could see the ground — fields, rolling farmland, woods, a town with a church with a tall, sharp steeple on it, on which I was sure I was about to be impaled. I tried to spill my chute enough to change my course but the silk fluttered a little and I got scared and stopped. I was afraid I would spill the whole thing. Fortunately I missed the steeple and the town and wound up in an open field about a mile from town. I looked around for a place to hide but there were no buildings, no woods, no place to hide, just rolling farmland. Then, eight or nine peple, men and women, closed in on me from different directions. They searched me, taking everything I had in my pockets including my escape kit, my parachute, and medical pack and then they took me to a nearby road. Before nightfall I was moved about, each time with more and more other shot-down crewmen. We were finally placed in a barn along with 33 other American fliers. Of the 33 men only 2 of us were not wounded.

About four hours after I jumped, I began to shake uncontrollably, I couldn't stop for quite a while. Finally the shock subsided and I remained calm.

I was sent to Stalag Luft No. 3 at Sagan for a few months I remember I arrived there on Thanksgiving Day. I was placed in the most western of the four or five compounds. Col. Luper and Major Kriehn were in the adjacent compound. I understand that Col. Luper left a trail behind him, like our own Col. could. I heard lots of stories about his stay in Germany as a prisoner, all hearsay, however.

Eventually we were moved to Mooseburg, on a hike I would just as soon forget!

We were liberated on the 29th of April 1945 by the 14th Armored Division of Lt. Gen. George S. Patton's Fifth Army. We were moved by C-47 to France and then arrived by ship, on 29 May 1945, in the good old U.S. of A.

Mission No. 143
2 November 1944
Target — Merseburg/Luena refinery

Crew of B-17G, No. 43-37766

1st Pilot	1st Lt.	Earl M. Morrow	
Co-Pilot	2nd Lt.	William M. Stemach	Wounded
Nav.	2nd Lt.	George J. Schaffer	
Bomb.	F/O	Samuel J. Lisica	
Engr.	T/Sgt.	Clifford A. Upton	
Radio Op.	T/Sgt.	Charles E. Lindquist	KIA
LW Gun.	S/Sgt.	Joseph P. Salerno	KIA
B. Turret	S/Sgt.	Robert H. Koerner	KIA
Tail Gun.	S/Sgt.	Harold W. Pannell	

Brig. Gen. Clifford A. Upton's story of the 2 November 1944 mission to Merseburg, Germany.

I just should not have been around on 2 November 1944. If I had gotten back from that mission I would have completed two tours of combat: one flying the 'Hump' in China and all but one mission in England. But it was not to be!

I was in the pilot class of 42J, the first class in which men were graduated as Flight Officers. They went down the roster through 'S' and made them Flight Officers. The rest of us remained as 'Flying Sergeants,' the rank we held as we were going through training. So, it was out of fighters and into multi-engine C-46's and C-47's. I then flew a tour in the China-Burma-India Theatre as the pilot of a C-47. When I returned to the States to be re-assigned, the powers to be did not know what to do with a pilot who was not an officer – a 'Flying Sergeant.' I was sent to the 'pool' in Salt Lake City, was assigned as an engineer on Lt. Earl M. Morrow's crew of a B-17, and was sent to the 457th BG at Station 130, England.

On 2 November 1944, we had some bombs hang up in the bomb bay, which we got rid of. But while that was being taken care of, the No. 3 enginee was hit by flak that started a fire, which was whipping up into the bomb bay. We closed the bomb bay doors and had the fire partially out when the fighters hit! We were hit by 20mm cannon fire which killed three of the crewmen and set three of the engines on fire. Morrow hit the bail-out bell and those of us still alive got out 'OK.' When I opened the chute I found that 20mm cannon fire had cut the harness on my parachute, which flipped me over when I hit the ground. I came down in a plowed field and the wind caught my chute and dragged me, so that when I hit on my right shoulder and head I guess it knocked me out. When I regained consciousness, a big fat German was sitting on me and I was covered with mud from head to toe. The tail of our airplane had fallen not more than 100 yards from me.

When they took me into town they put me in a yard with enough 457th BG men to run another mission. That began my stay as a guest of the 'Third Reich': Frankfurt, Oflager 64, Stalag Luft IV, and the 86 day 'Death March.' I was liberated on 2 May 1945.

Condensation trails. Nearest A/C flying on 3 engines.

1st Lt. Earl M. Morrow's story of the 2 November 1944 mission to Merseburg, Germany, given to the 457th BG Association news letter.

We were on the 2 November 1944 mission to Merseburg mission, when we were hit by waves of German fighters. We lost our tail and stabilizer, about six feet off of the left wing, and two 20mmm shells exploded in the cockpit setting us on fire. T/Sgt. Clifford A. Upton, the engineer, used up all the fire extinguishers and could not get the fire out. I gave the bail-out signal and was the last to go out the front hatch. I had to push Bill Stemach out, because he was badly wounded. As I dropped clear of the plane, it blew up! Three of the crew, Robert Koerner, Charles E. Lindquist, and Joe Salerno were killed by 20mm shrapnel. The others on the crew parachuted to the ground successfully. We were all brought together in a village house back-yard. A few days later Bill Stemach was brought in. He was in pretty bad shape but survived the war and died from heart failure while playing golf.

Mission No. 143
2 November 1944
Target — Merseburg/Luena refinery.

Crew of B-17G, No. 43-106998

1st Pilot	1st Lt.	Graeme L. Bow	KIA
Co-Pilot	2nd Lt.	Donald Allen	
Nav.	2nd	Lt. James F. McGee	KIA
Bomb.	2nd Lt.	Richard T. Hibschman	KIA
Engr.	T/Sgt.	Cheston H. Hall	
Radio Op.	T/Sgt.	John C. Bruggeman	
LW Gun.	S/Sgt.	Joseph Naverro	
B. Turret	S/Sgt.	Chester L. Spurrier	KIA
Tail Gun.	S/Sgt.	Robert P. Robinson	KIA

T/Sgt. John C. Bruggeman's story of the 2 November 1944 mission to Merseburg, Germany.

Looking back (I'm not superstitious), the events were strange from the time of the briefing. We were assigned to fly the 'kite,' 'Paper Doll' that day. I had flown my first mission with an experienced crew to the same target, Merseburg, in that plane. Our crew had not been assigned to fly again in that plane until the 2 November 1944 mission. When I arrived at the plane I found that I had forgotten my pencil and I had to 'scrounge one up.' I was the scribe, radio man, and as you recall we were required to 'log in' every half hour, under heavy penalty, with a time 'hack' and a number.

Lt. Graeme Bow and I had flown one more mission than had the other members of the crew, as he too had flown one mission with an experienced, operational crew before our crew was declared operational. We were flying our 26th mission on this day. The tail gunner, S/Sgt Joe Navarro, had been sick on a day we had flown a mission and he had one less mission than did the others on the crew. We were a very 'close' crew, then, I guess most crews were like that, and I remember the harmonious incidents with relish. I do not believe there is a time in one's life when a man is as close to a group of men, as he was as a member of a bomber crew in combat! Even though the mind tends to hide in its deep recesses, malevolence, I do not recall any serious disputes among the members of the crew.

There is not much to tell about the battle because it seemed it ended soon after it started! As I was in the radio room, I did not see a 'Jerry' fighter at all, when we were pummeled by 20mm cannon fire. I think it was the first shot that was fired that hit me. Our plane was the element lead of 'purple heart corner,' and as you know, that is where the wave of fighters hit the low squadron. As a position in the formation, "You can't get much lower than that." Robinson, the tail gunner, called out on the intercom, "Here they come; Lt. Bow, start evasive action; and start shooting!" That is an actual quote. All guns, ie, tail gunner Robinson, top turret Hall, and ball turret Spurrier, all 'opened up.' The plane was riddled with 20mm shrapnel on the first pass by the fighters through the formation. A fire was started and was burning in the wings and spreading into the bomb bay. Lt. Bow rang the bail-out bell and ordered everyone to abandon ship! Navarro opened the waist door and jumped. I saw his chute open as he fell away from the plane. I opened the bomb bay door and found it to be a blazing inferno. I again closed the door and headed for the rear of the plane where I could jump out the waist door. On the way, I helped Spurrier out

A wall of 'flak' to fly into.

of the ball turret and handed him a walk-around oxygen bottle. For some unknown reason he 'hooked back into' the main system and stood looking out the left waist window.

I proceeded back toward the waist door and, before I jumped, looked in the direction of the tail gunner, Robinson. While it was difficult to see into the tail clearly, I could see no movement and felt sure that he had been riddled with 20mm shrapnel. At this point I jumped from the airplane through the waist door. You recall, we were trained to delay opening the chute until you had cleared the plane and to fall to a lower altitude where the oxygen is somewhat more plentiful. Don't you believe it! When that tail 'skidded' by, my chute was open. I did not carry the oxygen bottle with me; however, I did not lose consciousness from anoxia on the way down. The 'float' down was uneventful, except that I had a P-51 circle me, between the first and second cloud layers. When I came through the second layer he circled me again until he could see where I was going to land — in a pasture near a small farming village, where I landed directly in a pile of cow manure! It's hard to hit a small target like that from 5 miles up, but I did it on the first try! Having lived in a small agricultural community most of my life I was accustomed to the odor.

I had no idea what was happening on the flight deck or in the nose during the short time between the fighter attack and when I bailed out. However, that night the 'Jerries' had rounded up survivors and taken us to a barn (near Eisleben), and most of the 751st Squadron were present. Lt. Don Allen, our co-pilot, Cheston Hall, engineer, and Joe Navarro, waist gunnner, were there. The others, Lt. Graeme Bow, pilot, Lt. George McGee, navigator, Lt. Richard Hibschman, bombardier, S/Sgt. Chester Spurrier, ball turet, were not there. We were optomistic but fearful, and of course we had heard nothing. A conversation between Allen and Hall, who were both in the front of the plane, said that the last they saw of Bow, Hibschman, and McGee, they were attempting to open the nose escape hatch but that it seemed to be jammed or frozen up. They also said that the plane had exploded shortly after they had jumped from the ship. As I told you earlier, I opened my chute as soon as I jumped from the ship and when I looked back and tried to locate the ship, I could not find it. There was debris falling but fortunately I was not hit by any if it. We assumed that the plane was demolished. Navarro and I were wounded. I was fortunate to receive some treatment, that night, when they removed some pieces of shrapnel from my butt and leg. Navarro did not receive any treatment and still has some pieces of shrapnel in his shoulder and leg.

Hall and Navarro were sent to a Stalag in East Prussia, very close to the Polish border. After sixty days in the hospital I was sent to Stalag Luft No. 1 where I stayed until I was liberated by the Russians on 1 May 1945.

The year 1986 proved to be a very memorable year, as three of us who survived the Merseburg mission met in Chicago, Illinois, at the Vietnam recognition parade. We ancients rode in a Cadillac convertible near the front of the parade and received a warm reception.

Col. Harris E. Rogner and staff watching return of A/C from mission.

748th Squadron flying staff. Left to right rear: Capt. James Kincaid; 1st Lt. Marsh Calloway; Major J. McGavock Dickinson, C.O.; Capt. Shelby Bale; Capt. Irwin Rosen. Left to right front: Capt. Douglas Deal; 1st Lt. Roland Byers; 1st Lt. Louis Mueller, 1st Lt. Kenneth Taylor.

Mission No. 154
30 November 1944
Target — Bohlen synthetic oil plant.

Crew of B-17G, No. 42-xx583

1st Pilot	2nd Lt.	Lauren Spleth
Co-Pilot	2nd Lt.	John F. Welch
Bombigator	2nd Lt.	Ted Braffman
Engr.	T/Sgt.	Robert Haynes
Radio Op.	T/Sgt.	Edward Grybo
B. Turret	S/Sgt.	John Briol
Tail Gun.	S/Sgt.	Harry Cornell

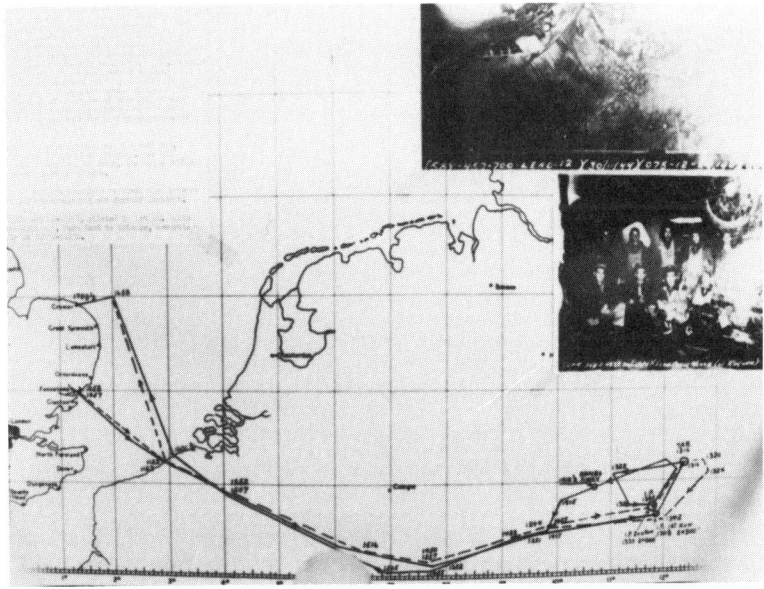

Track Chart, Mission No. 154, 30 Nov. 1944

457th Bomb Group Mission Narrative

Oil was again subjected to attacks by most of the Eighth Air Force today, with the synthetic oil plant at Bohlen as the primary target of the 457th BG Col. Rogner was A/C and led the take off at 0930 hours. Assembly was carried out at 8,000 feet on the Glatton buncher as briefed. The route over England was flown on time and on course.

After division assembly the formation flew the route over the continent approximately as briefed, although they were three minutes late because the winds were not as briefed.

The turn at the I.P. was made 5 miles south of the briefed course. On the first run the lead bombardier was not able to locate the target because of haze and smoke. The group leader ordered a second run and made a 360 over the I.P., again. The lead plane incurred flak damage on the run and the lead was turned over to the deputy lead ship. The group was about 3/4 of the way down the second run when an unidentified group interfered from the southwest, forcing the 457th to turn away to avoid a collision. The high squadron continued on to the target and bombed it visually. Smoke interfered with the sighting and the bombs were dropped 5 miles southwest of Bohlen.

After turning away from the bomb run, the lead and low squadrons turned left in search of a target of opportunity. At 1348 hours, the bombs were released on the town of Gotha, the bombs falling on a residential area in the northeastern section of town.

The lead and low squadrons joined the bomber stream in the vicinity of Folda and returned to base without further incident.

Two a/c, one No. 42-107026 piloted by Lt. White and the other No. 42-31505 piloted by Lt. Frechette, were lost to intense and accurate flak.

Col. John F. Welch's (Ret.) story of the 30 November mission to Bohlen, Germany.

An account of Lt. Lauren Spleth's crew's flight on the 457th BG mission No. 154 on 30 November 1944, in B-17G No. 42-xx583.

Target: Synthetic oil refinery at Bohlen, a few miles south of Leipzig.
Position in formation: Lead of the high element of the high box.
Recorded by 2nd Lt. John F. Welch, co-pilot.

Mission No. 154

B-17 on fire — one of the crewman's greatest fears.

This was my 24th mission. The target was the synthetic oil refinery, approximately 10 miles south of Leipzig, Germany.

As usual, Spleth, the 1st pilot and I spelled each other off, flying formation until he took over for the bomb run at the I.P. Up to that point, everything had been routine.

On the bomb run we saw the lead box picking up flak, but it was not much of a problem for us. Col. Rogner, in the lead ship, called on command radio and directed the group not to release their bombs because his bombardier had not been able to locate the target due to smoke and haze, and announced that we would return to the I.P. for a second run. Shortly thereafter he directed the deputy lead to take over the group lead for the second run, saying he had battle damage, with one engine out, and was returning to base.

The second run was 'wild' with deadly flak! Our box became separated from the lead box, because of interference from another group. The bombardier for our box took over the bomb aiming for our formation. During the bomb run we were struck by two or three very close bursts of flak, which did a lot of damage to our ship.

The number 1 propeller ran away — I could hear it going — it revved up like a 'bumble-bee.' In accordance with our crew SOP, I identified it by a glance at the tach, yanked the throttle away from

Spleth, and hit the feathering button — to no avail; it kept buzzing. The tach continued indicating 3700 to 3900rpm, and a severe left yaw developed. We didn't realize that Spleth's right rudder pedal was out of commission, so I wasn't helping with right rudder correction.

Ted Braffman, the 'bombigator,' called on the intercom, sounding pretty panicky, to ask if we pilots were OK.

"I see a lot of red stuff running down here."

We assured him that it must be hydraulic fluid and that we were not hurt.

The No. 1 engine spun freely for a while, but it caused so much drag we had to drop out of the formation, because we were unable to keep up. Then the engine obviously ran out of oil and began to seize, causing severe vibration, The planetary gears began cutting through the nose case and the whole front of the engine glowed red. The airplane shook more and more violently. I heard the tail gunner, Harry Cornell, banging against the sides of his compartment whenever he talked on the intercom, so I told him to get out of his position and come forward to the waist. I tried to call John Briol to tell him to get out of the ball turret, but the other gunners told me he was already out. Spleth alerted everbody to be prepared to bail out.

The engine gearing finally tore loose, leaving the now-stopped crankshaft speared into the freely spinning hub of the flat pitched prop. The vibration died down but the drag continued to be very bad. We thought that if we could slow, or yaw, the airplane, the prop might pull itself off and spin away from the airplane. But we didn't have electrical control of the flaps and gear, or enough variability of yaw control, so we couldn't slow down quickly enough.

The tremendous drag caused us to burn a lot of extra gasoline, just to stay in the air and we soon realized we would not make it back to the base in England. We gradually traded altitude for some air speed and fervently hoped we wouldn't encounter fighters or more flak.

The 'Gee' box had failed early in the flight, while climbing out to assemble in the formation. Battle damage, beside the failed No. 1 engine, included Spleth's rudder pedal, the brake hydraulic system, the gear and flap control wiring, and the wiring to the pilot's command radios. Our radio operator/gunner Ed Grybos couldn't get out on his radio, either. We also had a lot of flak holes in the airplane, none of which seemed to be in vital places. None of these items were of immediate concern, except for the Gee box. Of course we were out of our normal range anyway, but we thought it would be helpful when we came closer to base. The other airplanes in our formation had long since vanished, and we had a solid undercast. So all that Braffman had to navigate with was D.R.

We kept asking him for refined headings and to tell us when we were definitely over friendly territory. After what seemed an eternity, he finally announced,

"We should be over Belgium — I think."

"Are you sure?"

"Well, pretty sure."

About that time I spotted what appeared to be an opening in the undercast, ahead and to the right. We flew in that direction and looked down through it. There was a beautiful runway, with P-47's parked on the field. As we circled down to approximate traffic pattern altitude, we tried calling on every frequency we knew. Command radio was definitely out; no answer.

Bob Haynes, top turret/engineer, started cranking furiously on the landing gear, finally getting an indication it was down and locked. By now, the folks were firing green flares from both ends of the runway. Spleth told everyone to assume crash landing positions.

The landing was pretty good, but we soon found out we didn't have much directional control and had no brakes at all. The airplane drifted off the runway to the left, aimed directly at the 'follow me' jeep waiting to lead us to a parking spot. I have never seen a jeep move so fast!

Once off the hard surface of the runway into the soft grass, the airplane slowed abruptly and the No. 1 prop fell off, jabbing one blade into the ground. It just stuck there, upright.

There was a row of 2x4's standing on end, parallel to the runway. Our drift continued across them, knocking several of them over. The airplane came to a stop left of them. After we cut No. 2, 3, and 4 engines, the jeep pulled up off the right wing and the driver yelled over.

"That area past the 2x4's has not been cleared of land mines as yet. "Good luck!"

As we walked through the waist to leave, I noticed the entry door was missing.

"What happened to the door?" I asked.

"Oh that!" one of the gunners replied. "Back there when we were alerted to bail out, we pulled the hinge pins. The door fell off on the final approach to landing."

We had landed at a forward fighter base near Mons, Belgium.

We went over and looked at the prop. There was a flak hole in the prop dome, about an inch across. No wonder it wouldn't feather.

We managed to get a message off that evening, telling the 457th BG where we were and the condition of the airplane.

The P-47 outfit served much better meals than we usually got at Glatton: swiss steak and even fresh white bread. By Lend-Lease arrangements, we stayed two nights in a hotel in Mons. A troop carrier, C-47, crew in fatigues carried us to a base in France. There we switched to another C-47. The Air Transport Command on it were wearing Class A's. What a way to fight a war.

When we arrived back at Glatton, we found out that all our gear had been impounded. So, while never reported down or missing, we were at least briefly, and at least administratively, considered MIA—missing in action.

The 748th Squadron engineering officer presented Spleth and me with a 'bill.'

One (1) each, B-17G $306,000.00

Thunderbolt-P-47—'Little Friend'

Mission No. 172
10 January 1945
Target — Euskirchen airfield.

Crew of B-17G, No. 44-46088 "Rattlesnake Daddy II"

1st Pilot	2nd Lt.	Frederick C. Gauss	KIA
Co-Pilot	2nd Lt.	Ralph Gray	
Nav.	2nd Lt.	Bart Rizzo	
Bomb.	2nd Lt.	Arthur Fitch	
Engr.	T/Sgt.	Jack Woodford	
Radio Op.	T/Sgt.	Robert Pinkney	KIA in Miss Ida
LW Gun.	S/Sgt.	Robert Glenn	
B. Turret.	S/Sgt.	Walter McGuire	
Tail Gun.	S/Sgt.	Harold Reid	

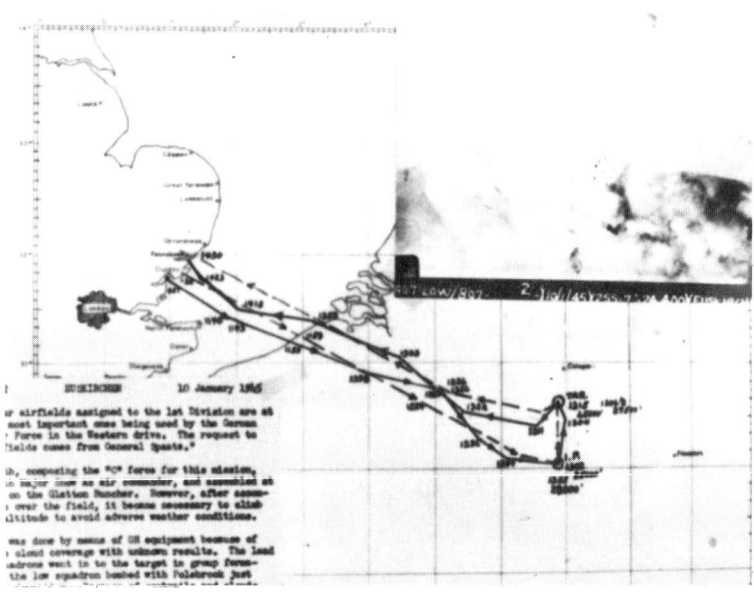

Track Chart, Mission No. 172, 10 Jan. 1945

457th Bomb Group Mission Narrative

The four airfields assigned to the 1st division are at present the most important ones being used by the German tactical air force in the western drive. The request to bomb these fields came from General 'Tooey' Spaatz.

The 457th BG, composing the 'C' force for this mission, took off with Major Wilbur D. Snow as A/C and assembled at 16,000 feet on the Glatton buncher. However, as assembly was made over the field, it became necessary to climb above this altitude to avoid adverse weather conditions.

Bombing was done by means of 'GH' equipment. Because of 10/10ths cloud coverage, the results were unknown. The lead and high squadrons went into the target in group formation, while the low squadron bombed with Polebrook (351st BG), just ahead in the formation. Because of contrails and clouds the group was 3,000 feet above the briefed bombing elevation. A short time before the BRL the target area opened up momentarily, but the mickey operator made a large correction, which prohibited the bombardier from taking over the run. The bombs in the left rack of the lead ship 'hung up,' and had to be toggled instead of salvoed.

Weather conditions made it impossible to follow the briefed route back to base. The lead and high squadrons returned to base individually, due to weather and contrails. Once over England the weather improved somewhat and landing was achieved without incident.

One a/c, that of Lt. Woods, was damaged and the crew chuted into allied territory in Europe.

Lt. Arthur Fitch's story of the 10 January mission to Euskirchen, Germany (His story previously appeared in the 8th Air Force Historical Society Newsletter).

It was cold — it was dark! The date was 10 January 1945. It was England — it was wartime.

We had been awakened at about 0500 hours and our crew had to report to the briefing room for orders for our first combat mission.

Now, 41 years later, I will try to recall some of the events of that day and the week that followed.

I would say that I was nervous, apprehensive, excited, and scared. Looking around the room at all the men making up the bomber crews, getting ready to go to war five miles up over Germany, I suspected all were feeling varying degrees of the same emotions, while trying to act as if we were going for a short, enjoyable flight in our B-17 bombers.

The target for the 'Mighty Eighth' that day was the area in and around Cologne. Brussels had been liberated, the 'Battle of the Bulge' was history, but fighting still continued in eastern Belgium.

Bombs had been loaded, fuel tanks had been filled, ground crews had worked through the night, and an added factor, about six inches of snow had fallen over night and the plows had been clearing the runways. The whole airbase was a 'beehive' of activity.

After briefing, I went to get my equipment and I recall that the parachute issued to me that morning (backpack) did not seem to fit me very well. I couldn't adjust the harness so I asked for, and received, another chute which seemed to be much more comfortable and easy to adjust. Along with an extra oxygen mask, I brought my G.I. shoes, which was a recommended procedure.

I thought we had a great crew. We had all originally met in Sioux City, Iowa, about four months earlier and gone through our transitional training in a professional manner, completing our requirements and developing a comfortable feeling with each other and a knowledge that each person did his job well and that we had a great all-around team.

I cannot remember much about the take off, the assembling of

A/C 44-46088, 2nd Lt. Arthur Fitch's plane.

the group, or of getting into the bomber stream and crossing over the North Sea. All the months of training had brought us to this point in time.

We were closing in toward the target area and up to then I had not seen any enemy fighters and very little flak. The first trouble seemed to start when the left outboard engine (No. 1) suddenly stopped, after which the co-pilot feathered the propellor. Shortly thereafter, engine No. 3 stopped and we began to drop behind the formation.

I stepped up on the navigator's table to look back through the astrodome toward the flight deck and could immediately sense the pilot and co-pilot were concerned.

Suddenly, as I looked out, engine No. 4 was ablaze and fire was streaming back over the wing and beginning to burn part of the tail section. The co-pilot had pulled the fire extinguisher but to no avail. At this point the pilot announced, over the intercom, that engines, No. 2 and No. 3 were out and No. 4 was on fire, out of control, and that he would try to dive and put the fire out. We made a turn away from the target area, back toward friendly territory, but the flames did not die.

Because we had originally hoped to make an emergency landing, the crew in the back of the ship had left their positions, had removed their earphones, and had not heard the order to abandon ship. However, the pilot had pushed the bell that was the signal to bail out and I had gone as far back as the bomb bay. Because all of the compartment doors were open, I motioned to the crew and watched as they all went out the waist door in tandem-like fashion.

By the time I returned to the escape hatch in the nose, it was open as the co-pilot had already jumped. I observed the chutes of the crew members that had gone out the waist door and now the pilot was coming off the flight deck preparing to go out behind me.

I remembered to tie my G.I. shoes to my harness at the last second and I estimated we were down to about 9,000 or 10,000 feet. All I remember was the flash of the tail section over my head and my G.I shoes swinging through the air and hitting me squarely on the nose. I don't even remember pulling the rip-cord — but there I was, after the noise — seeing the fire, the confusion of what was going to happen next, and all of a sudden the silence and floating earthward, in the winter air.

Now, at this point, a very strange thing happened. My thoughts shifted entirely from the burning aircraft and the exciting events of the previous few minutes, to thoughts of home. Jean and I had been married about one year and the expected arrival of our first child was 10 January. It flashed through my mind that this could be happening right at the very moment that I was floating toward the snow-covered earth. I made careful note of the exact time on my watch. I smiled as I thought, "What a coincidence it would be if our first child came into the world at this moment!" My strange sensation, my thoughts, and hanging in space seemed to suddenly end as I noticed I was rapidly approaching the ground, as visions of nearby trees went by.

Thud! I hit hard and fell backwards, cushioned somewhat by the new snow, and as the chute continued to fall in front of me, all was quiet and I was in a valley and in a pocket of fog. Where was I? My thoughts returned momentarily to the birth of our child — something I did not find out about until two weeks later.

I sat in the snow, released the harness and the chute, and covered them with snow. Now, which direction would I go? It really didn't make much difference. If my calculations were correct, my location was about 15 or 20 miles west of the fighting and somewhere west of Louvain, Belgium. However, at this point I was very much alone in this snow-covered field in a pocket of mist — or fog, very strange and quiet.

So I started to walk and probably went only a quarter of a mile, uphill and out of the local fog and into the sunshine. And then I began to hear voices — very far away — like children playing. Then I could see part of a small village and the voices were real — children playing games — probably at school recess. Soon, two of the small boys saw and ran toward me — shouting to me. They escorted me to the nearest house at the edge of the village and into a bright kitchen. By this time there were over a dozen young people, all talking at once, though none spoke English. I could tell they were giving me a warm reception and certainly understood right away how I had 'arrived.' Next, a bottle of cognac appeared from a cupboard and was placed before me, for me only!

Needless to say, by this time I felt the need for a drink and, though not familiar with cognac, it sure warmed and relaxed me in a hurry. After a time an older person came and said to me. "Military police," and then, "Follow me." Out we went into the warm afternoon sun — made even warmer by the amount of cognac I had consumed. The children were all dancing around me and I remember saying, "I am the Pied Piper — let us sing and dance down the street!"

Shortly we came to a halt as the man who had asked me to follow him raised his hand and asked me to follow him into his house. He introduced me to his wife, who immediately went into her kitchen to make a plate of ham and eggs. "Great American dish," she stated as she brought out the welcome food.

Shortly, an American ambulance arrived with a major and a sergeant. Now I had someone I could really talk to. "Where are we going?" "Have you found any of the others in my crew?" They had picked up others that day but could not identify them for me. They took me to an airfield. It was dark by this time and it was a base just taken by the RCAF back toward the area where the fighting was still going on.

The 'visit' lasted less than 30 minutes. I was then taken to a mess hall, a very temporary and dark structure (due to the complete blackout of the area), and I actually did not receive anything to eat. No sooner than we were inside than there was an air raid and we all scrambled under the nearest tables, while the Luftwaffe dropped a few bombs on the field. As soon as possible, along with about a dozen others, I was put in a truck and transported 25 or 30 miles back away from this area. We traveled without lights and several times during the dark, cold ride, we ran off the road and had to help get the truck out of the ditch.

Our destination was the village of Zaventam, about six miles east of Brussels. We arrived at an old school house about 2300 hours that night.

I signed my name to a pad of papers, received a blanket and fell into a bunk. The next morning I was surprised to find our co-pilot and four other crew members had been brought to the school house, along with about 100 others who had bailed out or were forced to land in Belgium the previous day. This was a sort of a 'clearing house' for downed airmen which had been hastily organized by the Air Force.

B-17 spinning down on fire.

We learned that our pilot had been killed when his chute had failed to open and the major in charge of our temporary billet assigned a jeep and a driver and arranged for us to view unidentified persons whom they thought might be our pilot. Unknown to us (until we returned to the States), he did have identification and was buried in the American Cemetery in Holland.

About three days later, on a visit to a cafe in Brussels, we met up with our three missing crew members and a joyous reunion followed. They had been picked up by the RAF and had been placed in a local hotel.

The cafe became 'our place' for the next week. The girl vocalist, Marianne, wanted the words to many of our popular songs and among us we were able to provide her with the 'hits' of the day, which she quickly learned and sang to us each night.

We also managed some meals and at least one over-night at the Hotel Metropole, which was a fantastic place even in wartime.

Everyone treated us kindly. You would have thought that we personally had liberated Belgium.

Finally, one day a C-47 flown by the RAF came into the field nearest the school house, picked up our crew, and flew us back to our base in England.

Epilogue

Our daughter had arrived on 27 December 1944, and not the 10th of January as I had envisioned!

Mission No. 228
10 April 1945
Target — Oranienburg M/Y

Crew of B-17G, No. 44-8368

1st Pilot	Capt.	Melvin M. Fox	
A/C	Lt. Col.	Roderick L. Francis	
Bomb.	Capt.	Charles E. Musgrove	
Nav.(lead)	1st Lt.	Beverly C. Robertson	
Nav.(D.R.)	2nd Lt.	Paul L. Bernstein	
Nav.(Mickey)	1st Lt.	Gerald Zelikosky (Selig)	
Engr.	T/Sgt.	Lloyd J. Blood	KIA
Radio Op.	T/Sgt.	Adrian A. Belanger	
LW/RW gun.	S/Sgt.	Alvin P. Prukop	
Tail Gun.	Capt.	Monroe J. Hotaling	

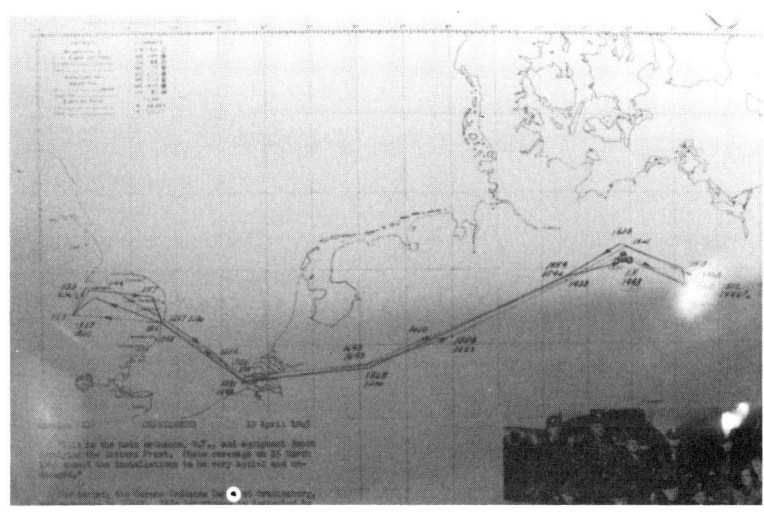

Track Chart, Mission No. 228, 10 April 1945

457th Bomb Group Mission Narrative

This target is the main ordinance, M.T., and equipment depot supplying the eastern front. Photo coverage on 15 March 1945 showed the installations to be very active and undamaged.

Our target, the German ordinance depot at Oranienburg, was requested by SHAEF. Its importance is indicated by the fact that seven other groups of the 1st division are being dispatched to hit it. It is the only primary of this type being attacked today, all others being A/F's.

Lt. Col. Francis, in the lead ship of the group, and the wing assembled the 457th BG's planes on the Glatton buncher at 5,000 feet, as briefed.

The group swung about five miles north of the briefed I.P., in order to permit squadrons to trail on the No. 1 target of Oranienburg. Cloud cover on the target was nil. The general target area was located by check points, and bombardiers were able to identify the MPI about three minutes before bombs away. Some interference was caused by 'prop wash' from preceding groups. The C-1 functioned normally for all squadrons and the mixed load of GP's and IB's were dropped at 1453 hours, from 25,000 feet.

Bomb results today were excellent as indicated from the strike photos. The lead plane's bombs hit 690 feet to the right of the M.P.I., with the balance of the squadron's bombs extending from the M.P.I. to 1,000 feet beyond. The low squadron's bombs, although obscured somewhat by smoke, covered almost the identical area. There should have been very effective damage by both of these squadrons. The high squadron's bombs fell, without causing any damage, in a lake beyond the target area.

Just after bombs away, the group was attacked by three or four Me-262's and one a/c was lost. The lead a/c was forced to leave the formation and turned the lead over to the high squadron leader. Slight confusion followed, forcing the formation to deviate from the briefed course just after bombs away. The squadrons rallied shortly thereafter and rejoined the wing formation. The return route was flown much as briefed, in trail of the division bomber stream. A normal let down was accomplished and the group returned to base.

Capt. Fox's crew preparing for take-off. Lt. Col. Francis with back to camera.

Lt. Gerald Zelikofsky (Selig) story of the 10 April 1945 mission to Oranienburg, Germany M/Y.

The mission to Oranienburg was delayed about two hours, due to an errant gunner carelessly spraying the hardstand area with .50 cal. bullets. Luckily no one was injured; however, an investigation followed.

The crew included Capt. Melvin Fox, pilot, Lt. Col. Roderick Francis, A/C, and me the PFF navigator. The briefing was CAVU, with no apparent problems on the way.

The mission was a 'milk run' all the way to the target, with the usual bomb run. "Bandits at two o'clock high!" screamed Capt. Hotaling, the tail gunner. It was all over in a flash! Those Me-262's could hit you, spray you with 30mm cannon shells, and be gone before you had a chance to shoot back. Radio operator T/Sgt. Lloyd Blood called Capt. Fox, informing him on intercom that the two engines on the left wing were on fire!

Capt. Fox immediately radioed the deputy lead a/c to take over the formation and we peeled off to the left and departed the formation. Capt. Fox then asked the lead navigator for a heading to the nearest Russian lines. I left my position, looked at the fire in the wing and reported to Fox that, in my opinion, the airplane was beyond saving, as the fire was very near the gas tanks. "Prepare to bail out!" came the order from the airplane commander, Capt. Fox, so I opened the door into the waist section of the airplane (the 'Mickey' navigator is seated in the radio room where the radar set is positioned) and saw the waist door was open and Capt. Hotaling poised at the door ready to jump. He jumped and at that time the plane peeled off into a spin. The centrifugal force of the spin threw me to the floor. The waist gunners and I had buckled on our chutes but were unable to get to the door because of the force of the spin. I remember the tremendous effort of crawling toward the door, of getting as far as where I had my head out the door, and then the lights went out!

The next thing I remember was the shock of the chute opening and of the ground coming up fast to meet me! Then the lights went out again! When I opened my eyes, I was lying flat on my back and as I looked up, I could see white cumulous clouds, on a sunny day, drifting by. Strangely, my first thought was of my missing the dance at the officers club that night.

S/Sgt. Alvin Prukop came running over to me and asked me, "Do you have a gun?" I looked at him and asked, "What happened?" He answered, "The ship blew up. You and S/Sgt. Blood were unconscious on the floor and I rolled you both over the side before I

Crew preparing for mission. Lt. Col. Rod Francis at left.

Capt. Fox's A/C No. 44-8368 over Germany.

jumped." (I have been unable to locate Sgt. Prukop since World War II and I would sure like to find that man.)

A large patrol of German soldiers, carrying automatic weapons, circled us cautiously and then approached us. We surrendered and were searched and stripped of everything we had in our pockets. We were offered no medical assistance, even though I had two bad head lacerations and was bleeding rather profusely from the wounds. We were taken to a nearby farmhouse where we were interrogated but they received no more information than our name, rank, and serial numbers. We were taken to what appeared to be the local jail, where we were placed in separate cells until the following morning.

I was awakened by shouting in the hallway outside my cell. "I demand to be taken to an American P.O.W. camp." a man shouted in English. Yep, you guessed it, Our noisy prisoner was Lt. Col. Roderick Francis.

S/Sgt. Blood's parachute never opened and from what the Germans told us he landed in the middle of a small lake and died. I have never heard whether any of the others in the airplane made it out alive or not. To this day I have no recollection of how I managed to get my parachute open as I do not consciously remember pulling the ripcord.

What happened from then, until the end of the war, is another story.

Mission No. 228
10 April 1945
Target — Oranienburg M/Y

Crew of B-17G, No. 43-38606

Pilot	2nd Lt.	Thomas P. Thompson	
Co-Pilot	F/O	Max E. Felder	KIA
B-N	F/O	Charlie P. Keith	
Engr.	S/Sgt.	Thomas L. Smith	KIA
Radio Op.	S/Sgt.	Keith V. Shinault	
Chin T.	S/Sgt.	Alfred F. Waichunas	KIA
LW Gun.	S/Sgt.	William A. Peltoma	
B. Turret	S/Sgt.	Walter J. Basara	KIA
Tail Gun.	S/Sgt.	John V. Lewis	

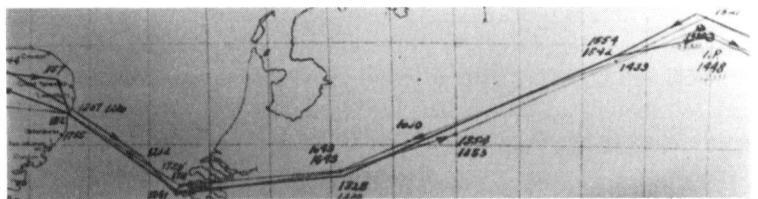

Track Chart, Mission No. 228, 10 April 1945

Major Ralph H. Hall's (Ret.) story of the 10 April 1945 mission to Oranienburg.

The above listed crew was that of 2nd Lt. William C. Moses who, at the time, was in the Base infirmary. Lt. Ralph H. Hall, the regular navigator on the crew, was on detached service attending G-H school. The crew was flying its seventh mission and was shot down by an Me-262 jet fighter near Berlin. Four of the crew were killed in the attack.

In 1989, at the 457th BG reunion in San Diego, CA, Norman Menard, who was flying in the formation at the time, observed that following the attack, the A/C exploded and the fact that any of the crew escaped was indeed fortunate.

The following story was provided by Col. Douglas Pitcairn, a member of the German Air Force, the Luftwaffe, during World War II.

Col. Douglas Pitcairn

"You can imagine the apprehensive feeling, I would have flying on a collision course with a formation of American bombers, into a heavy rain-shower of bomber .50 calibre guns! You are sure the whole armament of guns of all the bombers in the formation is directed at you, flying as the leading airplane."

"While you experienced some fear before take off, you'll know I'm sure of the inner calmness during the flight — almost a curiosity. Then as you attack the bombers and are busy using the gun sight of the 20mm cannon, you think of completing the pursuit curve and after the closest approach, only for the smallest instant, of seeing the crew's faces! Then you must react, strong and fast, as your reactions correspond to the controls in order to avoid a collision. Then to turn in a collecting curve and reform your unit and try to attack the bombers from behind. Then if the enemy fighter escort does not interfere, to attack the bombers again and possibly again!"

These are the words written to the author by a German Luftwaffe fighter pilot, who consented to provide a brief description of his experiences during World War II.

Col. Douglas Pitcairn was an officer in the German Air Force, the Luftwaffe. He was born in February of 1913, growing up on the Baltic Sea and East Prussian lakes, in summer on the sail boats; in winter, ice sailing and skating on the big lakes.

Flying started in 1932 at the Lufthansa training school; 1933 in the UDSSR (6 months clandestine fighter training); 1934/35, officer training in the Reichilehr; 1935, Luftwaffe Lieutenant in the Richthofen Wing, Aircraft-Heinkel, He51 (2 guns — undercarriage not retractable); 1936/37 in the Spanish Civil War, Adjutant, Squadron Officer, later Squadron Commander, Fighter Group 88; A/C-Heinkel — He51 missions after heavy losses by Soviet 'Rata's' (4 guns, retractable undercarriage), faster, more than 100 km/hr; Missions of close support for the Spanish, Nationalist army troops on all fronts; 1937/39, Squadron Commander; 1940, With Messerschmidt, Bf-109, the same unit one more year into the war.

First kill, Curtis, P-36 of the MER, Aerobatic Squadron (French). 6 kills, 4 confirmed by air witness.

1 P-36 French fighter.
1 Morane-Soulnier, French fighter.
1 Hurricane, British fighter.
2 Spitfires British fighter.
1 Beaufighter, Bristol, British, Recon. and light bomb.

After an alert take off against Beaufighters, my wing-mate crashed into my hood and I was badly injured in the head. It was the sixth mission that day, during the 'Battle of Britain,' which decided the unlucky fate of the Luftwaffe, fighters included. The British fighters, the Spitfire and the Hurricane, won the 'Battle of Britain.'

I spent many months in the hospital, followed by an assignment as Commanding Officer of a fighter training school in Germany, trying to regain my flying ability (lack of balance with head pains after take off) and finally, after recuperation, back to my fighter group.

I was assigned the responsibility of creating a small fighter unit to fly a 250KG bomb, attached under the fuselage, over London at

B-17 exploding during attack of fighters.

a low level to avoid the Dover radar net. We were called light bombers and invaded the London area by day. We had very high losses to our bomber units, from interception by British fighters. During these days I was shot up badly and made three forced landings on the French beach and just in the hinterland. So in the long run, after the failure of the light bombers to achieve any effectiveness, I rejoined the fighter division and then assigned to undergo the General Staff training. Because I had been hit in the head in the crash, I was assigned as Operation's Officer. Later I was assigned as Chief of Staff of the Rumanian — later Balkan — Air Defense.

After the collapse of southeast Europe, I was assigned to the 'REICHSVERTEIDIGUNG' during 1944-45 as a fighter pilot, with leading responsibility of young and inexperienced pilots and former bomber pilots (numbers of bomber units were obsolete because of the war picture and change in aircraft construction emphasis). You can imagine the effectiveness of this flying disaster! The young ones were lost after the first attack. The bomber pilots went crazy because of the narrowness of the Bf-109 and their own complete opposite mentality. I think the bomber crewmen will understand what I mean.

I became Chief of Staff of the Air Defense of Germany in the spring of 1945, and ended the war by similar functions, as second in command of the 'Molders Wing,' having flown missions repeatedly in East Prussia and Pomerania on the Baltic Sea.

I was then for three years 'Guest of the Queen' (British POW) and was released in February of 1948. I joined the Bundes-Luftwaffe in the spring of 1954, commissioned as 'Liaison and NATO Official with the US/British/Canadian/German/Italian Air Forces.' I retired in 1972.

During my military career I held the following military ranks: 1935, Lieutenant; 1937, 1st Lieutenant; 1937, Captain; 1942, Major; 1945, Lt. Colonel; 1964, Colonel.

Attended the following schools during my tenure with NATO; 1958, CSS Course, Maxwell AFB, Alabama; 1961, NATO Defense, College of Paris.

Thoughts about World War II:

1. Convinced by Nazi propoganda and no admission to political sources outside Germany, and as a soldier by profession, I had to fight and defend my country against the Anglo-Saxon capitalists and communism.

2. Nevertheless, the experiences during the Spanish Civil War did make us former 'Legion Condor' members pessimestic and reserved. The loss of the 'Battle of Britain' added to this judgement.

3. The overwhelming number of United States bombers, later on followed by unattainable numbers of escorting fighters and our own high losses of experienced crews in the European war theatre, together with as the fast progress of Soviet armies, made clear to us that we had to fulfill our duties as best as possible. So we had to stand a most impressive hail of bullets from your tight-flying formations of bomber aircraft. We had fear before take off, but never during the attack.

4. We had no hate against our air enemies. We shot at aircraft, not on crews, during bomber flights of U.S. planes crossing the Balkans, on their way to Vienna (Austrian industries). We never shot at crews hanging in parachutes. I took part repeatedly on fighter defense missions in that area and burned Goering's order, as Chief of Staff, to shoot crewmen in parachutes.

5. I will never forget both our's and the enemy crews shot down, as they were usually the best crews we had which were killed in action.

German Air Defense System

The whole German Air Defense System, was developed during the 'Guerre de Drole,' (Funny War), in August 1939-May 1940, following the Rhine River. We learned to perform 'Alert — take-off's,' as intercepts of French Recce a/c on Recce fighter formations from Mer. My first kill, in August 1939, was a Curtis (P-36, US) fighter of the French aerobatic flight stationed at Mer.

The air defense system developed a tight net, stretched from the English Channel over the occupied countries of France, Belgium, and Luxemburg, up to the areas east of Berlin and east to Vienna, Austria (see sketch A). The whole net was based on the closest cooperation of 'radar stations' and radio intercept units organized by signal units under fighter division staffs, that put together all detail reports, on a huge glass table, in order to show the leading officers a complete air situation picture currently changed by new reports. So the responsible officers in 'charge' informed the fighter units (leading pilots, all of them) in the air as neighbor fighter divisions by telephone, teletype, for 24 hours, because of day and night raids; the United States 8th Air Force by day and the British Bomber Command by night. The whole sketch is limited on the day-fighter organization, because only the fighter division are responsible for day and night fighter defense.

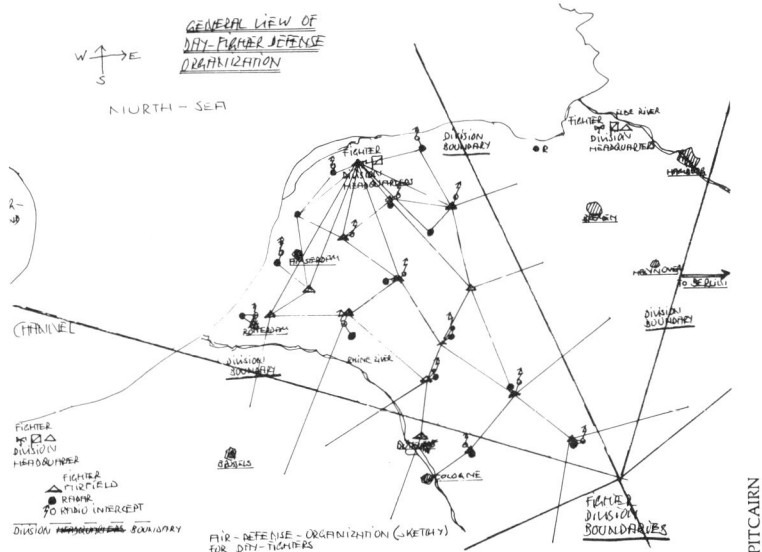

Sketch of German air defense system.

The night fighter control system consisted of a tight net of circular areas, inside of which are 1 or 2 and sometimes 3 fighters equipped with on-board radar were informed by ground radar stations about the course of the bombers, so they became able to pick up their goals by their on-board radar. The system became a bit complicated but never the less effective.

The average flying time of the day fighter, without reserve tank, was between 60 and 90 minutes, depending on whether they intercepted the bombers. The disposable reserve tank could increase the flying time to just over two hours and had to be jettisoned before joining the bomber interception.

Distributed about the whole area to be defended — east of Berlin — south of Munich — the whole of Germany — were over 100 airfields where fighters could land, refuel, and take off, in order to again attack the same bomber formation on its way into Germany and then on its way back to England. So during the whole flights of your bomber units, it became often possible to be subjected to continuous fighter attacks.

Very often the collection of large fighter formations became infeasible because of weather conditions and incorrect data of the air situation information, radio stations. This caused the creation of a small number of fighter units who crashed their planes into the bombers, but we didn't call them 'Kamikaze.'

The overall day fighter strategy consisted of:

a. Information about the air situation (early preparations of your bomber units by radio intercepts): Weather conditions, degree of alert status, etc.

b. Full alert given by fighter divisions of fighter wing commanders, or squadron commanders, depending on the fighter distribution on different airfields. Take-off time, collecting areas, and heights of flying levels came from continuous orders by telephone and radio.

c. Collection of fighter units into great formations for mass attacks, a most difficult task for all unit leaders. The whole collection phase took at least 20 minutes, about 1/3 of the flying time, air battle included, without a tank under the fuselage.

d. Attacks of the 1st phase were led by wing commanders: from above, from below, sidewise and on collision courses. The second phase, was developed to become attacks by smaller units, groups or squadrons, repeatedly as long as flying time allowed. The third phase was refueling on the next airfield and take off in the direction of the next bomber units — courses and heights given by radio. Fighter units now small, squadrons (9-12), or flights (4), and very often got into battle against small bomber units, flying home after fights against other fighters.

e. The fourth phase was returning to home airfield, where the whole fighter force of one of the fighter wings has been stationed. Single fighters flying home were forced to refuel on another airfield.

f. Personal experiences: As squadron commander I did fly in the Balkans, once over Silesia and Dresden, during the U.S. attacks after the terrible British night attack. Back from the Balkans, where we met U.S. fighters famous because of the black fighter unit (99th) consisting of young, aggressive, black pilots.

Goering gave the order to shoot down American airmen who are descending in parachutes. No German pilot ever did so to my knowledge — that were under my command. I tore up the order and burned it.

B-17 crash landing.

Critique of book *Flak Dodger*.

The author first met Col. Douglas Pitcairn (Ret.) when he gave a lecture to the ROTC, at the University of Idaho, Moscow, Idaho, in 1988. He had traveled to Moscow to visit Lt. Col. Raymond Proctor (Ret.), a history professor who had written a book about the Spanish Civil War, a war in which Col. Pitcairn had participated. This author had previously written the book *Flak Dodger* about experiences during World War II, as a member of the 457th Bombardment Group assigned to the 8th Air Force, stationed in England. This author talked with Col. Pitcairn and autographed a copy of the book and presented it to him, asking Col. Pitcairn for any comments he might have after he had read the book. The following are those comments:

Regarding *Flak Dodger*, resuscitates a decisive part of my life, and more and more coming to an end of this touching record about flying men 'of the other side of the hill' causes my reactions in commenting on the story of the 457th Bomb Group (H). Unforgettable memories of dangerous and successful situations and the adventure of the help to survival unknown until that time: Comradeship in the blue and on earth the indestructible basis of lifelong friendship between men.

So, in following the different chapters of your book, let me state once more the decisive difference within the characters of bombing and fighter pilots: The bomber pilot very quiet, imperturbable and maybe stolid; the fighter pilot mobile and aggressive; the bomber crews able to communicate in the air and to see each other, in all normal and exciting situations in the air; the fighter pilot alone in his small cage without any direct contact with his wing-mates, a positive and sometimes negative fact, shouldn't be underestimated.

'Bandits' the name you gave us German fighters, did surprise us. We never gave any of our enemies such humiliating names! May I add: We German fighters did in no way hate our enemies, in spite of official Nazi authorities' attempts to implant hate into the troops. They never succeeded in the GAF. In summer of 1944, I was responsible for the air defense in the Balkans as Chief of the Air Defense Staff (day and night fighters) in the vicinity of Beograd. From the highest authority of the Luftwaffe, I received a direct order to inform all of our pilots to shoot bomber crews hanging in parachutes. I destroyed this paper. No German pilot did ever shoot on crews hanging on parachutes in following this awful order, I'm informed after the war. We did not hate you. We had to destroy enemy aircraft and never thought during the attack on the human beings inside the fuselage. You had to destroy targets of every type and killed civilians without hesitation, so these facts are examples of our similar reactions and behavior. Many cases may prove this statement.

Training of German fighter pilots: I'm sure you never heard about the low grade of the fighter training before the war that took place after the first part, in fighter schools within the active fighter units (wings, groups, and squadrons). In the summer of 1939, I took my squadron up to 7,000 m (about 21,000 feet) for the first time in the Messerschmidt 109 E using oxygen masks--we put them on our faces at 4,000 m — and we talked about this experience hours after the flight. The main difficulty was in getting the whole bunch (12 Bf-109s) together in the right formation. I'm sure you had the same problem in your training flights. By the way, one of our most dangerous problems consisted of the inability of the so-called 'blind flying,' flying in the clouds or through the clouds. At the end of the war, a multi-engine a/c led us through thick layers of clouds by following the 'savior' in close formation flight, with the leading edges of the wings 6 to 9 feet behind the rear edge of the big bomber or recce a/c (He 111 or Ju-88). In addition, we had no navigational aids (devices) in the a/c's, to get to our home airfield.

In trying to comment to the content of your book, I always come back to the ways to compare your situation to ours. The military ranks of the German fighter pilots did cover from private first-class up to full colonels. Within a squadron, the commanding officer would be a lieutenant or captain, with two or three 1st lieutenants along with the other 9 to 12 pilots, at lower ranks. Normally, groups were composed of three squadrons and were commanded by majors: Wings, composed of three groups, were commanded by lt. colonels, or colonels.

Also in concern of the next fact, no difference shows between our common conviction: Complete confidence to every wing-mate became the basic phenomenon which caused the effectiveness — victories, of even the smallest fighter unit (2 a/c). No. 1 was the shooter, No. 2 was the so-called, 'Holzauge' (woodeye) He had to survey first of all the rear space above the shooter, because the view in that direction was very poor for the No.1. The structure of squadrons and wings followed this basic, smallest fighting unit.

We always admired the ability of your 'little friends' to stay airborne for so many hours. We lost innumerable pilots because of the limited flying time of our fighters, which averaged 1 hour and 20 minutes without a reserve tank and 1 hour and 55 minutes with a tank. Very often the red light shone on the way back across the English Channel and these a/c and crews never came back. It happened in most cases during missions in order to protect our bombers over England. By the way, as fighters we stayed in different grades of alert during the summer months, from 0400 twilight hours to 0900 hours at dawn. I remember seven missions during the 'Battle of Britain' when, because of the effectiveness of the British fighter defense, the Germans had to stop the day bombing of Britain.

May I direct your attention to the last ways the German fighters tried to stop the overwhelming waves of your bomber wings: The so-called 'Ramms-Geschwader' (ramming wings), fighter a/c that flew into the rudders and ailerons of the enemy bombers. The fighter pilot had to parachute in case the aircraft became disabled. On top of tactics the attacks became real 'kamikaze' flights. I did attend one of the briefings before one of the missions because we had to escort these special small units in order to attack your bombers ourselves, regularly from behind or in front. In addition let me say that all ramming a/c pilots were volunteers. The main reason for this was the fate of the pilot's relatives, families, wives, children, and friends killed by bombs during the raids, or as men in action. Desperation followed by self sacrifice.

I agree fully with your statement of the decisive role of the ground personnel, in all its activities. Without its dedication and real patriotism we could not have been airborne. Often your bomber groups would start with 36 a/c. This shows remarkable performance of your technicians.

B-17G A/C 'Snicklefritz.

Bits and Pieces

Capt. Clarence E. Schuchmann, a lead pilot who was a member of the 457th Bomb Group during its gestation and who fought successfully through some of its roughest missions, epitomizes the men of the United States who were willing to endure, to defend the principles of freedom they stood for, as have millions of other American men and women over the centuries.

The following are some of his thoughts about his service as a member of the 457th Bomb Group, flying strategic bombing missions against German industry, transportation, and instruments of war to reduce to impotancy, and thus force the surrender of, Adolph Hitler's and the German people's 'Third Reich.'

Capt. Clarence E. Schuchmann

Lead crew to Epinal—Capt. Clarence E. Schuchmann's crew. Left to right kneeling: Schuchmann, Goff, Smith, Blachley, Marra, Byers (author). Standing: Hibbs, Smith, Thorpe, Lanzoni, McMullen.

After you flew a mission or two, you decided there was no chance for you to finish a tour. As rough as those early missions were, I didn't see how in the world a crew could finish twenty-five missions. When they raised the number to thirty five missions, I was sure we couldn't! We talked about our chances of finishing a tour when we were losing long-time friends every day, some on each mission. Seventy-two crews had made the trip to England as part of the original combat crew complement and by the time the first crew had completed a tour of 25 missions, nearly one of three of the original crews had been lost in combat.

I can remember vividly the men in the 'Q hut' talking in their sleep— of my waking up in the middle of the night and hearing someone 'calling out' fighters, or talking about throwing out 'chaff.' Then when you have flown all but four or five missions to complete your tour, you begin to think, 'By golly, maybe I will make it through.'

Fear was with you all the time, I guess, even though you did not show it outwardly. Even with the outside temperature at 50 below zero, and looking ahead at the flak coming up that you knew you were going to fly through, you would feel the sweat running down your sides from your arm pits.

The flying condition that I despised more than anything was 'fog.' There were many collisions between airplanes resulting from flying formation in the 'fog.' Being shot at by fighters and flak guns was bad enough without having weather to fight as well. And let me tell you, we had our share of bad weather. The fog seemed to press in on you—you had no margin for error and the slightest mistake resulted in disaster! Assembly was particularly difficult, for as you circled the Glatton buncher you invariably ran into someone's 'prop wash.' Such a case was that which happened to Lt. Owen Coffman when he pulled out of severe turbulance, too sharply in the fog, and broke off the tail of the airplane.

I don't recall which particular mission we were flying, but Lt. Col. Tom Goff says it was on 4 March 1944. Anyway, at the time we were flying at about 25,000 feet, well above the Sandhill cranes and storks. I was leading the high squadron, and we were in the soup!—the fog. It had been a difficult day, as we had assembled in the soup and now were trying to fly a mission that took us in and out of fog banks. At one point we made a course change to the left and after turning and when rolling out of the turn, my right wing man did not roll out as quickly as he might have and 'Crash' Marra—yes, that was his name and he got it in flying school!—well anyway, Crash looked out his right window and saw the end of a wing heading for him. He yelled something and pulled the stick back in his lap! I disconnected the auto-pilot as quickly as I could and can remember pushing the throttles as far toward the fire-wall as possible. So we went as near straight up as a bomber full of gas and bombs can climb. We stalled out—and fell off—one way or the other, I don't remember which way, into a spin! I can recall the safety belt tightening around my lap. One of my wing men saw all of this happen and said to his co-pilot, "Well, I guess that is the last we will ever see of Schuchmann!" So he was real surprised when he arrived back at the the base and we were already there. Anyway, we leveled out after spinning down to about 12,000 feet. I think Tom Goff, the navigator, recorded our elevation to be 10,000 feet. Well, it had been 'touch and go' there for a bit. I reached across and 'clipped' Crash on the chin to make him let up on the stick and then I gradually eased back on the stick so as not to shed the wings. Then I called Tom Goff and asked him for a heading for home. I'm sure he placed his hand on his map and said, "Go west, young man." I guess in some respects we were glad the fog was as thick as it was, as we had no difficulty with fighters all the way home. At one point we did come out of the fog and there were three German fighters, close enough we could see the 'swastika.' I don't think they saw us, for they made no attempt to attack us. We headed for the nearest cloud bank however, at full throttle. We dropped our bombs on an airfield in Belgium and were home one-half hour before the group returned.

On one mission we had a 20mm shell go through the vertical stabilizer. Had it hit us a little farther back we would have lost all the tail surfaces and it would have been doubtful we could have made it back to base. The target was Augsburg, and when we dropped the bombs only part of them released from the shackles and we could not get the bomb bay doors closed. The increased drag of the bomb bay doors slowed us down and we were dropping behind the formation. I called one of the armorer-gunners and asked him to see if he could alleviate the situation. He and T/Sgt. Joe Hibbs, the engineer, plugged into walk-around oxygen bottles, climbed into the bomb bay, and were able to pry the bombs loose. They then cranked the doors closed and by pulling 60 inches of mercury we were able to catch up and stay with the formation. I was not sure how badly we had been hit and at one time stalled out the plane to see if it would hold together in the landing. It did hold together and we were able to return to base with the formation.

Incidentally, M/Sgt. Harold Wiseman installed a new tail on the airplane. He and his two assistants replaced the vertical

Capt. Schuchmann's lead crew, Oschersleben Mission.

Tail of Schuchmann's B-17, Augsburg Mission.

stablizer in less than 24 hours! One of his assistants quit — or attempted to. He said he would never work that hard again in his life! I can't remember where I first met Wiseman, I guess it must have been at Ephrata, Washington — Wiseman was one of the original members of the group who had been at Rapid City AAB and had traveled down to Florida when the cadre did some early training there. We were being assigned new airplanes — B17s — I believe we were at Wendover, Utah, and Capt. J. 'Mac' Dickinson, the operations officer, asked if we would care to pick out a crew chief for our airplane. The crew chiefs had already selected the crew they wished to crew for and Wiseman had selected our crew. The way I had come to know him was on a training flight. He was the crew chief of the training plane I was assigned to fly one day and as we took off I looked at the airspeed guage and it was registering '0.' Well, fortunately we got off the ground and made a quick circle and, by the seat of my pants, landed the airplane without knowing how fast we were flying. As I remember we came in a little 'hot.' When we landed he turned his butt toward me and said, "Kick me as many times as you like." He had forgotten to take the cover off of the pitot tube, one of his responsibilities. However, I did not kick him, as one of the responsibilities of the pilot is to walk around the airplane and to check for just such oversights, and to make sure the aircraft is airworthy.

We had a very good relationship with the crew chief. Later on, however, when flying lead PFF ships, I never knew who the crew chief might be on the airplane I was required to fly.

On our second mission we hit a target north of Paris and over the target we were hit by flak which knocked three engines out.

Only engine No. 1 was still running. We had taken a direct hit and the airplane was badly perforated with shrapnel. There were five different holes in the plexiglass nose as well as holes throughout the airplane. I had 'Crash' Marra call on VHF for fighter escort, as we dropped behind the formation almost immediately. We were leaking gasoline through the holes but the airplane did not catch on fire. With only one engine running we had to transfer gasoline to that engine as we headed for home. We were fast losing altitude; however, we made it across the English Channel and into England with enough altitude to probably make it to home base. We came down through the overcast and Tom Goff, the navigator, had brought us near the base. As I turned on a heading Tom had given me for home, I pushed forward on the throttle and the one engine that was running, quit! It had burned up! We were right over an airfield so we shot off some flares and I made a turn and landed — dead stick — downwind. Fortunately no one was coming from the other direction. I was afraid the airplane would blow up and I cut the switches on the landing descent. Joe Hibbs said, "Sir, you know the brakes will not work with the switches turned off, don't you?" Well, there was an emergency lever overhead, but I had never used it so I did not know whether it would work! Well, I turned on the switches again and the plane did not blow up and the brakes did stop us. The ground crew brought out a 'cleat track' and pulled us off the runway. One of the ground crew said, " Your airplane is shot up more than any plane I have ever seen." We had landed at Polebrook, the base of the 351st BG, one of our sister 94th wing members.

Anyway we were taken to the mess hall and then were interviewed by the base commander. When we went back to the airplane to retrieve our belongings, it had been stripped bare. We learned a little about life in the Air Force right there.

Mission No. 234
18 April 1945
Target — Freising M/Y

Crew of B-17G, No. 44-8557

1st Pilot	2nd Lt.	William T. Thistle
Co-Pilot	2nd Lt.	Joseph Taylor
Nav.	2nd Lt.	Roy M. Truda
Bomb.	2nd Lt.	Craig S. Winters
Engr.	S/Sgt.	John T. Miller
Radio Op.	S/Sgt.	Louis E. Domato
LW Gun.	Sgt.	Luther N. Smith
RW Gun.	Sgt.	Harvey C. Henkel
B. Turret	Sgt.	John M. Taylor
Tail Gun	F/O	William W. McIntosh

2nd Lt. William T. Thistle and his crew had the dubious honor of being the last crew from the 457th BG to be lost to enemy action during World War II. The target to which the 457th Bomb Group flew on 18 April 1945 was a marshalling yard and railroad bridge in the town of Freising, Germany.

The author of this book previously wrote a book with the title Flak Dodger a story about the 457th Bomb Group. One of the people who read the book sent the following letter to the author, describing how it felt to be on the receiving end of a bombing raid.

6 July 1986

Dear Col. Byers:
I have just finished reading your book *Flak Dodger* which I obtained from the local library. I found it most interesting, and although memory does become less clear with the passage of time, nevertheless, I remember only too well what it was like to be on the

receiving end of the U.S.A.F's bombs. I was in Freising on the afternoon of the 18th of April 1945 — and it occurred to me you might be interested to read my impressions of an air raid which warranted only a line or two in your book. Quite right, too. The mission to Freising was insignificant compared with other missions (or 'Operations' as we in the R.A.F. called them) and I have to agree with the bombing results classification of 'excellent.'

I joined the R.A.F. at the end of 1940 on the day following the first blitz of Manchester, and trained as an 'Observer.' In those days an observers main training was in navigation and bomb-aiming plus a full air gunners training and was also required to receive and transmit Morse Code at 12 words per minute by wireless and 6 words per minute by Aldis lamp. With the introduction of four-engine bombers, the trade of the observer was divided into navigators and bomb-aimers, but I managed to persuade my pilots if I had the hard work of navigating to a target, I was entitled to the fun of aiming the bombs. After a short tour in 'Lancasters' with 83 Squadron, I was posted to 149 Squadron at Lakenheath, where I became the navigator/bomb-aimer of Flight Commander Squadron-Leader 'Hutch' Hutchings D.F.C. When deputizing for an indisposed navigator of another crew, I was shot down on 10 September 1942 en route to Dusseldorf, Germany, on an operation.

I spent most of my time as a prisoner of war at Stalag VIII-B in Upper Silesia, but near the end of the war was evacuated on the 'march' when the Russians approached the River Oder in January 1945. I marched for over 200 miles, then started to use my head instead of my feet, and then 'scrounged' transport, to arrive at the P.O.W. hospital at Freising in February 1945. Most of the patients at the Freising P.O.W. hospital were men recovering from wounds received in Germany and Italy — the majority were British and American, in fairly equal numbers with some Italians, French, and Russians. I don't think it was a large hospital, but of course I was in a sick room and I did not see much of the 'surgical' side. I think I was admitted to the hospital because I had a very bad cold and weighed less than 8 stone (110 pounds).

The town of Freising was built on two levels. The hospital was located in some medieval buildings on the edge of an escarpment some 100 feet higher than the rest of the town where the River Isar and the railway station were located. From our room we could see a terraced garden leading to a small tributary of the Isar, then across the plain to Munich and the Alps Mountains beyond. It was very pleasant. The walls of the hospital were 2 feet thick and I think the whole complex had been, or still was, the home of some religious order, as we were nursed by nuns in addition to the Ger-

Thistle's last mission, A/C No. 44-8557.

man, British, and French medical staff. Compared to the P.O.W. camp at Stalag VIII B, this was heaven: Red Cross parcels from Britain and Canada to supplement the German hospital rations: real beds and clean sheets; a lovely view; and the added interest of watching Munich being bombed some 20 miles away. We also watched our 'Spitfires' and your 'Mustangs' and 'Lightnings' strafe some unseen target.

We had no news of the progress of the war at Freising. Winter gave way to spring and then winter returned for a few days, then spring returned. My cold was better and I regained most of my former weight, so that in the morning of 18 April 1945 the German doctor had pronounced me fit to be transferred to Stalag VII A at Mooseburg. I was to be escorted to the railway station that afternoon to travel by train the few miles nearer Regensburg. It was a lovely sunny day, and just after noon I was lying on my bed, by the window, wearing only pyjama trousers, hoping to get a bit of suntan with the sun shining through the open window. We were on the third floor, and I had watched some contrails appear, then smoke, dust, and the noise of distant bombs to the south-east. I had settled back in the sunshine when one of our soldiers cried out to me, "Hey, they've dropped one of the smoke things over here!" There was a tremendous roaring noise of falling bombs and I tried to dive under the bed, but glass, window frame, and myself were hurled to the other side of the room. Part of the ceiling came down as the whole building shook. The noise of the explosions ceased but we could hear more aircraft approaching. The soldier and I ran out into the corridor with the idea of going down to the air-raid shelter, but the roaring noise came again and Corporal Howle, an American Staff Sergeant and I tried to make ourselves very small under a large oak table. The three of us managed to get to the air-raid shelter before the next wave attacked, but this time the bombs were nearer and, by a freak of blast, the door of the coal cellar blew off and we were covered with coal dust. The noise of the aircraft diminished and we returned to our third floor room to look out over the little town.

Half of the town was on fire (or so it seemed), the sun still shone palely through the smoke and dust, the railroad station (less than half a mile away) was a ruin, and a train of freight cars was smashed and burning on a siding. The new spring leaves on the trees in 'our' terraced garden had been blasted away, and what we thought was a sack, blown up into a tree, turned out to be one of the priests. There were only minor cuts and bruises amongst the prisoners of war, but other wounded started to come to our hospital for treatment. There were no guards or prisoners now — only air-raid victims.

Six of us British P.O.W's, three American soldiers, a Scottish medic, and a French Army doctor tried to help where we could. We helped to dig 25 nuns out of the destroyed nunnery. The Scot and a German guard and I took a horse and cart out into the country to bring milk into the town from the surrounding farms.

There didn't seem to be much in the town of Freising of a military nature, but the railway station and the junction were destroyed. I counted six bomb craters in the terraced garden in front of our room, and there were a couple of craters in the courtyard at the rear. There was no electricity for two days and no more air raid warning system. One of our chaps had washed his haversack prior to the raid, and had hung it out to dry from his window catch. It had gone, and he cursed the 'Yanks' for having blown away his haversack. He found it at the foot of the wall — damaged and containing a piece of the railway line which must have been blown some 400 yards, straight into his haversack! One good thing about this air-raid: I could not be transferred to the camp at Mooseburg now. Not by rail, that's for sure.

Freising was taken by the United States troops on 29 April 1945. This forward detachment of U.S. troops pushed on toward Munich, leaving us with a radio, arms, and a locked-up small German garrison. I found myself to be the senior combatant rank amongst the prisoners. There was a Major Darling and a Captain Church, but both were medical corps, and there were also field rank officers who were patients in the hospital.

For a couple of days, only small units of American troops came through the town (An artillery battery came in to silence a German '88' that had been firing at us), then the armour came in, and what a sight that was. Marvellous! There was a General who came into the town square in a 'jeep.' I was introduced to him, and having inquired if we were okay, he told one of his officers to give me some cigarettes. This general had three stars and there was a white helmet in the back of the 'jeep.' I had never heard of General Patton, but I have often wondered if I met him that day in Freising.

Our common denominator is that we both served as navigators in the bombing of Germany and we both experienced the same airraid. Your losses were one aircraft on that day, and a German doctor told me there were over 800 people killed and some 1400 injured in Freising. I do wish that leaders of nations, great and small, would realize the cost and futility of war.

My best wishes to you,
Alan Yates
(ex-Warrant Officer, Royal Air Force)

The following diary of completed missions was provided T/Sgt. Robert H. Prisk, a radio operator who flew missions between 25 April 1944 and 3 August 1944, when assigned to the 749th Squadron of the 457th Bomb Group.

25 April 1944 (Nancy/Essey)
My first mission today. Up at 0300 hours, ate, briefing at 0400 hours and take off at 0600 hours. Target was an airfield at Nancy, France. On oxygen for 6 hours at an altitude of 22,000 feet. Saw no flak or fighters. Had P-38, P-47 and P-51 escorting fighters. Circled target three times, clouds about 9/10ths. Dropped no bombs. Returned to base with all 18 planes. The mission was a real easy

one and we were lucky. I wasn't as excited as I thought I would be. I wore my flak suit all the mission however. Landed at 1330 hours, was tired and glad to get some sleep.

27 April 1944 (No Ball)
Flew my second mission today. The target was a 'No Ball' [Ed. German V-1 launching platforms] on the coast of France near St. Omer. Was a short mission of only 4 hours, but rugged. Met no enemy fighters and saw no escorting fighters. But flak was heavy over the target, 'Those boys were really checked out down there,' plenty accurate. We were No.6 in 'Purple Heart Corner.' Luck was with us again and we had only one hole in the wing. Some of the boys were shot up plenty, but we did not lose any airplanes. Saw my first flak. Have still to see my first 'Jerry' fighters.

1 May 1944 (No Ball)
Made our third mission today. Was up at 1130 hours Sunday night. Took off at 0400 hours and flew over England to reach an altitude of 25,000 feet. Over the target at 0950 hours which was an enemy fortification, probably rocket emplacements. Circled target three times and hit it hard on last run. Bomb load was six, 1000 pounders. Blew the place to hell. Target was located near Hasen, France, about 20 minutes from the coast. Flak was heavy from the I.P. to the target. We had holes in the navigation dome, one landing light and a few small holes, made by flak. Was a rough mission but landed at 1230 hours.

4 May 1944 (Berlin)
Were on our way to Berlin today. Up at 0200 hours, took off at 0700 hours. Target was the heart of Berlin. We were flying C.B.W. spare No. 1. Filled in No. 3, second element, lead box with the 401st BG. Got within 55 minutes of Berlin and were recalled for some reason. Flew over Belgium and Holland. First time over Germany for me. Our group saw very little flak and it wasn't a bad trip at all. Bombed a secondary target, a German airfield on the coast of the Zieder Zee, Holland. Hit it square with 1000 and 500 pound incendiaries. Made a real mess of the place. Landed about 1300 hours. Still want to get to Berlin.

7 May 1944 (Berlin)
Got there today. Big 'B' Berlin. A tough one. Took off at 0600 hours and landed at 1400 hours. On oxygen for six hours. Flew at 27,000 feet, 47 degrees below zero! Had flak most of the way and real heavy over the target, but not very accurate. Some at the coast, very accurate. Saw no fighters, had good escort, 51's, 47's and 38's, glad to see them. This was No. 5, only 25 to go. Target was the

A/C No. 297571 landing at Glatton AAB. Note farmhouses in center of airbase.

heart of the city. Clouded over, 10/10ths. Bombed with PFF, 500 pound incendiaries, couldn't see results. Saw more B-17's in the air than I had ever before seen, about 750. Still have not seen a German fighter yet.

8 May 1944
Nothing much today. Flew as spare to French coast and returned.

9 May 1944 (Luxembourg)
Went to Luxembourg today. About an 8 hour mission. Target was a R.R. marshalling yards at outskirts of the city. Flew at 20,000 feet. Saw my first German fighters today. Two fighters came through our formation, I didn't see them myself. Saw some wonderful dog fights at a distance. P-38's and FW-190's. Fighters didn't score any hits on any of us, the P-38's took care of them. Wasn't bad for flak, saw very little. Bombed visually, hit target. Pretty good mission, not too rough.

13 May 1944 (Politz)
Went to Politz, Germany a port on the Baltic Sea. Trip took 9 hours, longest flight yet. Crossed the North Sea, climbed to altitude over Denmark, bombed at 18,000 feet. Plenty of flak, found two holes in the floor of the radio room, came too close for comfort. About 35 enemy fighters attacked us over the target. Our formation was very tight and the fighters did not bother us much. Our ship was struck by one of our smoke bombs at bombs away. We thought we were on fire at first, ruined the nose of our ship, filled the plane with smoke, however no one was hurt. Our bomb load was 38, 100 pounders. I believe we missed the target, a synthetic oil

plant. Hit the city of Stettin instead. It was fairly cloudy over the target. This was mission No. 7, sweating out No. 8. We flew in the second element of the lead box. Lots of escort, P-38, 47 and 51's. They looked good to us.

19 May 1944 (Berlin)
Berlin again. It was the toughest, roughest mission yet. We were in the air for 9 hours. Left at 0900 hours and returned to base at 1830 hours. Route was over the North Sea, Denmark, Baltic Sea, and into Berlin from the north. Target was the center of the city again. Hit it with 100 and 500 pound incendiaries. Saw more flak and fighters than ever before, mostly Me-109's. Had a good escort of P-51's. Saw some good dog fights. We had very little battle damage, a hole in the top turret, Vince was lucky, and another piece of flak came up through the radio room floor next to the ball turret. There were also some holes in the wings. Came home over the North Sea about 150 feet above the water. It was a tough mission. Guess I am lucky I can not see too much from the radio room. That was No. 2 to Berlin. Not anxious to go back again soon.

23 May 1944 (Epinal)
This was No. 9. Flew across the Channel into France. Target was the R.R. marshalling yard at Epinal in southern France near the Switzerland border. Mission took about six hours, saw no flak or enemy fighters. Had P-51, 47 and 38 escort all the way. Was a fairly easy mision. Flew in 'B' CBW, No. 5 low box, saw bombs hit the target for the first time.

27 May 1944 (Ludwigshaven)
Can truly say, today will live in my mind forever. This was the toughest mission in the history of the group and squadron. Took about 8 hours in the air, oxygen for 5 hours, altitude 25,000 feet. Target was the R.R. marshalling yard in the city of Ludwigshaven, Germany, near the border of France and Switzerland. We flew a nine man crew for the first time today, one man for the two waist guns. One hour from the target we were jumped by 30-40 Me-109's. 'Tex' was first to fire from the right waist gun. I left the radio and took over the right waist gun. Tex took the left waist gun. Shot at my first enemy fighters. Really poured the lead at them. The Me-109's made four passes at us. Tex, Vince and Brownie each claimed one Me-109. I can't say I hit any for sure, but think I should have put a few holes in some of them. They came in from the nose, went under our right wing, couldn't miss. It was a real thrill! I was plenty excited. Flak over the target was heavy and accurate. I saw everything that went on today. Spent three hours in the waist and

relieved Brownie in the ball turret for one hour. Our ship was hardly touched, only a few holes from flak. The group lost several ships today, but we also shot down plenty of German planes. Was a very tough trip, but I got a real thrill, was too excited to be scared. We flew No. 5 in the low box.

29 May 1944 (Sorau)
Off to Germany again today. Bombed the FW-190 airplane factory. About a seven hour mission, altitude 23,000 feet, 24 below zero. Flew No. 5 low element, lead box. Had a nine man crew again. Jordon didn't fly. Alford took the tail. Had a good escort, saw a few fighters way out, but they didn't hit our group. Flak was very heavy before target, missed MPI first run, made 360, came back for a second run. Was at right waist gun when fighters were around. Thats No. 11 in 33 days, will be going home at this rate, very soon.

3 June 1944 (Dannes-Nesles)
There's No. 12-A, very easy mission, took off about 1200 hours and were back by 1600 hours. Target was German fortifications on French coast near Calias. I.P. was the English coast, saw no flak or fighters. Altitude was 20,000 feet, flew as spare No. 1, filled in low box No. 4

4 June 1944 (Paris)
That was No. 12B (13), a little different from the usual run. Didn't take off until 1530 hours. The E.T.A of return was 2230 hours. Target was M/Y south of Paris, France. I saw Paris for the first time. Bombed from 22,000 feet, results good. Hit the target with 12, 500 pounds GP's. Saw a little flak over the target and some on the French coast on withdrawal. Our base was closed by weather and we were diverted to a B-26 base about 40 miles north of London. We spent the night there and flew home the next morning. We flew our own ship, 'Hells Belles,' today. We all like her. Well we are over the hump and will be finished soon.

6 June 1944 (D-Day)
The 'big works' began today. We were up at 1130 hours Monday night, had only 30 minutes sleep. We were briefed on our target, which was enemy gun installations and pill boxes on the French coast. Took off at 0445 hours and formed at 17,000 feet and flew across the English Channel. We flew in 12 ship squadrons. We were in 'D' dog, 748th Sqdn., the first 457th squadron and the 18th to bomb. We knew of the invasion before take off. Hoped to see ground action but the clouds were 10/10ths over channel and target. Bombed PFF with 42, 100 pound GP's super sensitive bombs. Flew 9 man crew, took over right waist over target. Saw no

fighters or flak, saw some rockets in the distance. Saw more B-17's in the air than ever before. They were strung out behind us as far as I could see. Looked like the whole 8th Air Force was out. We were back at base at 0930 hours and stood by all day until 1830 hours at night. We were in on the invasion, bombed the target 10 minutes before ground troops landed. That was mission No. 14 for us.

8 June 1944 (Etampes M/Y)
Off we go again today. Up at 2400 hours and took off at 1430 hours. Went over Channel at 13,500 feet to a target which was a R.R. marshalling yard south of Paris. There was 10/10ths clouds all the way, did not bomb and flew all over France looking for a place to drop our bombs. Returned with bombs. Flew right over invasion battle, saw lots of smoke and hundreds of boats crossing the Channel, it was my first look at the big battle. Very accurate flak over the target area, biggest burst of flak I have ever seen. Landed about 1100 hours and was briefed to return again in the afternoon, but mission was scrubbed before take off. Really flying hell out of us lately, rough war, plenty tired too. That is No. 15, but we just keep going now. No limit when we finish up! [ED. For a time the length of a tour was deemed to be indefinite; however that too was changed and later a limit of 30 and then 35 was established.]

12 June 1944 (Vitry-en-Artois)
Went over France again today to an airfield near Vitry, south of Paris. We were loaded with delayed action 250 pound bombs. Mission was for about five hours, flew our new ship for the first time. She seems to be all right, like her fine, lots of soup. We hit target right on the M.P.I. Saw some flak over the area, accurate but no great amount.

14 June 1944 (La Bourget A/F, Paris)
This was another day I will remember for a while. Went to another airfield near Paris. Took off at 0500 hours, flew at 22,000 feet, bombs were 20-250 pound GP's. All went well until we made a 360 over the target because of cloud cover. Ran into some awful flak. I was on the waist gun as we had seen some Me-109's just before we made the 360. One flak burst hit the oil cooler on engine No. 1 and a piece of shrapnel came through the side of the airplane in back of the ball turret that blew a hole about 4 inches in diameter in the airplane. An ammunition can deflected the piece and saved me from getting a purple heart. We came home on three engines with one prop feathered. Our group lost several ships, some blew up in the air. It was a damn rough mission, as rough as they come. That is number 17.

B-17 hit by bombs from A/C in group.

16 June 1944 (Angoulene)
Was lucky again today. Went to Angoulene, France, after a German Panzer division, which was at a railroad yard on a 30 car train. Took off at 0400 hours and was over the target at 0900 hours and bombed from 20,000 feet. Right after bombs away our No. 4 engine blew three cylinders, which blew the cowling off the engine. Pilot feathered the prop but we dropped out of the formation and lost some altitude. We took off by ourselves around the Bay of Biscay, and the Brest peninsula. We were really sweating it out and were ready to bail out a couple of times. Our gasoline was low but we made it back to England, we landed at Predannack, Cornwall. We were about thirty miles from St. Just and near Penzance. Missions are getting rougher all the time. Hit the target, probably wiped out 15,000 German soldiers. That's 18.

18 June 1944 (Hamburg) Off to Germany today, target was a big oil plant in Hamburg. Was the first time we hit the Reich for some time, and the first time we have hit Hamburg for over a year. We were expecting a lot of flak so flew at 27,000 feet. Flew No. 6 in the high box, was on oxygen for at least four hours. We were lucky again today as we saw little flak. The other wings flew through a lot of it. We sure hit the target, an explosion threw smoke 10,000 feet into the sky, through the overcast. That one made No. 19.

19 June 1944 (Landes de Bussac)
Today made 8 days in a row we have been up for missions, sure flying the hell out of us. Today we are flying to a tactical target in sup-

port of the ground troops. Flew to an airfield in Bordeaux, France, and not much happened to us. Flew at 20,000 feet, was real soup up there for a time, sure sweat out the formation flying. Mission took eight hours, oxygen five hours, hit target with good results. Hoping to get some rest soon. That made 20 for me.

21 June 1944 (Berlin)
Target Berlin, our third trip to 'Big B.' Flew over target at 28,000 feet in position No. 6 in high squadron. Mission took over nine hours. Target was underground railway station in center of city. Bomb load was 8-500No. GP's and 2-100No. incendiaries. Flak was intense, we had No. No. 3 engine knocked out and several holes in the airplane, some close to me. Airplane inside was black with flak smoke. We had to drop out of the formation, propeller failed to feather when all the oil ran out and she quit. We sweat it out, came home on QDM's, I had a good workout with my radio. Getting to be a habit this No. 3 engine stuff. Smoke and flame was pouring out of Berlin when we left it. Can't see how there is much left of the place. That's 21.

23 June 1944 (No Ball)
Hit a no-ball target on the French coast today. It was a rocket installation for German pilotless planes — the doodle-bugs. Took off at 1030 hours and was back at 1500 hours. On oxygen four hours, altitude 20,000 feet. We were expecting lots of flak but saw very little, none close to us. I broke my former 'chaff' record today, threw out 8 boxes in 15 minutes. Going on 48 hour pass tonight, we sure need it. That's 22.

28 June 1944 (Laon-Cauvron)
Went after a German airfield near Laon, France, today. Our first mission in five days. Took off at 0430 hours, over target at 0800 hours. On oxygen for four hours, flew at an elevation of 25,000 feet, 45 degrees below zero. Flak was moderate but very accurate over target. We got some awful big holes in the ship but no one was hurt. We had to land at a B-24 base on our way home as our base was 'socked in.' We were there for only two hours and then we were told our base had opened up. Old, 111 won't fly for a few days, raids are not getting any easier. I have 23 real missions and 26 under the new set-up, have 9 more to go. We were hit by a smoke bomb again today, made a 10 inch hole in the bomb bay and holes in the rudder and other places on the ship. Ship is in sub-depot for a time.

At home in 'Nissen Hut.'

13 July 1944 (Brionne Area)
Today was our first raid in over two weeks, longest we have gone between missions. (Note added, 8 Nov. 1989. While we were on a 7 day leave in Edinburgh, Scotland, our ship 'Hell's Belles' was flown by Lt. Kozel's crew and was landed in Payerne, Switzerland. B-17G No. 44-6111) Target was Munich, Germany. Made three days in a row our group has gone there. We were No. 2 flying spare and filled into the high box at No. 5 position. Was on oxygen for 8 hours, and although the flak was heavy we received no damage to the ship. 8 more missions to sweat out.

16 July 1944 (Munich)
Off for Munich again today. Mission was about the same as Thursday's mission. Overcast over target, bombed by PFF, flew at 27,000 feet, No. 4 low box, low squadron. Flak was quite heavy and there were German fighters in the area. Escorts took care of the fighters. Flak didn't bother us much. Saw the Swiss Alps and also several of our 'Forts' going for Switzerland after being damaged. One ship blew up from flak near the French coast. Have seven more to go, hope our luck holds out.

18 July 1944 (Peenemunde)
Off for Germany again today. Target was plant manufacturing concentrated hydrogen peroxide near Peenemunde. Mission took over 9 hours, on oxygen four and one-half hours. Plenty of accurate flak over target but we were not hit. Flew at 25,000 feet. Had a good look at Sweden and Denmark today. Believe we hit target today, saw plenty of smoke and flames. Had the best fighter escort

we have ever had, place was alive with P-51's, 47's and 38's. Saw no enemy fighters at all. That makes 26, 6 more to go.

21 July 1944 (Schweinfurt)
There's another one I won't forget for awhile, one of the roughest missions I have ever been on. Went to Schweinfurt to one of the ball bearing plants. Did not see much flak until we turned at the I.P. then we ran into one of the worst flak barrages I have ever seen. Can't figure out yet how we got through and never got a scratch. Bombed visually with 1,000No. GP's, don't know the results. Had good escort again today. Trip took 8 hours, at 25,000 feet, on oxygen 5 hours. That makes 27, 5 more to go.

24 July 1944 (St.Lo Area)
Went after a real living target again today. It was a maximum effort for the whole 8th AF. Went after a German troop concentration, and tanks. It was area bombing with fragmentation bombs. As far as I could see, there was nothing but B-17's. Went in at 16,000 feet. Took off at 1000 hours, returned to base at 1500 hours. 4 to go.

25 July 1944 (St. Lo Area)
Went German hunting again today. Back to about the same place we went yesterday. Flew in high box at 13.000 feet, did not go on oxygen. Saw no fighters or flak. 3 more to go.

31 July 1944 (Munich)
After five tries, 4 scrubs and one late take off, I finally got in No. 30. The mission was a rough long one, took 10 hours, at 25,000 feet, 7 hours on oxygen. Saw plenty of flak, did not get hit with any. Saw a German 'Scare Crow,' a big ball of fire and a big cloud of black smoke. There were some German jet fighters in the vicinity but we did not see any. Bombed through the overcast. Have two more to go.

1 August 1944 (Chateaudun)
Our mission to Chateaudun airfield was rather easy. Me-262 fighters were stationed at this airfield. Mission was 6 hours and we bombed at 20,000 feet. Saw no flak or fighters. Missed the target. That's 31, one more to go.

3 August 1944 (Strasbourg)
Made my last mission today. A marshalling yard in Strasbourg. Took about 6 hours, on oxygen 4 hours. This was the 100th mission for the group. We didn't get hit by flak, and did not see any fighters. Feels good to finish up. It took me 93 days to fly 32 missions. That completed my tour in the E.T.O. and I feel real fortunate to finish.

Listed below are the crews which were lost or missing, ditched or crash landed in England or on the Continent, that were assigned to the 457th Bombardment Group(H) during World War II. Ninety-five crews were shot down or the A/C was so badly damaged that the crew could not return to base. Seventy-two crews were shot down over enemy territory. Five crews were interned in either Sweden or Switzerland. Eight crews ditched in the North Sea/English Channel. Four crews crashed on take off. Six crews crash landed in occupied Europe and returned to base to complete their tour of missions.

Mission No.	Date	Name	1st Pilot	Target
1.	21 Feb. 1944	2nd Lt.	Llewellyn Bredeson	Lippstadt
3.	24 Feb. 1944	2nd Lt.	Max R. Morrow	Schweinfurt
4.	25 Feb. 1944	2nd Lt.	James R. Chinn	Augsburg
4.	"	2nd Lt.	Archie F. Bower, Jr.	"
8.	6 March 1944	2nd Lt.	Eugene H. Whelan	Berlin
8.	"	2nd Lt.	Roy E. Graves	"
13.	16 March 1944	2nd Lt.	Lewis W. Lennartson	Augsburg (ditched)
22.	29 March 1944	2nd Lt.	Lewis W. Lennartson	Waggum
23.	9 April 1944	2nd Lt.	Amos W. Shepard	Gdynia
23.	"	2nd Lt.	Robert K. Walker	"
23.	"	2nd Lt.	David P. Parks	"
24.	10 April 1944	2nd Lt.	Adrian W. Seabock	Brussels (5 of crew jumped)
29.	20 April 1944	2nd Lt.	Walter S. Milne	Gorenflos
—	21 April 1944	2nd Lt.	Owen B. Coffman	(crash on take-off)
32.	25 April 1944	Capt.	Edward M. Bender	Nancy
44.	12 May 1944	2nd Lt.	John Akers	Lutzkendorf
46.	19 May 1944	2nd Lt.	Phillip H. Birong	Berlin
50.	24 May 1944	2nd Lt.	Harry Stafford	Berlin (ditched)
52.	27 May 1944	2nd Lt.	Artie J. Whitlow	Ludwigshafen
52.	"	2nd Lt.	William E. Dee	"
52.	"	2nd Lt.	Roger W. Birkman	"
53.	28 May 1944	2nd Lt.	Rudolph M. Stohl	Dessau
53.	"	2nd Lt.	Clyde B. Knipfer	"
53.	"	2nd Lt.	Emanuel Hauf	"
66.	14 June 1944	2nd Lt.	Roy W. Allen	La Bourget
66.	"	2nd Lt.	Malcolm E. Johnson	"
66.	"	2nd Lt.	William F. Rogers	"

66.	"	2nd Lt.	Charles R. Blackwell	"
66.	"	2nd Lt.	James LaPaze	" (ditched)
71.	20 June 1944	2nd Lt.	William G. Bomar	Hamburg
73.	21 June 1944	1st Lt.	Robert G. Krumm	Berlin (Sweden)
73.	"	2nd Lt.	Hershel Wilson	"
77.	25 June 1944	2nd Lt.	Scott B. Ormsby	Montbartiers (4 men)
79.	29 June 1944	2nd Lt.	Albert Gumuslauskas	Leipzig
79.	"	2nd Lt.	Norman Breit	" (3 men)
83.	7 July 1944	2nd Lt.	Jack B. Owens	Leipzig (ditched)
86.	11 July 1944	2nd Lt.	Jack W. Gazzales	Munich (over England)
87.	12 July 1944	2nd Lt.	Edward Kozel	Munich (Switzerland)
87.	"	2nd Lt.	Gerald L. Kerr	" (Switzerland)
87.	"	2nd Lt.	Robert L. Kaufman	" (ditched)
91.	19 July 1944	2nd Lt.	Noel A. Cunefare	Augsburg
93.	21 July 1944	2nd Lt.	Norris H. Gerber	Schweinfurt
98.	31 July 1944	2nd Lt.	Byron S, Schiffman	Munich
103.	5 Aug. 1944	2nd Lt.	Charles C. Canfield	Nienburg (ditched)
104.	6 Aug. 1944	2nd Lt.	Vincent L. Frost	Genshagen
112.	24 Aug. 1944	1st Lt.	Windred L. Pugh	Weimar
112.	"	2nd Lt.	Teddy G. Shaw	"
113.	25 Aug. 1944	2nd Lt.	Donald K. Goss	Peenemunde (Sweden)
120.	10 Sept. 1944	2nd Lt.	Homer M. Passmore	Gagenau
120.	"	2nd Lt.	Loren G. Hampton	" (2 men)
120.	"	2nd Lt.	Paul W. Gilbert	" (1 man)
121.	12 Sept. 1944	1st Lt.	Harry H. Selling	Ruhland
123.	17 Sept. 1944	1st Lt.	Douglas Grantham	Nijmegan
126.	26 Sept. 1944	2nd Lt.	Carl H. Gooch	Osnabrook
128.	28 Sept. 1944	2nd Lt.	Harold D. Gay	Magdeburg
128.	"	1st Lt.	Albert L. Sikkenga	"
128.	"	2nd Lt.	Charles J. Schultz	"
128.	"	2nd Lt.	Keylon C. Clarke	"
128.	"	2nd Lt.	Robert I. Ellsworth	"
128.	"	1st Lt.	Fred J. Lockwald	"
129.	30 Sept. 1944	1st Lt.	William A. Millea	Munster
133.	7 Oct. 1944	Capt. Col.	Alfred W. Fischer/ James R. Luper	Politz
133.	"	1st Lt.	William H. Flannery	"
133.	"	2nd Lt.	Vernon M. Moland	"
133.	"	2nd Lt.	Clarence R. Jennings	" (Sweden)
133.	"	1st Lt.	Ernest T. Salzer	" (ditched)
136.	17 Oct. 1944	1st Lt.	Norman M. Chapman	Cologne
139.	25 Oct. 1944	1st Lt.	J. Francis Angier	Hamburg
143.	2 Nov. 1944	1st Lt.	Earl M. Morrow	Merseburg
143.	"	2nd Lt.	Bruce F. Harrison	"
143.	"	1st Lt.	Gordon E. Gallagher	"
143.	"	1st Lt.	William J. Murdock	"
143.	"	1st Lt.	William A. Dawson	"
143.	"	2nd Lt.	James B. Corriher	"
143.	"	1st Lt.	Samuel H. Schimel	"
143.	"	2nd Lt.	Kenneth E. Guptill	"
143.	"	1st Lt.	Graeme L. Bow	"
145.	6 Nov. 1944	2nd Lt.	Edward P. McCroarty	Harburg

146.	8 Nov. 1944	1st Lt.	Arnet L. Furr	Merseburg
151.	25 Nov. 1944	2nd Lt.	Jack B. Wescott	Merseburg
154.	30 Nov. 1944	2nd Lt.	James (NMI) Wilson	Bohlen (in France)
154.	"	2nd Lt.	Lauren Spleth	" (in Belgium)
154.	"	2nd Lt.	Joseph C. Freschette	" (in France)
154.	"	1st Lt.	John W. White	" (in France)
159.	12 Dec. 1944	1st Lt.	Montell C. Higgins	Lutzkendorf
162.	24 Dec. 1944	2nd Lt.	Carl P. Sundbaum	Koblenz (take-off)
165.	30 Dec. 1944	2nd Lt.	William R. McCall	Kaiserslautern (in France)
172.	10 Jan. 1945	2nd Lt.	Frederick C. Gauss	Euskirchen
172.	"	2nd Lt.	Robert H. Woods	" (in Belgium)
173.	13 Jan. 1945	2nd Lt.	Irwin C. Popham	Maxmilliansau
178.	22 Jan. 1945	1st Lt.	Arthur G. Jellinek	Sterkrade
179.	28 Jan. 1945	1st Lt.	William P. Boyes, Jr.	Cologne
188.	16 Feb. 1945	2nd Lt.	Roland H. Brazier	Gelsenkirchen
198.	28 Feb. 1945	2nd Lt.	Roy E. Kirk	Soest (ditched)
212.	18 Mar. 1945	2nd Lt.	John W. Schwikert	Berlin
214.	21 Mar. 1945	1st Lt.	Craig P. Creason	Hopsten
217.	24 Mar. 1945	2nd Lt.	Sherrill R. Williams	Hopsten
224.	5 Apr. 1945	2nd Lt.	Donald L. Snow	Ingolstadt (take-off)
228.	10 Apr. 1945	Capt.	Melvin M. Fox	Oranienburg
228.	"	2nd Lt.	Thomas P. Thompson	"
234.	18 Apr. 1945	2nd Lt.	William T. Thistle	Freising

The editor/author of BLACK PUFF POLLY is Professor Emeritus of General Engineering at the University of Idaho, Moscow, Idaho from 1954 to 1981. He was a member of the faculty of the College of Engineering where he served as Chairman of the Department of General Engineering. While Professor Byers has had a distinguished career in engineering education and was selected by the University student body for the Outstanding Faculty Award on two occasions, his broad interests include Aviation, Northwest history — about which he has written three books — and Athletics. He served as University of Idaho Faculty Athletic Representative to the National Collegiate Athletic Association (NCAA) for sixteen years (1965-81). Byers is the author of seven books including FLAK DODGER, a story of the 457th Bomb Group in which he served two tours of combat and flew 38 combat missions, most of which were flown as the lead Navigator over Germany and occupied Europe. He was decorated with the Distinguished Flying Cross with cluster, the Air Medal and five clusters In 1967 he retired as Lt. Colonel USAFR, after seven years of active duty and twenty-six years of reserve duty, including service during World War II and the Korean War.